EXCELLENCE FOR ALL

EXCELLENCE
FOR ALL

How a New Breed of Reformers
Is Transforming America's Public Schools

JACK SCHNEIDER

VANDERBILT UNIVERSITY PRESS

NASHVILLE

KH

Library of Congress Cataloging-in-Publication Data

Schneider, Jack.
Excellence for all : how a new breed of reformers is
transforming America's public schools / Jack Schneider.
p. cm.
Includes bibliographical references and index.
ISBN 978-0-8265-1810-1 (cloth edition : alk. paper)
ISBN 978-0-8265-1811-8 (pbk. edition : alk. paper)
1. Public schools—United States. 2. Educational
change—United States. I. Title.
LA217.2.S345 2011
371.010973—dc22
2011008246

3/15/13

For Katie. And Annabelle.

CONTENTS

ACKNOWLEDGMENTS

No AUTHOR IS AN ISLAND, and a full geography of acknowledgment would make this a substantially thicker book. To all those who shared their insights and their time, and especially to those whose perspectives constitute a part of the work itself, I am deeply indebted.

I do particularly wish to thank a distinct subset of readers who, while leafing through this book, will be struck by a sense of familiarity if not complete recognition—those who encountered the work in various stages of its evolution and left indelible marks on it. This includes the publications staff at Taylor & Francis, Ltd., who granted permission to use an earlier version of Chapter 4 that appeared in the *Journal of Curriculum Studies* (2009) as "Privilege, Equity, and the Advanced Placement Program: Tug of War."

True thanks must begin, however, in the primordial soup, which my initial observations about the nature of modern school reform might accurately be likened to. David Labaree from the very beginning of this project was its unambiguous champion and, no less importantly, an unrelenting interrogator. Without him, this book would not exist. Others who encountered the work in progress and generously extended their scholarly friendship were also instrumental. Sam Wineburg, Larry Cuban, David Tyack, and Elisabeth Hansot each had important insights about the project, and each was a consistent source of wise and sympathetic counsel.

My colleagues Sivan Zakai, Noam Silverman, and Ethan Hutt did the repeated heavy lifting that one can count only on friends to do. As such, many of the words in this book are theirs. The final reading of this work, however, was left to my wife, Katie Henderson—the Platonic ideal of the "general reader." All those who helped shape this work were influential both personally and professionally, and obviously that is true in her case. But what is most true is that I wake up each day for her; for other reasons, too, but mostly for her.

Finally, as authors, like ideas, have their origins, I must thank my parents—a poet and a librarian who, though they plied other trades, always traded in ideas, language, beauty, and truth. And love.

INTRODUCTION

"We do not believe that a public commitment to excellence and educational reform must be made at the expense of a strong public commitment to the equitable treatment of our diverse population. The twin goals of equity and high-quality schooling have profound and practical meaning for our economy and society, and we cannot permit one to yield to the other either in principle or in practice. To do so would deny young people their chance to learn and live according to their aspirations and abilities. It also would lead to a generalized accommodation to mediocrity in our society on the one hand or the creation of an undemocratic elitism on the other."

—National Commission on Excellence
in Education, *A Nation at Risk*, 1983[1]

"And probably the most important thing we can do after growing the economy generally is how can we improve school systems in low-income communities. And I am very proud of the efforts that we've made on education reform—which have received praise from Democrats and Republicans. This is one area where actually we've seen some good bipartisan cooperation."

—Barack Obama, 2010[2]

"WE CAN'T CONTINUE LIKE THIS," President-elect Barack Obama observed in late 2008, announcing Chicago schools CEO Arne Duncan as his pick for education secretary. "It's morally unacceptable for our children and economically untenable for America." In order to build a "twenty-first-century education system," Obama noted, leaders would need to spur innovation, demand more reform, and foster the expectation that all children "graduate from college and . . . get a good paying job."[3] A few months later, in his first address to a joint session of Congress, he echoed the same message, calling for the expansion of "innovative programs" that would help Americans compete "in a global economy where the most valuable skill you can sell is your knowledge."[4]

In the early twenty-first century, the sentiment was commonplace: all children, regardless of socioeconomic status, needed to be prepared for college. The U.S. Department of Education, according to its website, sought to promote "Educational Excellence for All Americans."[5] The College Board, proprietor of the SAT test and the Advanced Placement Program, embraced a similar mission: "Educational Excellence for All Students."[6] Reform-minded organizations like Teach For America and the Bill and Melinda Gates Foundation articulated aims to provide "all children . . . the opportunity to attain an excellent education," and to ensure that "all people—especially those with the fewest resources—have access to the opportunities they need to succeed in school and life."[7] And, as a publication from the conservative Thomas B. Fordham Foundation put it, "a system characterized by equity and excellence: that's our dream and our mission, and we believe that nearly every philanthropist who gets involved in education reform shares it. *We also believe it is possible.*"[8]

By the end of the first decade of the new century, the aim of "excellence for all" in American education had developed a sort of obviousness about it, perhaps made most clear by the outlandishness of the linguistic alternatives: "excellence for some" and "mediocrity for all." In an era of political discord, "excellence for all" in American education was a distinct point of bipartisan agreement, and it had been for some time. And yet, as much as the aim of "excellence for all" may have seemed both timeless and indisputable, it was, in fact, neither. As Frederick Hess and Andrew Rotherham wrote in 2007, "there has always been an unavoidable tension between efforts to bolster American 'competitiveness' and those to promote educational equity."[9]

Resolution of that tension was hardly a foregone conclusion. Education reformers in the early part of the twentieth century pursued excellence, for instance, but only for the so-called best and brightest. Accordingly, they pursued policies like academic tracking that would raise the height of the nation's educational pyramid without any particular concern for the effects of such radical stratification on the wide base of students at the bottom. By the middle of the twentieth century, however, a newly influential group of equity-minded reformers began building on the momentum of the broader civil rights movement. Like equity advocates before them, they made the case that schools failed to meet the particular needs of low-income and minority students. But with allies in government, nonprofit organizations, and philanthropic foundations, these new activists were able to win significant policy victories. An increasingly formidable bloc in the world of education reform, they argued in favor of providing compensatory support for the less privileged—"the direct opposite of the emphasis on 'quality' or 'excellence'" as one pair of scholars put it.[10]

These two approaches to school reform, separately focused on excellence and equity, remained distinct and often in conflict with one another—that is, until reformers began to fuse them together in the early 1980s, at the dawn of the "excellence for all" era. In part, the impetus for such hybridization was pragmatism—scaffolding a larger tent for coalition building. But it was also the product of a new political context: a globalizing world economy that seemed to threaten the aims of both excellence and equity. Unless direct action was taken, critics contended, globalization would undermine national competitiveness and increase the disparity between the privileged and the less advantaged. Only greater educational achievement and attainment for all students could ward off this fate.

Still, while motivated reformers were united by a common aim, no consensus existed about how it might be achieved. But during a period in which entrepreneurship and the free market were routinely fetishized, a critical mass of policy elites began looking to what they saw as models of excellence, seeking to identify "what works" and take those solutions to scale. As an official at the Bill and Melinda Gates Foundation put it, the organization aims to provide the underserved with "the same kind of schooling that rich kids get."[11] As New York schools chancellor Joel Klein added, the challenge is to find schools about which it can be said: "This works. All we've got to do is replicate this." And, in voicing her approval for the selection of former Chicago schools chief Arne Duncan as secretary of education, Teach For America CEO Wendy Kopp declared that Duncan "just wants to find and scale the ideas that work, period."[12] In short, such leaders believed that an answer to the school problem existed and that if they pursued it aggressively enough they could transform the nation.

So what was the answer? Good schools—many of them the elite high schools that reformers themselves had attended—seemed to offer a clue. Maybe if public schools were smaller, some thought, they would start producing the kind of results top schools did. Or maybe they needed to have a particular theme like "high tech." Maybe the right lever was curricular, and programs like Advanced Placement or International Baccalaureate were the answer. Maybe a direct pipeline to college through something like the Early College program or a big scholarship fund like the Gates Millennium Scholars would do the trick. Maybe personnel reforms like Teach For America or New Leaders for New Schools would turn urban schools around. Or maybe the idea was still waiting to be discovered, requiring something like the $5 billion "Race to the Top Fund" included in the 2009 federal stimulus bill.

Whatever the solution, there was a strong sense among education reformers that a national network of high-performing urban high schools—an Andover in every neighborhood—was just on the horizon. The No Child Left Behind Act (NCLB), which some observers have framed as the signature reform of the period, did channel aspects of "excellence for all." Its name alone is evidence of that, and the law certainly garnered the lion's share of public attention. Much of that attention, however, was due to conflict and contestation over the law. Unlike purer expressions of "excellence for all," NCLB failed to capture the full spirit of the movement. It focused on adequacy rather than excellence, relied on mandates rather than innovation, and promised accountability rather than transformation. Consequently, as both Bush administration secretary of education Margaret Spellings and Obama administration secretary of education Arne Duncan observed, NCLB became a "toxic brand."[13] Within a decade, support for it unraveled and policymakers of all stripes began to discuss rolling back a number of the law's major components. Other reforms, meanwhile, were sweeping up and inspiring parents, educators, policy makers, and donors, all without generating an opposition.

As a reform vision, "excellence for all" was a consensus-building dynamo. It promised to address the needs of the underserved without interfering with private or suburban education; it promised major change without resorting to heavy-handed government intervention; it promised to meet the challenges posed by globalization; and perhaps most importantly, in identifying ostensibly "high-leverage" practices—often inspired by the work of top schools—and then reproducing them, it promised to work. Consequently, ideological adversaries found common ground, political opponents reached across the aisle, philanthropists opened their checkbooks, and school districts engaged in the disruptive and messy process of wide-scale change.

To be clear, education reform was no less diverse than in previous eras. But despite a variety of different visions, the most ambitious reformers were in agreement that the highest aim in American education was simple: excellence for all. In part, such consensus was the result of a powerful idea, perfectly suited to a particular historical context. Excellence for all tapped into divergent constituencies, capitalized on shifting political realities, and successfully played to the American faith in education as a panacea. But excellence for all was also the vision of a particular class of policy elites, who already shared a set of common backgrounds and experiences, moved through the same spheres of influence, and held similar assumptions about schooling and social change. Thus, while the inherent power of the idea was significant, it was no less important that it was favored by those with the biggest dreams and the deepest pockets—reform tastemakers and policy trendsetters—who possessed the power to change the educational landscape from the top down.

Educational policy elites in the last decades of the twentieth century and first decade of the twenty-first were not always coordinated in their actions. Sometimes they supported separate projects that, without widespread support, never gained substantial momentum. At other times, they worked at cross-purposes. But the idea of excellence for all continued to exert a magnetic pull, drawing reformers together around a common vision. In its purest form, through efforts to replicate aspects of elite schooling in low-performing and traditionally underserved urban districts, excellence for all was a rallying cry. Working together, leaders at think tanks and nonprofits, in foundations and government, and in state and district offices leveraged the resources at their disposal to generate national momentum. In turn, teachers and principals, parents and activists, politicians and community leaders threw in their lots with those leading the charge. Major reforms swept across American high schools.

Despite eliciting such broad support, the excellence for all movement has been plagued by significant challenges, unintended consequences, and mixed results. Yet setbacks have not undermined this distinctly modern vision of school reform. Instead, in the face of such challenges policy elites have redoubled their efforts. Education reform, after all, is only partly a matter of what happens in schools. It is equally about politics and faith— the product of coalitions and interest groups struggling to enact particular visions shaped by deep-rooted ideologies.

This book is about understanding the world of ideas in American school reform. It considers how history and current events, social conditions and political alignments, leadership and rhetoric collectively shape the educational policy-making environment and the individuals working within it. It explores why certain modes of thought become prevalent, and it looks at how particular school improvement efforts gain traction.

But this book is also about understanding a specific approach to educational change. Examining the excellence for all era, it aims to establish the ways in which this most recent period represents a departure from previous reform eras. In so doing, it identifies the unique characteristics of this vision that sought to remake urban public schools in the image of the private academy. Concerned with both the political successes and practical shortcomings of this highly visible effort, the work explores both the assumptions underlying the excellence for all approach and the tradeoffs required by it.

METHODOLOGY

This educational history explores the excellence for all era through three exemplary reforms: a facility redesign, a staffing improvement effort, and a curricular adoption. Beyond merely dividing up the complex package of formal education, such an approach examines the aspects of schooling—the school plant, the faculty, and the curriculum—that Americans believed would best promote universal achievement.[14]

Although intended to change different parts of the school, each of these cases reflects the characteristic approach of reformers in the excellence for all era: finding what works and taking it to scale. By identifying models of excellence and replicating their successful practices, reformers believed that they could achieve a kind of educational alchemy, transforming even struggling schools into high performers. This book, as it seeks to understand the essence of this approach to education reform, explores the vision not in its various guises, but in its grandest style. Consequently, it focuses most closely on efforts to remake large urban high schools—the so-called dropout factories that symbolized the nation's educational shortcomings and that were the object of reformers' greatest ambitions.

Before looking at particular reforms, however, this book explores the particular historical context that made such efforts not only plausible, but popular. As school reforms designed to promote excellence for all were the unique product of the late twentieth and early twenty-first centuries, this chapter seeks to outline the various concerns and interests related to schooling that developed prior to the era. It examines the social, political, and economic forces that shaped these often-divergent views about the preferred means and ends of school reform, the fractured policy-making landscape that this ideological diversity created, and, finally, the way in which different interest groups were brought together to form a broad national reform movement. By developing this context, Chapter 1 sets the scene for the case studies that follow it.

This book first examines reform at the level of the school plant, looking at the phenomenon of the small schools movement. Arguing that the comprehensive high school was no longer an appropriate model for American secondary education, small schools advocates compared the intimate and highly academic environments of top independent schools with nightmarish visions of large, violent, and academically abysmal urban public schools attended by less-advantaged students of color. Models of excellence like small private schools, as well as a number of small Catholic and charter schools, they argued, sent their students on to college, retained their talented and engaged faculties, and often attracted alumni back as teachers. All large urban schools, reformers argued, should be made small; Chapter 2 looks at that effort and its consequences.

At the school personnel level, this study explores the growth of Teach For America (TFA). Advocates of TFA, concerned with the disparity between the backgrounds of teachers in high-income areas and those in low-income areas, made the case that underserved schools were overwhelmingly staffed by teachers lacking content expertise. Private school teachers, by contrast, came from elite liberal-arts backgrounds, majored in content areas, and often pursued teaching as a means of staying connected with their fields. In this context, Wendy Kopp proposed "a new Teacher Corps" to help all American children attain "an excellent education." A year later, Kopp founded TFA to encourage undergraduates from top colleges to teach for two years in underserved urban and rural schools. Chapter 3 looks at the efforts of TFA supporters to turn around America's low-performing schools by placing Ivy League–educated teachers in them.

Finally, at the level of the curriculum, this study examines the expansion of the Advanced Placement Program (AP). Conceived of in the 1950s as a way of engaging and challenging the top students at the best American high schools, AP remained for over two decades a small, elite curricular program found only in top private and suburban schools. By the late 1970s and early 1980s, however, equity advocates were calling for expansion of the program into less privileged schools, and by the 1990s the federal government and major foundations were funding that expansion. Advanced Placement, they argued, fostered engagement, promoted academic rigor, and gained students a college admissions advantage.[15] Even better in the eyes of excellence for all reformers, the program could be transplanted. Consequently,

Chapter 4 looks at the growth of AP and the outcomes—intended and otherwise—of that growth.

The story of the excellence for all era is a national story. Therefore, much of it must be told from a macroscopic perspective. To keep the study grounded, this book emphasizes the experiences of three major American cities: New York, Chicago, and Los Angeles. Because each of these reform efforts targeted urban public schools, it makes sense to look at the nation's three largest school districts, which together educate over two million students each year. Additionally, because excellence for all reforms were particularly targeted at the underserved, it makes sense to look within high-poverty districts. Twenty-nine percent of the students in New York and Chicago public schools are classified by the National Center for Education Statistics as living in poverty, while the same is true of 31 percent of Los Angeles students—figures rivaled by few other metropolitan areas in the United States.[16]

These cities also represent fertile places in which to root this study because they have been particularly active sites of reform, as well as representative in the reforms they pursued. The largest of them, New York, has in the past three decades frequently been the launching pad for national reform efforts and has been called "super-typical" of American urban education.[17] The small schools movement, for instance, quietly began in New York with the founding of Central Park East Secondary School in 1985. A decade later, the first major philanthropic grants for the creation of small schools were given to New York, which subsequently adopted a citywide small schools strategy; others across the nation soon followed suit. New York was also the birthplace of Teach For America. Since its founding in 1990, TFA has expanded its New York program to one thousand corps members, making it the organization's largest placement area, and by 2010 the New York branch of Teach For America had three thousand alumni. Finally, New York has been a major site for expansion of the Advanced Placement Program, as well as for knee-jerk reactions to that expansion. In recent years, the city has received grants from a number of sources, including the U.S. Department of Education's Advanced Placement Incentive Program, with the aim of increasing participation by low-income students.[18] As a result of such efforts, AP has exploded in New York public schools. But as expanding access eroded the value of the AP credential, New York prep schools like Fieldston, Calhoun, Dalton, and Spence, along with the entire Scarsdale public school district, dropped the AP Program. In short, New York has been a leading city both in adopting AP and in dumping it.

The second of the three cities through which this book explores excellence for all reforms is Chicago. In the mid-1990s, before the Gates Foundation began pouring money into small schools in Chicago and beyond, the city was already embarking on an effort to create dozens of small high schools. Since then, Chicago has opened scores more and received tens of millions of dollars in grants from the likes of the Department of Education and the Gates Foundation to do so. Unlike New York, Chicago was late to partner with Teach For America. Still, the organization and the district have wasted no time in expanding the program. According to former Chicago Public Schools CEO Arne Duncan, Chicago "is committed to recruiting the best and the brightest to teach [the city's] students . . . [and is] thrilled that Teach For America corps members are teaching in our high needs areas."[19] By 2010, Chicago was one of TFA's largest placement areas. Finally, the city has been quite active over the past two decades in trying to expand its Advanced Placement offerings for low-income students. Between 1998 and 2003, the number of Latino and African American students taking AP exams in the Chicago public school system increased by 227 percent and 176 percent, respectively. According to a 2004 report, Chicago Public Schools sought "to help close the achievement gap by giving students of color in neighborhood schools more access to Advanced Placement. . . . As a result, Chicago is now a national leader in expanding access to AP."[20] Results, however—as in other places—have been mixed.

Los Angeles, like the other two cities, has been a major site of recent school reform, particularly the three reforms that this study examines. The small schools movement, for instance, took root in L.A. later than in New York and Chicago, but nevertheless has spread throughout the city and influenced dozens of schools at the cost of tens of millions of dollars. In 2005, the Los Angeles Unified School District became the first to mandate that all its large high schools be broken into smaller learning communities. Los Angeles was also one of Teach For America's initial placement locations, functioning as the site for the organization's first summer training institutes. TFA has received major support in Los Angeles, both from philanthropic organizations and from civic leaders like mayor Antonio Villaraigosa, who praised TFA as "a crucial source of talented leaders at all levels who work tirelessly for education equality in our city."[21] Annually, TFA affects an organization-estimated forty thousand students in Los Angeles Unified public schools. Finally, Los Angeles has been a hotbed of activity in the spread of the Advanced Placement Program, as well as the recipient of some unanticipated reaction to it. For decades, L.A. was a highly visible site of AP reform, largely because of Jaime Escalante's work at Garfield High School, publicized by education writer Jay Mathews and by the film *Stand and Deliver*. In 1999, L.A. and AP began making headlines once again when the American Civil Liberties Union filed a lawsuit on behalf of students at L.A. Unified's Inglewood High School, alleging that the school's three AP course offerings were inadequate and inequitable. Responding to such demands for program expansion, Los Angeles public schools have dramatically increased their AP offerings. The results of that growth, however, like the results of other excellence for all efforts in the city, have been uneven and often have been accompanied by unintended consequences.

THIS BOOK IS NOT an exhaustive history of educational policy shifts in the past thirty years. Instead, it is an exploration of a particularly powerful idea that has captivated the hearts and minds of a generation of school reformers. Although it is not a complete accounting of all educational change between 1980 and 2010, the story of the excellence for all era is nevertheless illustrative of what a nation wanted from its schools by the dawn of the twenty-first century, and of how policy leaders intended to provide it. This is a book about America's romance with school reform, and the shape that romance has taken in a distinctly modern period.

1

THE RIGHT TIME

1980–2010

By the time of Barack Obama's inauguration in 2009, the idea of excellence for all had been firmly established as the highest aim in American education reform. Equally well accepted was the notion that by taking an entrepreneurial approach to the nation's education problem, reformers could identify "what works" and replicate successful school models on a large scale. The result, its supporters argued, would be a nationwide network of urban academies, providing for low-income and minority students the kind of schools previously reserved for more privileged populations.

Like an invasive species with no natural enemies, the excellence for all movement became the dominant vision in American school reform efforts in the early twenty-first century. It so captured the imaginations of ambitious school leaders, politicians, and philanthropists that it swiftly became a widely accepted bipartisan rallying cry at the local, state, and national levels. But far from being a nonnative transplant to the American educational ecosystem, the excellence for all movement is a homegrown product—the unique result of particular historical circumstances.

In that sense, the story of the excellence for all era is also a story of evolution in the world of education reform. Excellence for all as a reform credo was not hatched into the world fully formed. Rather, it developed in response to unique environmental challenges, organically transforming and adapting in order to win constituencies, expand in appeal, and grow in influence. The education policy-making context of the twentieth century was fraught with tensions—between social efficiency and social justice, between pursuit of access and advantage, and between government and markets—and the aim of excellence for all unified a fractured landscape by offering something for everyone. In so doing, it won the day, if perhaps only politically.

STRUGGLES OVER THE SCHOOLS

Americans have long fought over the aims of schooling, variously expecting schools to maintain order, foster social mobility, strengthen the state, advance meritocracy, reinforce privilege, and promote equality. But while at the dawn of the twentieth century policy elites in the world of education reform tended to share similar concerns, that would begin to change over time.[1] Leaders representing a broader range of backgrounds and ideologies, and working in rapidly changing domestic and international contexts, would introduce new concerns and emphasize different aims in education policy making. And while some of these varied purposes would be compatible, they would hardly be mutually inclusive, eventually threatening to permanently balkanize American school reform.

Whatever policy-making divides might later emerge, early twentieth-century school reformers were in relative agreement about the means and ends of school reform. Driven by social efficiency concerns like social utility and administrative efficiency, they supported efforts that they believed would produce stability both in and out of the schools. Hoping to address the era's major concerns, they sought to create policies that would Americanize the immigrant, for instance, or modernize rural areas. And, in a period still characterized by local control and radical geographical differentiation in terms of educational standards and resources, they strove to consolidate one-room schoolhouses, to create teacher credentialing requirements, and to reduce the number of students repeating grade levels in public schools.[2]

Perhaps most emblematically, school reformers of the early twentieth century sought to make the schools more "socially useful" by creating alternatives to the academic curriculum for non-college-bound students.[3] Unlike future reformers who would define equity differently, these "administrative progressives," as historian David Tyack has called them, sought to serve each student according to his or her perceived needs.[4] As Boston's superintendent noted in 1908, the schools had previously offered "equal opportunity for all to receive *one kind* of education." But times had changed, and high schools were finding themselves serving an increasingly wide cross section of the American population. The remedy for such "democratization" of the schools, this superintendent proposed, was simple: provide the opportunity for students to receive an "education as will fit them *equally well* for their particular life work."[5] The college-preparatory curriculum, such leaders argued, was simply impractical, particularly in light of the rapid expansion of high school enrollment, and failed to educate most students for their likelier destination after high school—the workforce.

Exemplary among these early twentieth-century sorting efforts was the crafting of the Cardinal Principles of Secondary Education in 1918. The report, authored by a commission appointed by the National Education Association, established formal guidelines for the differentiated "tracked" curriculum and proposed non–college preparatory education for 60 percent of the American public.[6] Distinct from those like David Snedden, who favored dividing "the rank and file" into separate vocationally focused facilities, the Cardinal Principles report proposed differentiation within the same comprehensive high school.[7] Such sentiments were in congruence with the work of educational psychologists like Lewis Terman and Edward Thorndike, which suggested that inherited IQ scores marked people and groups for their stations in life and that differences between groups were products of heredity.[8] But unlike those who favored more direct social reproduction, the authors of the Cardinal Principles report sought to track people by perceived ability rather than by social class. While students in vocational tracks would still be drawn almost exclusively from the working class, such sorting would promote national strength without violating democratic principles. Armed with research that seemed to support such efforts, a coalition of policy makers and professional educators created a nationwide network of comprehensive high schools.

In the following decades, school reformers continued, in the name of practicality and a particular understanding of equity, to create disparate schooling experiences for students. In 1944, the Educational Policies Commission published *Education for All American Youth*, which stated that "differences in intelligence and aptitude will exist" and that such differences required "different educational procedures, content, and standards of speed and achievement."[9] Consequently, "life adjustment education"—as distinct from a classical academic education—was recommended for the majority of American students. Although such an approach perpetuated social differences, advocates portrayed it as a functional means of promoting social and economic stability for the nation and a suitable way of preparing students for their likely careers.

Given that little changed in terms of the class to which influential school reformers generally belonged or the social and economic tensions that shaped their interests, education policy remained relatively consistent through the early years of the Cold War.[10] In the wake of Sputnik, however, school reform efforts began to reflect an increased concern with "excellence."[11] Primarily as a matter of national security, reformers argued, the best students could no longer simply be prepared for college; they needed to be identified, paired with well-trained teachers, and driven to realize lofty goals. As former president Herbert Hoover observed in 1957, "our higher institutions of learning have the capacity to train the recruits we need." But, he added, "the harsh fact is that the high schools are not preparing youngsters for the entrance requirements which must be maintained by our institutions training scientists and engineers."[12] In short, if the United States was going to maintain its position of dominance, American schools needed to prepare scientists and leaders capable of outcompeting their Soviet counterparts.

But rather than challenging the accepted practice of providing different educational experiences to students of different backgrounds, the drive for excellence reinforced it, concentrating efforts to increase academic achievement on those identified as most likely to assume leadership positions. In 1958, for instance, Congress passed the National Defense Education Act, providing nearly $1 billion in federal assistance, the bulk of which was appropriated for two priorities: improving math, science, and foreign language instruction and providing low-interest loans to college students. No less importantly, however, Title V of the act established grants to state educational agencies to assist in establishing and maintaining programs of guidance, counseling, and testing—a means of identifying the nation's best and brightest and encouraging them to pursue rigorous coursework and postsecondary education. In a similar spirit, school reformers at organizations like the Ford Foundation poured money into programs like the College Board's Advanced Placement Program—created to promote rigor among college-bound high school students—as well as into masters of arts in teaching programs designed to prepare disciplinary majors in top colleges to teach.

Most students, meanwhile, were still seen as needing only "functional experiences in the areas of practical arts, home and family life, health and physical fitness, and civic competence."[13] As a consequence, reformers, most of whom still believed that student ability naturally distributed in a pyramid-like shape, continued to advocate for programs that served students according to their distinct needs and abilities. Few efforts reflected this perspective as clearly as that which sought to enhance and enlarge the comprehensive high school. The university-sized high school—backed enthusiastically by James Conant, former chairman of the National Defense Research Committee and past president of Harvard University—would more productively train some students vocationally, provide a general non–college preparatory education to most, and groom the minority for college by giving them access to the most talented teachers and the widest range of academic courses.[14] As Conant supporter John Gardner wrote in his 1961 book *Excellence: Can We Be Equal and Excellent Too?*, the only sense in which equality of opportunity could "mean anything" was by providing "each youngster with the particular kind of education which will benefit *him*."[15] In short, while reformers of the period were concerned with promoting excellence, their concerns were typically with increasing the height of the pyramid.

Though concerns like social efficiency would remain powerful undercurrents in reform, the decades broadly characterized as the civil rights era dramatically changed the context in which school reform was created. In this new situation, defending policies that could be attacked as racist, classist, or sexist became highly problematic politically. Equally important, this national shift in tone also allowed for the emergence of a generation of leaders concerned with the aim of social justice. Challenging policies ranging from the vocational tracking of working-class students to racially motivated boundary gerrymandering, these activists began to redefine educational equity. Equal access and educational self-determination, they argued, were the right of all Americans.

The push for greater opportunities in schooling, of course, was nothing new. For as long as formal schooling had existed, disenfranchised groups had agitated—often inconspicuously, in cases where open resistance incited disproportionate reprisals—for what they viewed as their educational rights. Even the pursuit of equal opportunity through the courts, a hallmark of the civil rights movement, began well before the 1950s and 1960s. Two decades before the *Brown* decision, for instance, Mexican American parents not only filed but won a desegregation suit in Lemon Grove, California.[16]

However, while the push for social justice may not have been new, its entrance into the mainstream was. As the post–World War II political agenda expanded in scope—at least among liberals who believed the forces of government should be marshaled to improve conditions for the greatest number of Americans—those concerned with social justice in education became more active, more visible, and better funded.[17]

Consequently, broader conceptions of educational equity began to shift by the 1960s. Earlier policies that provided differentiated experiences for students from different backgrounds, activists argued, were misguided. And equally important, such policies were far-reaching in their effects. A 1963 article in Atlanta University's journal *Phylon*, for instance, argued that inequitable opportunity structures had not only perpetuated social inequity, but had also produced among students of color a "damaged self concept," "inadequate motivation," "unawareness of employment opportunities," and "resistance by peers and community to self-advancement."[18]

Consequently, while some began to advocate for more equitable opportunities, others made the case that even more had to be done in the pursuit of social equity. Thus, as reformer Chester Finn recalled, the focus in education reform shifted to "helping disadvantaged children use education as an escalator out of poverty."[19] With cooperation from grassroots supporters, liberal whites, and progressive politicians, social justice–minded school reformers succeeded in winning a number of substantive policy changes—Title I of the Elementary and Secondary Education Act foremost among them—that they believed would more fairly allocate resources and serve the real needs of low-income and minority students.[20]

The social justice–tinged push for equity in education was not confined to the aim of better serving racial minorities and low-income students. Members of the women's movement, for instance, made the case that gender bias in public education had restricted opportunity for half of the American population.[21] Similarly, advocates of children with disabilities argued that despite compulsory education laws instituted in the early twentieth century, many children with disabilities were turned away by the public schools, leaving institutionalization as the only alternative to homeschooling. Consequently, women pursued a variety of reforms with varying degrees of success, and the work of advocates for special education resulted in a string of amendments to the Elementary and Secondary Education Act that eventually led to the creation of the Education for All Handicapped Children Act of 1975, requiring public schools to provide equal access to education for children with physical and mental disabilities.[22]

Such activists were concerned with education for its own sake but were also passionate about using the schools to remedy social inequities. The long struggle for equal education had fostered hopes about outcomes that extended far beyond what could be learned in school. School desegregation efforts, for instance, promised to transform educational opportunity in both the South and the North; more important, however, given the amplified rhetoric that accompanied these struggles, they also promised to transform the very nature of American race relations.[23] The *Brown* decision, most visibly, and new federal legislation and programs like the Civil Rights

Act and Head Start increased expectations that the schools would pave the way for a new, and more equitable, social order.

DIVIDES DEEPEN

Whatever social justice–oriented school reform efforts may have had the capacity to accomplish, they were met with varying degrees of opposition. Efforts to integrate schools and litigation around gender bias were criticized as distractions from the real business of education and as divorced from the actual educational needs of low-income, minority, and female students bound for lower-status occupations.[24] And in response to the push among equity advocates to include special needs students in traditional public school classes, policy makers focused on social efficiency and excellence frequently dismissed the special education movement as ideologically misguided.[25] Thus, ambitious Great Society programs "designed to promote justice and opportunity" were frequently met with opposition by more conservative groups who, according to historian Diane Ravitch, characterized such efforts as "utopian formulations" marred by "a stubborn unwillingness to acknowledge the limits of federal action in the American system."[26]

Still, although the pursuit of social justice and greater equity of opportunity through the schools was contested, the movement continued to gather political momentum through the 1960s and 1970s. Social efficiency reforms, for their part, could be framed as investments in human capital that would "pay bountiful dividends for the community as a whole and ultimately for each taxpayer."[27] Yet, as more and more Americans became at least marginally concerned with systemic inequities, a strict social efficiency approach to education reform looked less and less appropriate. Consequently, leaders in state and local government and at nonprofit groups and foundations understood that any significant school change effort would need to address the particular needs of low-income and minority students. The Ford Foundation, for instance, had supported reform efforts that reflected the national concern with what the foundation's Edward J. Meade called the "pursuit of excellence."[28] But as times changed, the foundation sought to place more emphasis on matters of equity and opportunity in its work. As Meade noted, "increasing awareness of the extent of inequality of opportunity in America's educational system and increasing activism on the part of civil rights groups made it clear that entirely different types of educational change would be necessary."[29]

Closely related to the push for equity and social justice in education, but distinct in its own right, was the drive for social mobility. But whereas the former largely represented a public good—education for the purpose of creating a fairer and more just society—the latter represented a private good—education for the purpose of getting ahead. By the mid-twentieth century, more civic-minded educational aims like fostering citizenship had long been eclipsed in the minds of concerned parents by the desire to use schools as a means of giving their children a social and economic advantage. In the early 1960s, John Gardner observed, a college diploma had become "firmly associated in the public mind with personal advancement [and] upward social mobility."[30] Reforms like school integration, then, stirred hopes among underprivileged families not only for fairness but also for personal opportunity.

Given its nature as a positional good, however, education has a market value only when consumed unequally.[31] Consequently, insofar as particular education policies promised to increase access and opportunity for some, they aroused opposition among those who felt their degree of privilege was threatened. Thus, because increased opportunity for some meant declining opportunity for others, such reforms also produced anxiety among those who stood to lose their relative educational advantage—anxiety frequently translated into action.

Most often, such fears were articulated as concerns about declining academic quality. In a 1957 article in the *Journal of Educational Sociology*, one author described arguments against "equality of educational opportunity" as centering around the idea that such equality could only be achieved "by sacrificing existing educational standards and services," leveling the entire educational playing field downward. Parents expressed concerns that "'equalizing' the distribution of educational resources for all children" would result in a decline in "the quality of education offered in a particular school or school system."[32] This opposition, in turn, inspired more aggressive efforts to integrate schools in fifteen hundred school districts from Charlotte to San Francisco, bringing about interventions like redistricting and busing plans.[33] But though some efforts, like Charlotte's, were relatively successful, most achieved neither integration nor a greater degree of educational equality.

Whatever their success, educational equity efforts of the 1960s and 1970s inspired a great deal of resistance and hostility, inciting an opposition that threatened to abandon city schools, even at the personal cost of private school tuition or residential relocation. Racism, certainly, played a part in this. But such opposition was as much, if not more, about the use of public dollars to undermine educational advantage. As sociologist Arnold Rose put it, while some parents were "motivated by racial prejudice," others were "merely status-conscious."[34] And as Richard Nixon wrote in 1972, "there may be some doubt as to the validity of the *Brown* philosophy that integrating education will pull up the blacks and not pull down the whites."[35] Metropolitan busing efforts, for instance, were often opposed by parents on the grounds that such plans took their students out of the neighborhood schools they had carefully sought out for perceived quality. Other reform efforts that promised to expand access to quality schools, like the move to equalize school funding, for instance, aroused opposition among those concerned with their property tax rates and the funding allocated to their own children's schools.[36] The pursuit of educational equity, they seemed to believe, was a zero-sum proposition that threatened to draw resources away from more privileged schools in equal proportion to any infusion of resources in struggling ones.

The 1960s marked the rise of social justice proponents and buoyed the hopes of working-class and lower middle-class parents for greater educational opportunity. Particularly in the broader context of the civil rights movement and Lyndon Johnson's War on Poverty, many began to believe that equity was within reach.[37] Yet as much as such moves created a sense of optimism among some, they raised concerns among others, exacerbating the classic American tension between government intervention and the free market. Conservatives in the 1960s, as historian Lisa McGirr writes, were increasingly "united in their opposition to liberal 'collectivism'—the growing tendency of the state to organize social and economic life in the name of the public welfare and the social good."[38] Perceiving a decline in religiosity, morality, individual responsibility, and family authority, all of which seemed to coincide with the growth of centralized federal power, they sought to limit "the intrusiveness of the nation-state."[39]

Not surprisingly, resistance among those who maligned the intrusiveness and heavy taxation of "big government" soon manifested in fights over public education. Struggles over school funding, of course, were nothing new to American education.[40] In the 1970s, however, antitax advocates in favor of local control had powerful allies in various levels of government. Further, the movement had an increasingly wide appeal as the escalating costs of education placed a growing financial burden on the state, and as conflicts over the purpose of public schooling polarized voters and taxpayers on education issues. Ultimately, in what constituted the movement's clearest act of resistance, the taxpayer revolts of the late 1970s—exemplified by Proposition 13 in California and Proposition 2½ in Massachusetts—slashed the flow of funding to public schools by strictly limiting property-tax increases. Such actions delivered a message that the voting population had its doubts about the work of government and even the merits of public schooling.

Clearly, by the late 1970s there were serious divides in the world of school reform. The convergence of tensions like disagreements over the purpose of schooling, competition for its rewards, and conflict between the ideals of personal freedom and equality turned education policy making into a veritable minefield. In 1977, for instance, the federal government, at the behest of activists and advocacy organizations, decided to open an investigation into New York City's three most prestigious public high schools—the Bronx High School of Science, Stuyvesant, and Brooklyn Tech—regarding low enrollments of women and minority groups. Parents and school supporters strongly opposed the investigation, viewing it "as a threat to the preservation of high-quality education for the city's academically superior students" that would "spur the flight of middle-class families, both black and white, from the city" in order to preserve the relative advantages they had secured for their children.[41] Further, many saw the move as a heavy-handed intervention that failed to recognize the sovereignty of the family and the wisdom of the market. The same was true in urban districts across the United States, with a common result: privileged families exiting urban public schools.

One less contentious approach to social justice–minded school reform, and one less dependent on federal control, was the effort to create separate community schools. Such efforts avoided the controversial expansion of access to successful schools and promised to specifically tailor schools to the particular needs of the underserved. Unlike many other advocates for equity and access, community school activists believed that "different students learn best in different ways."[42] Further, they believed, as Jonathan Kozol wrote, that schools needed to be "in direct contact with the needs and urgencies of those among the poor, the black, the dispossessed"—students who he argued had been "the most clearly victimized by public education."[43] Echoing dissatisfaction with the American public school system, scholar Maurie Hillson had written in the late 1960s that "there is no question in the minds of observers and students of the educational scene that the school discriminates against lower-class students, minorities, and in many instances, any who deviate slightly from the established and imposed middle-class norm behavior patterns and performances."[44] Consequently, such reformers in the 1970s proposed to create alternative schools, free schools, and full-service community schools.[45] Such schools would exist outside of the public education bureaucracy, providing unique and different experiences from those of more privileged populations.

Community schools inspired less hostility, but they were still divisive. As conservative scholar Sol Stern would later write, "in their ideologically induced paranoia about America, the radical education theorists, like most ideologues, cannot see what is right in front of their eyes—that America and democratic capitalism are actually doing very well, thank you, but that the children of the minority poor are getting a lousy education because of the education establishment, and that teaching for social justice provides no solutions."[46] In other words, while such schools did not threaten the status of more privileged families, they were still perceived by some as anti-American threats to the economic and social order. Further, to conservatives concerned with equity, such schools seemed to do more harm than good.

The school reform landscape of the 1970s was marked by deep divides separating politically and ideologically distinct constituencies. Yet, the domestic and international context in which political factions operated was beginning to change, amplifying concerns about the need for education reform and, in turn, opening up opportunities for cooperation. Possession of a college diploma, for instance, was increasingly becoming the minimum standard for access to middle-class jobs. As the growth of postsecondary enrollment swelled—stimulated in part by the declining value of the high school diploma—high schools were increasingly expected to provide a college-preparatory curriculum and environment.[47] Middle-class parents were "beginning to worry" about the quality of public schools "because students did not seem to be adequately prepared for college," and those able to do so were increasingly turning to private and suburban schools to secure opportunities for their children.[48] Strengthening the college preparatory function of public schools was also a major concern of social justice advocates, who insisted that access to a college education be extended well beyond the highest social strata. Anything less, noted one author, "seems to many to be absurd at best, and racist or classist at worst."[49]

Yet in such a politically fragmented landscape, major school change could only be successfully pursued with the support of a broad coalition. As the Ford Foundation's Edward Meade wrote in 1972, "innovation and change need the broadest possible commitment of intellectual and financial resources. . . . [T]he commitments from multiple funding sources and especially from [school] districts are essential ingredients, not simply as they represent broadly based intentions to stay with the program, but also as they illustrate for staff and the public a budgetary and philosophical commitment to the concept."[50] Thus, the fractures that characterized education policy making toward the end of the 1970s—dividing social efficiency–minded reformers from social justice activists, access advocates from the privileged, and free market thinkers from those who favored government intervention—seemed to preclude a major national school reform movement. In the coming years, however, the sense of urgency around improving America's schools would only continue to grow, particularly as the impact of globalization became a reality. Further, new opportunities for cooperation, collaboration, and even consensus would continue to present themselves to ambitious reformers.

EMERGING OPPORTUNITIES

America in the 1980s, wrote journalist Haynes Johnson, "wanted to believe it had recaptured a sense of success. Success for the nation, success for the individual."[51] This national shift in tone presented an opportunity to begin thinking once more about improving the nation's schools. But it would not be easy, as such steps were not a part of President-elect Ronald Reagan's plan and the world of education policy was plagued by deep divisions. Still, opportunities for bridging such divides, for pursuing a national education reform agenda, for reaping a windfall of positive publicity, and for building a political legacy continued to present themselves and would eventually present too much of a draw to be ignored, even by Reagan. The result, as National Education Association president Mary Hatwood Futrell would recall, was that "President Reagan elevated education." Before the 1980s, she added, "we had never had that kind of visibility."[52]

An increasing national optimism was far from the only factor transforming the education policy-making context of the period and was arguably much less significant than the changing global economy. While justifications based in social efficiency and excellence had previously supported policies that tracked students and provided differentiated experiences, globalization appeared to be changing that. As markets continued to open around the world and barriers to trade continued to fall, the American education system came under fire for failing to foster competition and to prepare all children for the new knowledge-based, rather than industrial, economy.[53] Consequently, conservative education reformers found themselves more and more in agreement with liberals, at least on one point:

postsecondary opportunities had to be expanded for those who had traditionally completed their educations at the high school level.

Conservatives did not suddenly find themselves deeply concerned with issues of fairness and equity, much less with social justice. Rather, they tended to justify their policy recommendations by citing the need for the United States to maintain its world economic position and the need for American corporations to remain competitive in the age of globalization—an economic translation of the Cold War–era concern with military competitiveness. As a U.S. Chamber of Commerce report noted in 1982, the problem was straightforward: the American education system was unprepared to train workers for emerging white-collar "knowledge occupations."[54] Later reformers, somewhat more dramatically, would refer to the looming "national economic, civic and social disaster," citing the "national imperative that high school graduates attend college."[55] A college education rather than industrial training, they seemed to believe, would provide American students with skills safe from outsourcing while at the same time giving American corporations a global advantage.

Conservative reformers also made the case that the potential benefits to society of preparing all citizens for full civic and economic participation extended beyond the abstract idea of national economic competitiveness. Promoting greater educational opportunity, for instance, would also increase tax revenues, reduce crime, and limit dependence on welfare.[56] Further, increasing human capital, they believed, would produce greater prosperity, thereby alleviating social problems and providing a significant return on any investment in promoting postsecondary education.

Liberal education reformers, for their part, continued to focus on the concept of equity in agitating for increased access to postsecondary education for underserved students. And while social justice remained a core concept in liberal circles, many savvier reformers on the left began to adopt aspects of the arguments made by more conservative thinkers. If educational opportunity could be equalized, one author wrote, schools might "solve the dilemma of racial discrimination." He was sure to include, however, that they would also "teach children and provide the basic skills needed by a complex technological society."[57] Typical was the case made by Theodore Sizer, dean of the Harvard Graduate School of Education: the future economy would be "volatile and dependent on flexible workers with a high level of intellectual skills." Consequently, "the best vocational education"—something conservatives and social efficiency advocates had long been concerned with—would actually be a "general education in the use of one's mind."[58] Of course, many parents advocating for increased access to higher education saw a simpler equation: earning a college degree would increase the earning potential of their children. For the most part, however, they recognized the importance of appealing to more high-minded ideals rather than to personal gain in voicing their concerns.

Also important in the fusion of traditionally oppositional aims was the fact that, unlike the fight over increasing access to good high schools, the effort to increase postsecondary enrollment did not pose an immediate and intolerable threat to the already educationally advantaged. The push for integration had been met with strong resistance because many parents viewed it as a midgame change of rules—an unfair handicapping of white middle-class students that counteracted the decisions parents had made about schooling. The effort to increase access to higher education, on the other hand, aimed to level-up rather than level-down—helping the traditionally disadvantaged improve their college readiness rather than, say, pulling students and resources out of successful school districts.

At the same time, however, the push to expand college enrollment did not, as many equity- and social justice–oriented reforms had, promise to serve everyone. Instead, it sought to work toward the *future* goal of universal postsecondary enrollment, promising immediate benefit for only the academically able. Such an effort appealed to the American ideal of meritocracy while also more or less preserving the status quo. Finally, the move to expand college enrollment often manifested most clearly at the bottom rungs of the system—in community colleges and lower-status state colleges—which did not pose a direct challenge to more privileged families. Some exceptions, like the still-raging debates over affirmative action at schools like the University of California and the University of Michigan, are notable but nevertheless seem to prove the rule.[59]

If increasing access to postsecondary options was the aim, it only seemed to follow that secondary education would need to improve for a large cross section of American students. And this, under different circumstances, might have initiated renewed attempts to pursue controversial policies like reshuffling public school populations. But the integration movement had lost momentum because of strong opposition and limited victories, and the saga of metropolitan busing had alienated not only those who feared its impact but also those whose children it had promised, and so often failed, to help. Consequently, a new call arose for improving the existing schools, segregated or not, in low-income and minority communities, and particularly in building on the successes of alternative school pioneers. The effort to improve low-performing schools appealed to a wide range of constituencies both in and out of low-income urban neighborhoods, from black nationalists to conservative Republicans.

Some conservatives, as early as the late 1970s, had seen these windows of opportunity as means for undermining the political left. Seeking to "advance traditionally liberal ends by conservative means," they favored embracing the moral imperative of the civil rights movement and appealing more directly to the interests of low-income and minority communities.[60] In a widely circulated 1980 report, for instance, Michael Horowitz argued that conservatives needed to seek out "poor clients such as ghetto school children affirmatively interested in the maintenance of internal school discipline" and "ghetto public housing residents" who wished to "re-establish order in their neighborhoods."[61] But despite the resonance such arguments had in some circles, ideologically pluralistic views toward education reform came slowly and somewhat unnaturally to those on the right.

More prominent at the time, particularly after Ronald Reagan's landslide victory over Jimmy Carter in 1980, were those who saw the expansion of civil rights as external to conservatism and the Republican Party. Concerned more with issues like shoring up the nation's economic strength, right-leaning reformers were driven by a "lurking fear that America was slipping" and were alarmed that "many nations" appeared to be "doing better than the United States."[62] And unlike social justice advocates, reform-minded conservatives tended to see the United States as a fair and meritocratic place. As Reagan supporter George Gilder noted, "it would seem genuinely difficult to sustain the idea that America is still oppressive and discriminatory."[63] Still, conservatives were interested in increasing national academic achievement and attainment, which made them more receptive to efforts that would address the failures of schools in low-income and minority neighborhoods.

Although shifting views among conservatives were creating opportunities for bipartisanship, the right remained opposed to the kinds of large-scale government intervention that had long characterized liberal policy. The most vigorous opponents of such efforts were disciples of theorist Milton Friedman, who viewed the market as the most efficient and effective mechanism for social change and who saw in the nation's education system the failure of the "state monopoly" and an inflexible, inflated, and dysfunctional bureaucracy.[64] Such reverence for the free market had for decades been a fringe element of the right wing, but Reagan's election had brought an advocate of markets and privatization into the White House and, as scholar Peter Cookson later wrote, "legitimated a political philosophy."[65] As a result, this brand of thinking began to take root well beyond Pennsylvania Avenue. As the authors of the Carnegie Corporation report *A Nation Prepared: Teachers for the 21st Century* wrote in 1986, for instance, "markets have proven to be very efficient instruments to allocate resources and motivate people in many sectors of American life. . . . They can also make it possible for all public-school students to gain access to equal school resources."[66]

Although aspects of the conservative vision would eventually be accepted by the left, liberals did work to defeat a number of more radical propositions. On the issue of private school vouchers, for instance, a coalition of liberal politicians, educators, and activists rallied together to convince the American public that such a move would place public schools in jeopardy. Similarly, they presented a united front against Reagan's proposed elimination of the Department of Education, keeping him from realizing his campaign promise of transforming it into a foundation for educational assistance. Thus, although they lost the presidency and their majority in the Senate in the early 1980s, Democratic politicians and liberal activists—particularly through the House of Representatives, the American Federation of Teachers, and the National Education Association—were still a formidable opposition. In light of this, more pragmatic conservatives began to construct strategies that would appeal to centrist Democrats or that might circumvent the educational establishment entirely.

As the decade wore on, conservative policy makers refined their political rhetoric, though they continued to favor free markets and small government. Increasingly, they pursued policies in line with the conservative agenda but, as Michael Horowitz had advocated, employed the language of equity and access. Often disillusioned liberals themselves, they criticized the education establishment's "equity agenda" but leveled such criticisms not on the basis that equity was a problematic goal but that the left's methods were inherently flawed. Traditional equity efforts, wrote Chester Finn—a protégé of Democratic senator Daniel Patrick Moynihan—had "much to do with participation and completion rates . . . but . . . very little to do with how much people actually learn."[67] The result, he argued, was that they continued to fail to improve the lot of low-income and minority students.

Two trends, then, were orienting conservatives more toward reforms that at least acknowledged their more liberal counterparts. One was straightforward political expediency in an effort to create a degree of bipartisanship. The second, however, was a genuine belief that improving education for the traditionally underserved would bring about important national outcomes. As John Chubb later recalled, "even though the instrument was planned to be private, we all thought that disadvantaged students were the key group to reach if we wanted schools to make a contribution to the nation."[68] Such divide-bridging thinkers also believed that, given the power of the free market, school reforms targeted at traditionally underserved students could be pursued without threatening more privileged groups and resorting to heavy-handed government intervention. At the same time, they recognized that a large-scale reform effort could not too aggressively attack the education establishment or too clearly reflect ideological extremism. Reform efforts could not, for instance, threaten the existence of the public school system, however much the more doctrinaire among neoconservative free market thinkers would have been pleased with such an outcome. Emerging, consequently, was the idea of promoting excellence for all students via more entrepreneurial practices that would transform local public schools into college prep academies.

This budding approach to educational change was evidenced, though imperfectly, in the rhetoric of the decade's best-known reform document, *A Nation at Risk*. The report, for instance, artfully wove together traditionally opposing aims, promising efficiency and justice, excellence and equity, prosperity and access. "Our concern," its authors wrote, "goes well beyond matters such as industry and commerce." Improving educational outcomes was also essential for preventing the less privileged from becoming further disenfranchised from "the material rewards that accompany competent performance" and "the chance to participate fully in our national life." The answer to the nation's education crisis, they argued, was a higher level of achievement among all American students.[69]

A Nation at Risk was hardly alone in making such a case; a dozen other reports, while less heralded, echoed its findings.[70] Still, *A Nation at Risk* was by far the most visible, galvanizing attention and spurring politicians at the local, state, and national level into action. The original print run of the report sold out, newspapers printed its full text, and commission members were invited to speak on television talk shows.[71] And, though the report was largely a piece of rhetoric, it created, as one author observed, "a useful national debate on the quality of education."[72] Finally, for Ronald Reagan, who was beginning his run for reelection, it presented an opportunity to rebrand himself as an education-minded president. Consequently, he abruptly transformed into a reformer, winning the school issue for Republicans in the 1984 election and bringing educational improvement to the forefront of policy debates. When potential voters were polled in an August 1983 *Newsweek* survey, they ranked "the quality of public education" second only to "economic conditions in the country" among the most pressing issues facing the nation.[73]

A Nation at Risk, and the score of similar reports that preceded and followed it, called for action. And an emerging generation of school reformers was ready to answer that call, proposing consensus-building policy approaches that increasingly sought to "level-up" American public schools. As one New Jersey state senator griped in 1985, "in fulfilling the social mission of the '70s, the schools have failed as academic institutions." The only alternative, he explained, was simple: "excellence for all."[74] Others quickly adopted the phrase.

Reform-minded thinkers also began advancing a new vision for anti-bureaucratic educational change led by those outside the education establishment. The bottom line, according to Frederick Hess, was "that most of the educational establishment—districts, schools, textbook publishers, test companies, and colleges of education—lack[ed] the tools, incentives, opportunities, and personnel to survey the changing educational world and reimagine themselves in a profoundly more effective fashion."[75] Low-performing public high schools—"government schools" as some reformers deridingly referred to them—had failed and should be allowed to go out of business, not simply because they violated free market theory but also because they were failing the nation's neediest children. By that same logic, successful schools, like successful businesses, should be allowed to expand and assisted in replication, not only to better meet the needs of the underserved but to shore up national strength.

Entrepreneurial reformers found a broadly receptive audience in policy circles and, increasingly, among powerful philanthropists who thought about educational change in similar ways and who were willing to fund their efforts.[76] And, somewhat surprisingly, they found an audience among equity advocates frustrated by the long and often fruitless struggle to improve the nation's least privileged schools. Additionally, though much of the reform rhetoric was critical of public school insiders, the movement also found school leaders at the state and local levels who were open to major school change initiatives. Those leaders, after all, particularly in the wake of *A Nation at Risk*, were more than ever before faced with the challenge of improving low-performing schools. As American Federation of Teachers head Albert Shanker noted in 1985, schools were faced with fewer resources and greater demands for improvement—and that made them likely partners for reform efforts.[77] In short, conservatives had successfully expanded the appeal of their school reform movement well beyond the partisan divide.

Conservatives were not alone in reaching across party lines, at least rhetorically. More liberal thinkers in education reform circles, for their part, began to bridge the partisan divide by appealing to "excellence" in their reform proposals. In the Carnegie Foundation study *High School*, for instance, former Carter administration commissioner of education Ernest Boyer observed that "equity and excellence are connected." Expanding access was only the first step toward opportunity for all; the next, he argued, was advancing the quality of education for all students.[78] Others, like scholar Michelle Fine, even went so far as to promote market-oriented reforms—endorsing them and recasting them as tools of a "democratic movement for social change."[79] Both sides, it appeared, had something to gain from resolving historic tensions and creating a postpartisan national school reform movement.

Still, not all reform efforts in the wake of *A Nation at Risk* were consensus-building entrepreneurial efforts seeking to transform urban schools into college-preparatory academies. That vision was still a work in progress and many of the school reforms initiated in the early and mid-1980s remained ideologically skewed. The push for private school vouchers, for instance, had aggravated social justice advocates, access activists, and those skeptical about the beneficence of the free market. Consequently, the vouchers effort had met with great resistance from the more progressive camps in American education. On three separate occasions, the Reagan administration pushed for vouchers and tuition tax credits for private schools. But facing strong opposition, particularly from teachers' unions, the effort never got off the ground and voucher plans were consistently defeated in public referenda.[80]

Despite such fits and starts in the early years of the excellence for all era, intellectually agile policy makers and school reformers adapted both their proposals and the language they used to support them. Reagan's successor, George H. W. Bush, for example, continued to make arguments about the "damaging monopoly power" of the public schools and the benefits of a "marketplace of opportunities."[81] But Bush and his philosophical allies pursued bipartisan support, meeting centrist, market-leaning Democrats in the middle. Such members of the new left, like Arkansas governor Bill Clinton, bemoaned wasteful government and promoted tougher fiscal policies. Others more explicitly sought to "take a more rigorous, business-like approach to public problems by making 'critical infrastructure investments' capable of generating social returns."[82] Thus, as the left moved toward the center, opposition to more entrepreneurial and business-minded approaches to education reform began to dissipate. Leaders on the right, for their part, shrewdly continued to adjust their message and, when necessary, cut their losses.

Perhaps more importantly, the context for policy making continued to change in subtle ways, affecting the way a new generation of leaders would think about school reform. Globalization, once a speculative vision of the future, had become a clear and present reality, and the multidimensional importance of expanding access to higher education was also becoming so prevalent as to, in many cases, become common sense. By the early twenty-first century, for instance, the Phi Delta Kappa / Gallup poll of attitudes toward education found that 75 percent of Americans agreed that "a college education is essential for success in today's world"—a dramatic increase from 58 percent of respondents in 1983 and 36 percent in 1978.[83] Additionally, with each passing year the unrealized struggle for equal educational opportunity disillusioned more educators and policy makers, not to mention parents, with traditional approaches to reform. And, rhetoric about the power of entrepreneurism and the ineffectiveness of bureaucracy continued to shape discussions about the means of pursuing educational change.

Thus, as a new corps of leaders assumed positions of power in government, in nonprofit organizations and philanthropic foundations, and even in school districts themselves, they were remarkably in agreement about the future of American education. They lacked only a road map for how to realize their vision.

EXCELLENCE FOR ALL

By the dawn of the twentieth century's last decade, excellence for all had emerged as a compelling, if not yet coherent, vision among the nation's best-resourced education reformers. Like earlier reformers, they hoped to use schools as a means for solving problems not directly related to education. What distinguished them from their predecessors, however, was the fusion of multiple aims into an objective with no natural opposition—an objective as simple as it was extraordinarily ambitious. By harnessing the power of the market and of free enterprise to promote greater achievement and attainment, particularly among low-income and minority students, reformers believed they would unlock the power of education as a panacea.

Perhaps the clearest manifestation of the evolution of the movement was the revised push for educational choice. Vouchers writ large had failed.

But in a new twist on an old design, the Wisconsin legislature in 1990 approved the nation's first public voucher plan, giving Milwaukee's poorest families, though not their middle- and upper-class counterparts, tuition vouchers to be used in independent and parochial schools. Liberals, social justice advocates, and those striving for greater access could support the plan because it provided greater opportunity for low-income and minority students, while conservatives, social efficiency–minded reformers, small government advocates, and the entrepreneurially minded could support it on the grounds that, unlike busing, it was a market-oriented approach that would have little effect on white suburban families.[84]

As if to confirm the power of this new vision, Minnesota introduced the nation's first charter schools a year later, allowing independent providers to open publicly funded schools that would compete with traditional public schools. The Minnesota charter law cited the need to "provide more quality learning opportunities for more students," and an award subsequently received by the state praised Minnesota for working to expand the opportunities accorded "students of color, low economic class, or with special needs." At the same time, however, the charter law sought to address a threat to the state's economic welfare and received praise from free-market thinkers for circumventing the shortcomings of "the public school bureaucracy."[85] Witnessing Minnesota's success in enacting charter school legislation, dozens of other states soon followed suit.

For market advocates in education reform, voucher and charter school legislation marked major successes, building on successful school-choice experiments in places like Cambridge, Massachusetts, and New York City's District 4. Still, while these efforts engendered optimism, obstacles remained for those hoping to transform America's public schools. For instance, voucher programs, despite some political victories, remained heavily contested, particularly by the nation's largest teachers' union, the National Education Association.[86] While vouchers for low-income students were relatively uncontroversial, vouchers as a wider phenomenon represented a threat to public school funding and any attempt to expand them was certain to meet with major political opposition. Consequently, voucher efforts remained small, limiting their power to grow successful schools and put failing schools out of business.

Still, even if underserved students could be channeled into successful schools, such schools could not realistically accommodate all applicants without being completely transformed in the process. As education policy experts Paul Hill and Mary Beth Celio later observed, "the only way to make such schools available to all children is to create new schools."[87] Charter schools, which *were* new schools, aroused less fierce opposition. But though they infused market-style competition into the public education system and were praised for "cutting through red tape," charters were still faced with the same task as traditional public schools—creating schools that work. And while many charter schools were unquestioned successes, the overall results were highly mixed.[88]

Another potential solution for wide-scale school improvement was the establishment of curricular standards and clear accountability mechanisms. Though such an approach was tied to traditional bureaucratic practices, it nevertheless emerged alongside the voucher and charter movements as a potential means of promoting excellence for all. Like those more market-oriented efforts, the standards and accountability movement promised to serve all students and to strengthen national competitiveness in the process, all without redistributing resources.

Governors and state departments of education were the first to push for the development of curricular standards and accountability mechanisms. Although they initially developed such guidelines, as the Education Commission of the States put it, "primarily as a basis for textbook selection" or "minimum competency testing," they soon sought to "define a curriculum to achieve excellence."[89] As one pair of authors observed in 1986, "bellwether states such as Florida" were taking the lead in such efforts by "moving toward statewide standardization" of the curriculum.[90] Roughly two dozen other states, most of them in the South, also began work on broad comprehensive educational packages that included the strengthening of academic standards.[91]

The standards movement appeared to have traction. In 1986, for instance, E. D. Hirsch of the University of Virginia established his Core Knowledge Foundation under the assumption that the "universal attainment" of a "core of shared knowledge is a necessary step in developing a first-rate educational system."[92] A year later his book *Cultural Literacy: What Every American Needs to Know* became a national best seller. But despite the resonance of such calls to action, policy progress in the diffuse American system was slow.

The standards and accountability movement took a significant step forward in 1989, when President George H. W. Bush convened the nation's governors in Charlottesville, Virginia, to draft a set of goals for American education. What emerged was a plan that participants, including Arkansas governor Bill Clinton, believed would support work already being done at the state level around curricular standards and accountability tests. A year after the summit, the Bush administration announced a new education strategy—"America 2000"—that would, among other things, introduce voluntary American Achievement Tests at grades four, eight, and twelve.[93] In 1991 and 1992, the Department of Education funded efforts to draft national curriculum standards in several subject areas, while the Bush administration worked to move its America 2000 legislation through Congress. After a year of compromise and contention, however, the bill was killed in the Senate. "Republicans don't like 'national,'" reformer Chester Finn observed; "Democrats don't like 'test.'"[94] Perhaps believing that he would have a second term in office, Bush decided to return to the question of education at a later date.

The sinking of America 2000 legislation and George H. W. Bush's loss to Bill Clinton in 1992 did not mark the end of the Charlottesville goals, however. Seeking to create "a vision of excellence and equity" to guide all federal-level education-related programs, the Democratic Clinton administration proposed a state grants program that would support the development of curricular standards and assessments.[95] Framed as a means of serving the national interest as well as the disadvantaged, and designed for maximum spending flexibility, Clinton's "Goals 2000" elicited broad support from "virtually every major education and business organization."[96] In 1994 it was signed into law, providing roughly $2 billion in competitive grants to local school districts between the time of its inception and the end of the century.

By the dawn of the twenty-first century, most states had established content and performance standards, standardized assessments, and systems for data collection.[97] Building on this work and capitalizing on an opportunity to enact major legislation early in his tenure, incoming Republican president George W. Bush pushed forward a sweeping reauthorization of the Elementary and Secondary Education Act. The bill—"No Child Left Behind" (NCLB)—required that states build assessment systems to track the achievement of all students in reading and math standards, that they make "Adequate Yearly Progress" in helping all students meet proficiency goals, and that they report results publicly. Students in failing schools would have the option to exit, and schools that continued to fail would be reorganized or closed.[98]

At least at the federal level, NCLB had bipartisan support and was co-sponsored by Democratic senator Ted Kennedy of Massachusetts. Conservatives liked that the bill promoted curricular standards, encouraged school choice, opened doors for private and for-profit educational organizations, and worked through the states, which would be tasked with instituting statewide accountability systems. Liberals liked that it would continue to channel hundreds of millions of dollars into education, as well as the fact that it would target traditionally underserved groups by requiring that test scores be disaggregated by group based on poverty, race and ethnicity, disability, and limited English proficiency; it also required that low-income students from low-achieving schools be given priority in school transfers and supplemental services. And, unlike more open-ended bills like Goals 2000, NCLB tied funding to clearly delineated state responsibilities and strong accountability mechanisms.

Bush played on the political moment at a time when the idea of promoting excellence for all students had gained rhetorical prominence. But while NCLB won overwhelming support at the federal level—passing by votes of 381–41 and 87–10 in the House and Senate, respectively—it struck a sour note. NCLB, despite its strengths, failed to tap into the unifying vision of successful school replication. Unlike purer incarnations of excellence for all, NCLB promised only to establish a floor for performance, and one that would be measured by standardized tests at that. As Barack Obama's secretary of education, Arne Duncan, put it, "the biggest problem with NCLB is that it doesn't encourage high learning standards. In fact, it inadvertently encourages states to lower them."[99] Thus, by defining success so narrowly and by seeking to promote proficiency rather than "excellence," NCLB failed to galvanize widespread and long-term support.

With goals perceived as too modest and too specific, and accountability mechanisms perceived as too strong, NCLB was frequently viewed in the harshest possible light. Those on the right began to see the law as a clumsy federal intervention that failed to infuse schools with new ideas, talent, or leadership. As Diane Ravitch noted, "under NCLB, the federal government was dictating ineffectual remedies, which had no track record of success."[100] And as former Republican majority leader Tom DeLay grumbled, "I came here to eliminate the Department of Education, so it was very hard for me to vote for something that expands [it]."[101] Those on the left saw it as a punitive legislative mandate distracting from the real business of schooling. Rather than building capacity, NCLB merely threatened to close schools, demoralize teachers, and further widen the gulf between the privileged and the less advantaged. As a statement from the National Education Association framed it, NCLB outlined reasonable goals, but the "test-and-punish" approach" of the law "does not move us toward those goals."[102] A statement signed by 144 education-related organizations made the case that Congress should "replace sanctions that do not have a consistent record of success with interventions that enable schools to make changes that result in improved student achievement."[103] Whatever its strengths, NCLB struck the wrong notes with too many powerful constituencies and proved more divisive than unifying.

Meanwhile, however, other reformers were tapping into the heart of the era, capturing the spirit of the age. Their approaches were no more objectively right or wrong than NCLB; in fact, much of the rhetoric they employed was the same. But they were politically more apt. Thus, while educators and reformers were throwing stones over NCLB, a new core of entrepreneurially minded reformers worked in a virtually conflict-free—and thus, quieter—environment. They built powerful coalitions, launched nationwide initiatives, and began to shape the way future reformers would approach the question of school improvement.

Learning from the failures of voucher proponents, the limitations of charter schools, and the miscues of the standards and accountability movement, entrepreneurial reformers offered a different means of realizing the vision of excellence for all. Applying the concept of "what works"—an idea with free enterprise at its heart—they argued that the market would reveal the most effective mechanisms for improving schools. Focused on the language of consumer choice and "common sense," such a vision represented a distinct departure from a long tradition of legalistic and bureaucratic solutions to the nation's school problem. But their approach also had idealism at its core. The market would not simply let a thousand flowers bloom while some areas withered and died. Rather, it would function as a laboratory for reform-minded leaders willing to look beyond traditional approaches in order to find the key to school transformation. Consequently, unlike the standards and choice movements, this approach to reform appealed to educators because it promised to show them how to improve children's lives. Even better, it promised to make educators' jobs easier, their working conditions better, and their organizations more effective.

By looking at schools that worked, these entrepreneurial reformers reasoned, they could glean lessons that might then be applied in struggling schools. Such a straightforward approach, of course, was not entirely new. What was new, however, was the scale at which reformers intended to work. In the excellence for all era, any answer to the public education problem—portrayed as an imminent nationwide crisis—needed to be systemic, bringing about improvements not just in one school or for a handful of needy students, but for all students. Future education secretary Arne Duncan would later neatly sum up the scope of the mission: "the goal shouldn't be to save a handful of children."[104] Further, if the aim was to promote excellence among all students, reformers would need to determine what excellence looked like. The task was as straightforward as it was Herculean: determine the components of successful schools and implement them on a national level.

In search of scalable solutions, entrepreneurial reformers looked for "emerging models of excellence" in American education.[105] Research on effective schools had begun in the 1970s with the work of scholars like George Weber and Ronald Edmonds. Unlike many researchers in the wake of the Coleman report, they argued that the success of a school was in fact not always dependent on the socioeconomic status of its students.[106] Thus, by 1980, the new field of effective schools research sought to "ascertain if any truly exemplary schools exist after controlling for socioeconomic status" and, if so, "to determine what characteristics of these exemplars differentiate them from average or negative outlying schools." Such research further sought to determine if exemplary schools had "a consistent and generalizable pattern that accounts for their distinguishing characteristics"— findings that would be extremely useful to those seeking to replicate successful schools.[107] Still, such work had gone relatively unnoticed on the national policy level.

A separate branch of "what works" research focusing on the work of elite private schools went back even earlier than the 1970s. In the early 1950s, for example, school critics like Arthur Bestor had begun comparatively analyzing the work of public and private schools, finding the latter worthy of not only praise, but emulation. Bestor argued that policy makers needed to "learn to make comparisons, not with the wretchedly inadequate public schools of earlier generations, but with the very best schools, public or private, American or foreign, past or present."[108] Still, critics like Bestor, who saw great flaws in the public system, never went so far as to articulate lessons taught by the elite schools he praised.

By the 1980s and 1990s, however, the national education policy-making environment had shifted, becoming more receptive to market-based thinking and more oriented toward identifying models of excellence that could be taken to scale. Revealingly, more research began to directly examine what made certain schools effective. Even more telling was an emerging body of scholarship that studied what its authors often called models of excellence in plain view: America's independent and parochial schools. Decades after

Bestor published *Educational Wastelands*, dozens of studies by authors of various political leanings and employing a wide range of methodologies sought to find concrete lessons offered by private schools—lessons that might then be applied on a nationwide scale.[109] And in 1984, the U.S. Department of Education conducted its first annual "Exemplary Private School Recognition Project," which, according to Secretary of Education Terrel H. Bell, "distinguished schools that are doing an exceptionally fine job, so we can focus on what they are doing that is right."[110]

Although perhaps not immediately striking, the relatively sudden emergence of such work into the mainstream signaled a growing concern with finding replicable models of success, as well as an increasing willingness to look beyond district-run public schools for such models. By the dawn of the new century, references to models of educational success, many of them private schools, would be commonplace. As Tom Vander Ark of the Gates Foundation observed in 2003, his work in crafting reform efforts had been inspired by "pockets of excellence" in American education that included "a century of success in private education," the work of "urban Catholic schools," and "highly successful charter schools."[111] Public or private, entrepreneurial reformers were concerned with one thing: what works.

While such thinking arose organically out of the policy-making context of the century's last decades, it was advanced and accelerated by an ambitious group of philanthropists. Reform-minded billionaires such as Bill Gates, Eli Broad, and Michael Dell, like previous philanthropists, wanted to make tangible contributions to American public education. But while earlier philanthropic work in education had generally been devoted to "helping schools do what they were already doing," these "new" philanthropists—as journalist Richard Lee Colvin has called them—were more interested in disrupting the status quo.[112] Further, whereas earlier philanthropically funded efforts had been characterized by an "emphasis on piecemeal accomplishments," these deep-pocketed benefactors were more focused on "systematic impact and replicable models"—much as they had been in their work in the private sector.[113]

Worth noting is the fact that many of these increasingly prominent educational entrepreneurs, whether in foundations, think tanks, government, or school districts, had firsthand experiences with high-status schools. To be clear, they were no more likely to possess elite educational backgrounds than reformers and policy makers in previous eras had been. But in earlier eras such experiences had been irrelevant for reformers working to improve urban public schooling. They were not, after all, striving to transform schools for the underserved into high-performance college-preparatory academies, but rather to create "appropriate" schooling experiences for low-income and minority students. As reformers increasingly sought to erase the gap between privileged schools and their urban public counterparts, however, those experiences became more pertinent. Already inclined to see education through a corporate lens, many were also drawn to the idea that their experiences could be learned from and should be shared.

In the midst of an emerging consensus around the excellence for all agenda and the means of enacting it, there were those whose enthusiasm was tempered. Researchers, for instance, did not immediately or unequivocally jump on board: reproducing effective schools, they argued, proved no easy task in controlled studies. As one pair of authors noted in 1985, "many schools . . . need concrete, practical models for change." Yet, "the relatively small number of schools found . . . to exhibit extraordinary improvement indicate that necessary methods are neither very widespread nor obvious."[114] Another pair of researchers publishing in the same volume did find aspects that led to effective schooling. However, their expansive list consisted of thirteen different and "interrelated" aspects of schooling: no simple solution.[115] Such findings in education research often frustrated reformers. Some researchers would find particular practices effective, only to have others find them not to be. Or, more frequently, they would find effective practices but insist that they were contingent upon a swarm of other factors. Results were almost always mixed, or, if not, they were inseparable from a host of criteria like school leadership and parent involvement—aspects much more difficult to promote in schools than, say, curricular standards.

Many educational entrepreneurs found such complicated findings to be unhelpful. Frequently, they leveled the criticism that the educational establishment, particularly researchers in schools of education, had long proved ineffective at inspiring change. While some took aim at the methodological training of education researchers, others argued that the problem was with university settings where, as one pair of scholars put it, "new theory development is more valued than practical solutions to real problems."[116] As a consequence, entrepreneurial education policy makers concerned with getting to work on fixing America's schools saw research as, at best, a secondary factor in decision making and, at worst, an obstacle to be overcome.

Although educational entrepreneurs were not ideologically opposed to research, they did not intend to let a thin research base or inconclusive results prevent them from seeking solutions to school problems. Perceiving a gulf between the worlds of research and practice, they frequently turned instead to professional organizations, advocacy groups, and peer networks for ostensibly more practical, if less research-based, forms of evidence.[117] In cases where little scholarship was available, they often used observational research, citing the work of private, parochial, or charter schools in their calls for replicating successful models.[118] When they did use more formal education research, it was frequently as a means of justifying favored approaches, assembling a body of positive findings, as scholars David Cohen and Michael Garet once wrote, "to rationalize political life by providing evidence for decisions."[119] Ultimately, believing that "expertise, resources, and research offer no guarantees," educational entrepreneurs pursued their own "common sense" solutions without fear or hesitation.[120] As one venture philanthropist recalled, a fairly typical funding decision was made based not on research, but on belief. "When we made our first investment," she noted, "none of the research had come out."[121] Free from the educational establishment at last, excellence for all reformers planned to make their own distinct mark on the nation's schools. And with a big-tent message, they would.

A NEW REFORM PARADIGM

At the end of the twentieth century and into the early years of the next, the battle cry of America's most visible and best-resourced education reformers was "excellence for all." Having addressed most of the obstacles preventing major national school reform efforts, and having identified a means toward their ambitious end, entrepreneurial leaders advocated for and funded projects designed to bring aspects of elite-level education to distinctly non-elite populations. As one pair of researcher-advocates put it, "what historically we have asked for only a modest portion of students has now become a universal goal."[122] The message was infectious.

Many urban school leaders continued to do the day-to-day work they had always done, guided first and foremost by steady pragmatism. Nevertheless, they pursued the grants and resources available, particularly if they believed that such efforts would help them to fill classrooms, interest students, and send a message to parents to continue enrolling their children. Under pressure to increase performance in low-performing urban schools, many districts also began to seek out new kinds of leaders whose visions were as ambitious as those of outside reformers. With school districts across the nation willing to experiment, leaders in government creating capacity for large-scale change efforts, and billionaire philanthropists willing to fund high-impact ventures, the movement exploded.

With experiments evolving in urban districts across the nation and with educational entrepreneurs having assumed leadership positions in government, philanthropic organizations, and school districts, a new reform paradigm took hold. By the turn of the new century, the excellence for all movement was widely accepted, deeply influencing a new generation of educators, policy makers, and school reformers. Typical of this approach to education reform was the articulated mission of the Philanthropy Roundtable, an organization "committed to whatever works in raising the academic achievement of all American children, especially low-income and minority children." The organization's goal, like that of many other groups involved in education, was to achieve "systemic reform through competition and parental choice, freedom and accountability for schools, excellent teachers and leaders, and high standards and expectations for students of all backgrounds."[123] Excellence for all was at last a complete vision.

Reformers in the excellence for all era, whatever their particular ideologies, were remarkably united in their belief that America's urban public schools could be transformed into college preparatory academies—schools that would address the needs of both the nation and the traditionally underserved. "If your parents are poor, you need a good education in order to have the equal opportunity that our founders promoted for every citizen," Bill Gates declared in 2009. At the same time, he added, "we believe improving education is the key to retaining our position of world leadership in all areas, including starting great businesses and doing innovative research."[124] Committed to "what works" and seeking systemwide change efforts, the most ambitious reformers in the twenty-first century pursued the mission of excellence for all as if no alternative existed.

This work is the story, through three illustrative cases, of how a broad coalition of traditionally separate interest groups was united behind an idea—an idea uniquely suited to the needs and concerns of the late twentieth century and early twenty-first. The results would frequently be mixed, plagued by problematic consequences, and often revealing inherent challenges to the broader aims of excellence for all. But to the entrepreneurial reformers who led the push for excellence for all, such challenges were simply obstacles to be overcome, not indicators of any endemic flaws. Led by a dynamic corps of committed believers and characterized by powerful rhetoric that unified seemingly disparate groups, the movement continued to inspire visions of an America remade by its schools.

2

THE RIGHT SPACE

The Small Schools Movement

IN THE LAST DECADES of the twentieth century, education reformers made the case that America's urban public high schools had reached a point of intolerable failure. In an era in which higher education was being more frequently seen as a prerequisite for active economic participation, reformers bemoaned urban public schools as outdated and inadequate for the task. Achievement was down. Violence was up. Graduation rates hovered around 50 percent. And college-going rates, on which both social justice and social efficiency advocates had become fixated, were usually in the single digits.

The situation looked even worse when urban schools were measured alongside the nation's most successful high schools. Such schools graduated all their seniors each year and sent a wide cross section of them off to the Ivy League. And they did so for their tuition-paying pupils as well as for their low-income and minority students on scholarship. To the casual observer it seemed clear: some schools simply did it better.

Although top schools were different in a number of distinct ways from their urban public counterparts, the most obvious and stark difference—at least in the eyes of some—was the size of the facilities. While top private schools were characterized by intimate, nurturing environments, urban public high schools looked more like factories and prisons. Further, while elite schools served students by the hundreds, urban comprehensive high schools were populated by casts of thousands. In 1994, the average New York City high school had 2,200 students.[1] New York private schools Horace Mann, Dalton, and Riverdale, by contrast, had an average of roughly 600. Smaller elite New York prep schools, like Spence and Calhoun, had an average of 200.

Other differences clearly mattered. Top private schools, among other things, generally worked with highly privileged populations, which no

41

doubt accounted for much of their superior performance. Yet a number of urban parochial schools and charter schools were experiencing success while working with students quite similar to those found in typical public schools. And, like top private schools, they were often characterized by enrollments small enough that faculty knew all their students by name. Perhaps, some thought, many of the problems of urban public education could be traced back to the nature of their facilities.

The comprehensive high school, some reformers began to argue, was a vestige of a previous era and a flawed vision. Midcentury policy leaders like James Conant had pushed to create schools that would train some students vocationally, provide a general education to most, and prepare a small number for college—a once appropriate, if somewhat undemocratic, goal.[2] Large high schools would promote wider course offerings, greater opportunities for specialization, and, supporters claimed, economies of scale. By the 1980s, however, educators like Deborah Meier were arguing that whatever the comprehensive high school did well, its day was over. It failed to help all children learn.

The idea of creating smaller schools had a broad appeal. Liberal social justice advocates saw in small schools the potential to promote community, increase access, and advance educational equity. More conservative school critics, on the other hand, saw the chance to increase achievement and stave off the social and economic consequences of low school performance, all without resorting to contested methods like metropolitan busing. Thus, though its particular appeal differed from constituency to constituency, the small schools movement drew in supporters from both the right and the left while stirring little opposition.

Among those particularly interested in the potential of small schools was a new breed of reformers whose concern for democratic equity was not separate from the goal of workforce preparation. For them, fairness and national strength demanded the same thing: that all students be prepared for twenty-first-century jobs. In small schools they saw a chance to advance that hybrid aim, believing that such settings would raise student achievement and college-going rates by expanding a model its champions argued had long promoted excellence.

But small schools had an additional draw for educational entrepreneurs. Inclined to favor market-based solutions, such reformers saw small schools as antibureaucratic "start-ups" with a certain commonsense appeal. Further, they represented the sort of replicable model that scale-obsessed reformers were looking for. Although the initial research base on small schools was relatively thin, the small schools that existed—many of them highly regarded independent schools that reformers themselves had attended—functioned as concrete evidence of an imagined possibility: a nationwide network of top-flight public academies. Eventually more research emerged, though much of it was mixed; by that time, however, the notion that small is good had become something close to folk wisdom. With billions in financial backing, the movement swept across the nation.

At the end of the twentieth century and the beginning of the twenty-first, educational entrepreneurs pursued smaller schools with increasing aggressiveness, eventually creating hundreds of public high schools that looked like the successful schools they had been modeled on. And yet, despite their accomplishments, they were markedly less effective in bridging the achievement gap. Tens of thousands of students from underserved communities attended newly created small schools; yet big or small, the schools in urban areas continued to lag far behind.

This chapter examines the small schools movement from its origins in the alternative schools effort through its peak in the early twenty-first century. Why, it asks, did small schools become a cornerstone in the pursuit of excellence for all? What were the movement's shortcomings? And what does its story reveal about this unique era of school reform?

MODERN, EFFICIENT, BIGGER

Before it was associated with failure, the large urban high school symbolized progress. At the dawn of the twentieth century, thousands of schools were still small, and frequently one-room, facilities. But despite their long histories, such schools were portrayed with increasing frequency as impediments to development. They lacked systematic quality-control methods, they allowed untrained teachers to use outdated methods, and many were in states of disrepair.

The size divide, not surprisingly, broke along geographic lines, with urban schools dwarfing their rural counterparts. In 1914, public high schools in cities with populations of 8,000 or more had an average of 668 students enrolled, compared to high schools in municipalities with populations less than 8,000, which had an average of 62 students enrolled.[3] Urban high schools were better resourced, had teachers with more training, and were more effectively managed than rural schools, or so the argument went.

Consequently, emulating urban schools represented one natural solution to the perceived crisis in rural schooling.

Another major aim in consolidation efforts was the diversification of the curriculum to better prepare students for their future roles in life. Few were bound for college, which might demand knowledge of subjects like Latin and Greek; all, however, would go on to some form of work. In a 1912 speech before the U.S. Senate, Carroll Smalley Page made the case for social efficiency–minded education reform, stating that he, like many, "would have every boy thoroughly educated." Such a prospect, however, was inefficient if not impossible. Thus, he argued, "since this can not be, let us be practical . . . [and] teach him how to get a living."[4] Smalley's sentiment reflected widespread concern with the social efficiency aim of sorting students for their perceived futures—something small, locally controlled schools were failing to do.

Reformers agreed on a set of remedies for rural education problems, among which were moves to consolidate schools, transport pupils, and bring in expert supervision by county superintendents. Consequently, small schools, attacked as "inefficient, short-sighted, and unprogressive," began to give way to larger ones in the hope that the result would be something more modern, efficient, and socially useful.[5] District superintendents across the nation supported the consolidation of both schools and districts, and, in the decades that followed, rural schools began to resemble their larger urban counterparts.

In the wake of the Second World War, building larger schools became an urban concern. In part, this was driven by the need to accommodate higher enrollments, triggered by a larger youth population and a broader cross section of young people delaying work to stay in school. Yet the overriding aim remained that of social efficiency, which required that schools prepare students for the workforce. As one author reminded school leaders, for many students "high school is the last steppingstone before entering the work world," and only a large school could provide a differentiated experience to prepare them for their different futures.[6] Thus, reformers believed that big urban high schools needed to be made even bigger.

It was in this context that James Conant established himself as the ideological leader of the large schools movement. Conant, former president of Harvard University, was a strong believer in tracking, particularly insofar as it promoted social efficiency. In the context of the Cold War, he argued that even larger schools were required to serve low-achieving students by providing them a wide array of vocational training opportunities. Further, such schools would also better serve high-achieving students by providing them with an ever-wider range of advanced courses and access to the best teachers. In *The American High School Today*, Conant wrote that small schools were "not in a position to provide a satisfactory education for any group of their students—the academically talented, the vocationally oriented, or the slow reader."[7] The larger the school, the better it could perform this task.

Conant was not alone in calling for larger high schools, and within a decade such criticisms of smaller high schools became relatively common. Equity advocate Arnold Rose, for instance, argued in 1967 that in order to encourage integration, every high school should be excellent. Consequently, small schools would need to be consolidated into larger ones. The notion that "a good school is a small school," Rose wrote, "is patently untrue at the secondary level, where quality of education is associated with a wide range of course offerings and with costly equipment, both of which are feasible only in heavily populated schools." Small schools, he continued, "can claim no benefit toward quality education" and should be consolidated in order to "improve the quality of educational offerings and make it much easier to find the residential mix so as to break up racial imbalance in the schools."[8]

But hardly any research accompanied these arguments for larger high schools. In fact, in one of the few evidence-based attempts to gauge the impact of school size, Roger Barker and Paul Gump found little to support the expansion of the comprehensive high school.[9] Instead, they discovered that small high schools offered more than their size might have indicated. In terms of "interior characteristics not easily seen from the outside," they found that small schools were surprisingly similar to large schools and produced surprisingly similar experiences for students.[10] In the end, they concluded that the research available could not answer the many questions surrounding the school size issue. But that, of course, would not prevent schools from growing even larger. The movement was spurred not by evidence, but by a then-commonly held belief about the problematic nature of small schools.

Other reformers and practitioners continued to echo and answer Conant's call for the comprehensive high school. Between 1950 and 1965, high schools grew from an average of just more than four hundred students per school to more than seven hundred.[11] While the largest schools in urban areas had enrollments in the thousands as early as the 1930s, such supersized high schools became more common both in cities and out. Very quickly, students began to attend schools that were "large and complex organiza-tions," with "vice-principals, deans," and "heads of departments."[12] And, by 1980, 65 percent of the nation's public high schools had enrollments of more than one thousand students, 20 percent of which enrolled more than two thousand students. By contrast, high-performance private schools uniformly enrolled between one hundred and five hundred students.[13]

But facility size was not the only major change urban high schools un-derwent in the second half of the twentieth century. As urban centers in the 1960s and 1970s began hemorrhaging their white middle- and upper-class populations, the student population in urban schools became more and more uniformly low-income and minority.[14] In turn, comprehensive high schools were serving not only greater numbers of underserved students, but also higher concentrations of them. Not surprisingly, they developed the highest dropout rates, the lowest test scores, and the lowest rates of advance-ment to postsecondary education.[15]

Whatever the promise of the comprehensive high school had been, by 1980 it was the site of low achievement scores and large numbers of low-income and minority students. Consequently, large schools became a target for a number of reform efforts, few of which would be as visible as the effort to make big schools small.

SOCIAL JUSTICE IN CENTRAL PARK

By the 1960s and 1970s, an increasing number of educators concerned with social justice began to rethink the American high school. Rather than sorting students for their perceived futures, they were determined to focus on the unique needs of underserved students. Consequently, they sought to create smaller "alternative" schools that would provide an "articulate op-position to normal public and private school education."[16] According to au-thor and educator Jonathan Kozol, alternative schools would exist outside of "the public education apparatus," doing whatever it would take to help students who had slipped through the cracks in other schools.[17]

Made up of a broad and diverse group of educators, the alternative schools movement also contained within it those who aimed to promote social justice by focusing on academic rigor. Among the alternative schools with this aim, none would be more widely acclaimed than Deborah Meier's Central Park East (CPE) schools—an elementary school founded in 1974 and a high school founded ten years later with the aid of Ted Sizer's newly formed Coalition of Essential Schools.

Central Park East was a unique school that, like most alternative schools, did a number of things quite differently than comprehensive high schools. According to Deborah Meier, the school was "led by people who represent the values of the school itself . . . [whose] task involves raising issues, provoking reflection, inspiring people, holding up standards of work and competence."[18] CPE teachers were "instrumental in decisions about curriculum and assessment," were "involved in hiring their colleagues and providing ongoing support to them," and "kept extensive notes and records of children's work, continuously experimenting with better ways to keep and use such information."[19] Large urban public schools, by contrast, were organizationally complex bureaucracies with the least-experienced teachers and, by some measures, the least-engaging curriculum.[20]

Like other alternative schools, CPE was small, autonomous, democratically operated, and focused on the unique needs of the underserved. But Meier and her colleagues sought to promote social justice not only by reaching out to poor and minority students, but also by preparing them for college.

Such a vision had an obvious attraction for social justice advocates, but by the early 1980s it also began to resonate among those concerned with social efficiency. As the authors of the *A Nation at Risk* report had observed, "more and more young people [were] emerg[ing] from high school ready neither for college nor for work."[21] But even readiness for work was becoming dependent on possession of a college degree. Manufacturing jobs were being outsourced overseas while white-collar employment opportunities were expanding, and the American high school had not adjusted to that reality.

Despite the fact that schools like CPE were characterized by a range of unique characteristics, one difference was immediately obvious in comparison with large urban high schools: size. CPE worked with certified New York public school teachers, low-income New York students, and public school funding. Only two quantifiable factors distinguished CPE from typical New York City high schools—it was a fraction of the size of typical schools, and it produced remarkable achievement scores and graduation rates.[22] Meier was quick to point out the connection, believing that small schools were an "absolute prerequisite" for educating all students well.[23] And she was certainly not alone. Writing in 1991, for instance, education writer Thomas Toch observed that "the majority of the public junior and senior high schools in the United States are drab, uninviting institutions, almost prisonlike, with cinderblock walls and long, often ill-lit corridors that are commonly cordoned by heavy metal gates at the end of the day. The coldness and impersonality of such surroundings is heightened by the huge size of many schools."[24]

The Central Park East schools and a crop of similar "urban acade-mies"—many of which were supported by Sizer's Coalition for Essential Schools—soon began to attract the attention of education reformers. Such schools produced high achievement scores and college-going rates. They increased opportunity for the underserved without resorting to heavy-handed interventions. They promoted school choice. And, they seemed to have learned from America's most successful schools; as Meier put it, the Central Park East schools followed "in the tradition of many of New York's independent private schools, a tradition few believed was appropriate for public education."[25]

Perhaps most importantly, they seemed to simultaneously promote both social justice and social efficiency aims. As scholar Michelle Fine wrote, "many in the small schools movement originally conceived the schools as a movement for educational justice. Like the Mississippi Freedom Schools and the best of popular education, these small schools take questions of social justice and responsibility seriously, in the classroom and beyond."[26] At the same time, though, the small schools movement ignited the imagina-tions of those traditionally attracted to social efficiency–oriented reforms by promising to reduce social ills and increase American competitiveness.

Small schools, most of which were private schools or charter schools, also seemed to square with the antibureaucratic and market-oriented per-spectives of educational entrepreneurs. According to Deborah Meier, the small schools movement was a response to the "complex bureaucracy" in American education that promoted "a one-size-fits-all curriculum . . . [in order to] more easily grade, measure, and categorize" children.[27] And, as Michelle Fine observed, many began to see small schools as promot-ing "'educational entrepreneurship,' reflecting an assumption that public schools should become more like private businesses."[28] To market-oriented reformers, small schools presented an opportunity to advance "privatization and voucher schemes that seek to replace public education with a market system or turn schools over to for-profit management firms."[29] Small thus also became bound up with free-market ideas like competition and disdain for bureaucracy.

Though advocates like Meier and Sizer were strong supporters of scaling down the nation's high schools, they did caution against trying to replicate the small school model, which involved a number of complex factors. In the early 1990s Meier echoed her warning to those who would try to reproduce her schools, writing that they "are not meant to be copied piece by piece." Observing that "the current reform mood" offered an opening, she nevertheless maintained that educators must "resist the desire for a new 'one best way,' for new cookie-cutter solutions that can be easily 'replicated.'"[30] Stopping short of saying it could not be done, Meier explained that what made CPE a great school was not any one particular reform. Monumental school change required a range of factors such as a committed and involved faculty.[31] Still, she continued to promote size as a key issue in school improvement.

Sizer echoed Meier's stance that size was only a part of a larger whole. Good schools, he wrote in 1992,

> are thoughtful places. The people in them are known. The units are small enough to be coherent communities of friends. Amenities are observed. There are quiet places available as well as places for socializing. No one is ridiculed. No one is the servant of another. The work is shared. The entire place is thoughtful: everything in its routines meets a standard of common sense and civility. At such places do adolescents learn about the thoughtful life.[32]

Consequently, Sizer's Coalition for Essential Schools established a host of guidelines that included rules such as "teaching and learning should be personalized to the maximum feasible extent," "no teacher [should] have direct responsibility for more than eighty students," and "staff should expect multiple obligations . . . and a sense of commitment to the entire school.[33] In short, Sizer, the former headmaster of Phillips Andover, painted a picture of a typically successful independent school.[34] And, like Meier, he believed that smallness was a necessary, though not sufficient, condition for success.

Creating good schools, at least according to school leaders like Meier and Sizer, was complicated but not impossible. If the right personnel were paired with the right systems and structures, they argued, all children could achieve. But it was the structural element that would gain particular prominence in years to follow, perhaps because making schools smaller was so straightforward a proposition, or perhaps because the effect of school size seemed so easily observable. Large urban public high schools could be

frightening and dangerous places. On the other hand, small high schools—
private schools, small parochial schools, and emerging charter schools—
were intimate and caring settings, which also seemed to foster high achievement scores. For some the answer seemed obvious: make it smaller.

IN SEARCH OF EMPIRICAL EVIDENCE

Research on school size was limited in the 1980s and early 1990s, as it had
been in previous decades. Yet the few existing studies on size did generally corroborate common-sense notions about small schools. On the whole,
small schools seemed to be correlated with positive educational outcomes.

Many studies that found school size to be a salient factor were, in fact,
studies of private school effectiveness. Because most nonrural small high
schools were independent or parochial schools, conducting apples-to-apples
comparisons was a challenging proposition.[35] In 1982, for instance, sociologist James Coleman and his colleagues found private schools to be more effective institutions than public schools, and they noted size among the key
differences between private schools and their public counterparts.[36] Other
researchers exploring the effectiveness of private schools identified school
culture as a distinctive factor in student success and speculated that size
was a necessary requirement in crafting a thoughtful and supportive school
culture.[37] Still, despite the promise of many positive findings, the extent to
which they applied to public schools was questionable.

But there were also studies that looked specifically at small public
schools, many of which seemed to confirm the promise of size reductions.
Some researchers found that small schools could craft and maintain a common message about appropriate behavior more effectively than a large
school.[38] Other researchers found that small schools were associated with
factors like better attendance.[39] And some found higher levels of teacher
morale in small schools than in large ones.[40]

More importantly, though, some researchers, using a wide range of
methodologies, began to make the case that small schools increased student
achievement. Anthony Bryk and Mary Erina Driscoll, for instance, found a
correlation between greater gains in math and smaller high schools.[41] Mary
Anne Raywid found small schools related to greater student participation
and attendance, which she connected with the potential to "enhance academic achievement."[42] A handful of studies supported that belief, finding
small schools to be strongly associated with greater achievement.[43] Other

promising research found achievement effects to be particularly strong for students from disadvantaged backgrounds.[44] But perhaps most attractive of all was the work that found small schools to be correlated with higher graduation rates and matriculation to college.[45] For both social efficiency and social justice advocates, this represented the ultimate aim of late twentieth-century school reform.

Not all the research on small schools, however, was positive. Analyzing data from the National Educational Longitudinal Study, Valerie Lee and Julia Smith found that schools with six hundred to twelve hundred students showed slightly higher gains in reading and math achievement than schools that were smaller or larger. Schools with enrollments less than six hundred—enrollments small schools supporters were advocating—were too small, they found, to offer substantial curricular diversity, even if they had lower dropout rates.[46]

Small, in short, was good—except when it was not. Other research told a similar story. According to Kathleen Cotton's 1996 review of previous work on the subject, "about half the student achievement research [found] no difference between the achievement levels of students in large and small schools." Consequently, Cotton warned that "achievement may not only be a result of smallness, but connected to other variables such as environment and attachment."[47] These findings are particularly notable given the fact that Cotton's study is the foundational piece of research for a number of small schools efforts. The Chicago Public Schools website, for instance, notes that each section of its "Small Schools Research" page begins "with an excerpt from Kathleen Cotton's 1996 review of research to provide a summary of small schools findings."[48] Needless to say, the excerpts used are those portraying small schools in the most positive light possible.

A number of studies found small schools relatively ineffective at promoting achievement. None, however, found that small schools had a dramatically *negative* effect on achievement. Consequently, many small schools supporters felt comfortable saying that student achievement in small schools was at least equal to, and often better than, achievement in large schools.[49]

But for many reformers, research was a secondary issue. They did, of course, begin to reference an empirical basis for their efforts; doing so, after all, had become a requisite move in establishing outward-facing legitimacy. Yet advocates could often find at least one piece of research to support whatever claim they wanted to make. More influential, it seems, was the fact that creating smaller schools was becoming a matter of common sense.

GOING SMALL

Small schools advocates had a number of reasons to believe in their effort. Many already had positive feelings about small schools, rooted in observations of and experiences with America's successful private and parochial schools. Added to any such sentiments were widely publicized examples of successful small public charter schools, not to mention the body of research indicating that size did matter. Acting on their beliefs, a coalition of social justice–and social efficiency–motivated leaders took action with the support of entrepreneurial foundations and school district leaders. In so doing, they created dozens of small schools or schools-within-schools— semiautonomous units within large comprehensive high schools—in the 1990s.

Some of the earliest advocacy for small schools as a means of promoting excellence for all took place in Chicago. In 1991 William Ayers and Michael Klonsky secured foundation support to found the Small Schools Workshop at the University of Illinois at Chicago. The workshop's goal was to support "Chicago's reform-minded teachers" with information and assistance "as they tried to create new, smaller learning communities in an environment that was historically toxic."[50] According to Ayers and Klonsky, the small schools movement was "connected with the issues of social justice, equity, and community . . . [and] offered a strategy for engaging teachers, students, parents, and whole communities . . . in a movement for democratic education."[51] With the help of the Quest Center, the professional development arm of the Chicago Teachers' Union, the Small Schools Workshop began bringing activist educators and principals into the movement.

But advocates like Ayers and Klonsky were not simply promoting community building. Small schools also meant increased achievement. And, insofar as that was the case, members of Chicago's business community took interest. Soon, reform groups like Leadership for Quality Education and Business and Professional People for the Public Interest (BPI) began looking more deeply into small schools. Alexander Polikoff, head of BPI at the time, visited several small schools in Harlem and was won over. They served low-income and minority students, they got results, and they were small. "Logically," he recalled, "it made good sense." Under Polikoff, BPI joined community groups in advocating for small schools and soon began sponsoring teacher and principal trips to visit model schools in New York.[52] Along with the Small Schools Workshop, the Quest Center, and several other organizations, they formed the Small Schools Coalition to mobilize further support for small schools in Chicago.[53]

Support for the creation of small schools also came from district leadership. In 1994, Polikoff and other reformers delivered a report to the district and requested formal backing for small schools. Although the group found a receptive audience, it was not until the passage of the Chicago School Reform Act a year later that policies began to change. The act gave Mayor Richard M. Daley control over the schools, and Daly responded by appointing a new five-member School Reform Board of Trustees and a management team led by Chief Executive Officer Paul Vallas.[54] Small schools advocates moved quickly and called on new School Reform Board president Gery Chico to support their efforts.[55] That same year, the new board issued a resolution stating its commitment to small schools: "Whereas, both educational literature and experience in other school systems, as well as some early experience in Chicago, establish that Small Schools are a hopeful avenue for the improvement of urban public education at both elementary and high school levels . . . the Trustees are committed to the goal of assisting the formation and strengthening of Small Schools in Chicago."[56]

The board's resolution was followed by a request for proposals, and it subsequently awarded twenty-four grants for the planning and start-up of new small schools. A year later, in 1996, the state of Illinois passed charter legislation to create new public schools free of all central office mandates other than accountability in finance and performance. The new law made it even easier to start new small schools. All that the district needed was a grant large enough to begin going to scale.

New York's experience was quite similar to Chicago's, driven by a combination of grassroots social justice advocacy, top-down pressure on the school district to turn around failing high schools, and foundation funding for what seemed to be a common element of effective schools. In 1990, Deborah Meier formed the Center for Collaborative Education, which along with its partners worked to promote small schools in the city.[57] Then, in 1992, a school shooting in Brooklyn concentrated political pressure on then-chancellor Joseph A. Fernandez, who turned to small community-controlled high schools as a potential solution. "Our high schools were just too large, and there were a lot of problems with kids not feeling people even knew who they [were]," recalled Fernandez in 1995.[58] And while Fernandez saw them as primarily about safety and community control, his support lent tremendous momentum to those who believed that small schools could also bridge the achievement gap.

Despite the fact that the next chancellor, Ramon C. Cortines, was not a major supporter of small schools, the movement continued to make progress. Warning that small schools were not a cure-all, Cortines—who would later run L.A.'s schools—made the case that a number of the city's large high schools like Stuyvesant and Midwood still functioned well. Further, they still served a majority of the city's public school students.[59] But others in the district were more hopeful about small schools. "We don't want to say that smallness is some miracle panacea," noted John Ferrandino, the board of education's chief executive for high schools, "but they're showing some nice success."[60] What the district needed, Ferrandino and others argued, was funding to create more small schools.

Fortunately for New York's small schools advocates, private foundations were willing to fund further experimentation with the model. One early financial backer was the Aaron Diamond Foundation, the board of which, according to former executive director Vincent McGee, wanted to aid the traditionally underserved. "Early on," said McGee, some board members "wanted to focus on increasing minority enrollment in prep schools and elite institutions of higher education." But Irene Diamond, Aaron Diamond's widow, wanted to make a wider impact on the city, promoting opportunity for all students in New York. Consequently, the Diamond Foundation began to explore funding small school conversions throughout the city. "Our thinking," noted McGee, "was that by doing something to improve the system, we could help many, many more students and raise the level for everybody."[61] In small schools they saw a chance to promote excellence for all.

Other organizations followed in funding small high schools as a means of creating systemic change. In 1994 the Annenberg Foundation, through the Annenberg Challenge, granted a half billion dollars to American public schools. Among those grants was $25 million to build fifty small schools in New York City. The goal in doing so was to provide greater individual attention for students and to focus on community projects or vocational specialties.[62] This justification for the grant was relatively modest, as was the size of the grant given the costs associated with building and staffing new schools. And, according to then-superintendent Rudy Crew, small schools, though "sexy" as a reform concept, were difficult to replicate in a cost-efficient way that produced increased student achievement results.[63] Further, as Chester

Finn would later comment, the small schools movement "professed no one model for a good school nor any uniform standards by which to appraise efforts to create more of them."[64] Nevertheless, it represented a major step forward for small schools supporters, who over the next decade would push size onto the national agenda.

Foundations like Annenberg's supported small schools for a number of reasons, but significant among them was the influence of an overlapping network of reformers. In the case of the Annenberg Challenge, some of the most prominent small schools advocates served as advisors to the foundation. Ted Sizer, for instance, was named the first executive director of the Annenberg Institute for School Reform, which was created by the grant. And in the case of municipal-level work, Deborah Meier advised New York City schools during the implementation of their Annenberg Challenge grant. Writing later, during her tenure at the Annenberg Institute at Brown University in 1996, Meier noted that "small schools come as close to being a panacea for America's educational ills as we're likely to get."[65] Clearly, there were others who believed the same.

By the late 1990s, leaders in the federal government began discussing the effectiveness of small schools. Though their reasons for supporting small schools varied, a number of members of Congress began proposing federal grants that included funding for small schools initiatives. In his 1997 proposal for a National Dropout Prevention Act, for instance, New Mexico senator Jeff Bingaman argued that small schools could keep students in school. Citing George H. W. Bush's standards-focused Goals 2000 plan, Bingaman noted that "we are much closer to the year 2000, but we are nowhere near the goal of graduating 90 percent of our students before they drop out of school." His bill would have created a new $100 million grant program to reach the thousand schools across the country with the highest dropout rates. "With these funds," Bingaman argued, "schools would be able to try proven strategies that have been shown to work—strategies like breaking larger schools down into smaller learning communities."[66] The bill did not pass, but it was a harbinger of things to come.

Small schools, it seemed, offered something for everyone. Those looking to promote student achievement pointed to the size of successful schools as evidence that small was good. Those concerned with better meeting the needs of low-income and minority students made the case that large schools were dehumanizing dropout factories and that size was a crucial issue. Even school choice advocates and critics of bureaucracy saw something to like in small schools. Thus, with no natural opposition, the idea of making high schools smaller continued to spread, moving from an article of faith among supporters to a widely accepted truism.

Over the course of the last decade of the twentieth century, small schools supporters secured district support and enough foundation funding to enact their vision, building dozens of new small schools in the nation's largest districts. In New York alone, they created more than one hundred small schools in a five-year span between 1991 and 1996. But these successes did not represent a capstone in the small schools movement; rather, they opened the door for efforts on an even wider scale. At the dawn of the twenty-first century, when major funders like the federal government and the Bill and Melinda Gates Foundation began looking for education reform projects to fund, small schools were at the top of their lists.

THE SMALL SCHOOLS GIANT

The new century ushered in the ascendance of the small schools movement. While advocacy for small schools continued without any particular breakthroughs in research, two contextual factors changed. The first was the passage of the No Child Left Behind Act (NCLB) in 2001. NCLB, a reauthorization of the Elementary and Secondary Education Act, established accountability measures that would punish low-performing schools, threatening persistent low performers with state takeover. With this heightened sense of urgency, district and school leaders at low-performing schools became even more receptive to reform than they had been previously, searching for solutions to their persistent problems. Along with accountability, NCLB also emphasized the implementation of "proven methods," which small schools supporters believed they had firmly established.[67]

The second, and more influential, change of the new century was the entrance of the Gates Foundation onto the scene. The foundation, which would provide roughly $2 billion for small schools, transformed the small schools movement into a national phenomenon. Formed in 1994 as the William H. Gates Foundation with an initial stock gift of $94 million, it was renamed the Bill and Melinda Gates Foundation in 1999. The foundation's endowment steadily grew through 2006, when investor Warren Buffett doubled Gates's holdings through a record-setting gift of roughly $30 billion. Despite the resources at its disposal, the Gates Foundation focused on only two initiatives: world health and American education. Through school improvement efforts, leaders at the foundation believed they could aid both the nation and the underserved, promoting both social justice and social efficiency aims. They were determined, by 2025, to increase the percentage of low-income and minority students prepared to enter college from 20 to 80 and to double the number of low-income and minority students graduating from college.[68]

Leaders at Gates were drawn to small schools for most of the reasons that other education reformers were. Like many other small schools advocates, for instance, key stakeholders at Gates tended to favor entrepreneurial market-based solutions, and many of them were themselves former corporate executives. As Director of Evaluation, Policy, and Research David Ferrero put it, "that Chubb and Moe argument [in favor of markets and choice] was pretty heavily influential to us as well as to a lot of business reformers."[69] Underlying much of the small schools work that the foundation did was the idea that small schools were "antibureaucratic" and maximized corporate values like "leanness, efficiency, [and] buffering from government." It was, Ferrero added, "almost axiomatic."[70]

As was the case elsewhere, support for small schools at the Gates Foundation was also shaped by personal relationships. Educational initiatives at Gates during this era were spearheaded by Tom Vander Ark, former superintendent of the Federal Way school district in Washington State, and upon accepting his position at Gates Vander Ark quickly named Tony Wagner as an advisor. Wagner, a faculty member of Harvard University's Executive Leadership Program for Educators, was a believer in small schools and had worked with Vander Ark in Federal Way. In his new role, Wagner, who was affiliated with a group of small schools supporters, steered Vander Ark toward the movement's philosophical leaders like Deborah Meier and Ted Sizer.[71]

With encouragement from this new network, Vander Ark spent his first six months on the job in 2000 touring successful schools, both public and private, in an effort to determine what made them work. And, like many small schools advocates before him, he saw something those schools held in common: their size. David Ferrero recalled Vander Ark making the case as follows: "Look at what private schools are; they're small." There was also, he noted, "kind of an Arthur Powell dimension" to the argument for small schools among leaders at Gates, the root sentiment of which was "let's make public schools more like private schools."[72] Scholars like Powell, author of *Lessons from Privilege*, made the case that public schools were too big and that their size was a major factor in their ineffectiveness. Independent schools, on the other hand, tended to be "places where teachers and students knew each other well, and no one could slide by, or even disappear, without notice."[73] The nation's best schools, Powell noted, were small by design.[74]

Leaders at Gates, many of whom were graduates of small private schools, also had personal experiences that reinforced these claims. Tom Vander Ark and his wife, for instance, attended small private high schools in Denver. According to Vander Ark, the experience set him "on a journey of discovery . . . to figure out what it is about schools like Denver Christian and Denver Lutheran . . . that make them work so well."[75] Bill Gates himself, for that matter, attended Lakeside School—an exclusive independent school in Seattle with a high school enrollment of roughly five hundred students. Lakeside, Gates noted in 2009, "made a huge difference in my life"—a claim he supported by continuing to make generous contributions to the school.[76] Whether or not those experiences shaped policy is unclear; what is clear is that leaders at the foundation strongly believed in the small private schools they had attended.

Preferences for private schools at the foundation were supported by observations of small urban Catholic and charter schools. Private schools were small and successful, but they tended to work with a less than representative population. Small schools like Central Park East and many low-cost Catholic schools, however, were also successful, and they worked with traditionally underserved students. Reflecting on his tour of high-performing schools, Tom Vander Ark cited three "pockets of excellence" that had resonated with him: "A century of success in private education, particularly urban Catholic schools; the small-schools movement that began in New York City in the late 1970s; and innovative and highly successful charter schools." What they had in common, Vander Ark argued, was size.[77] Despite the fact that many large public high schools were by a variety of measures quite successful, that many Catholic high schools were quite large, and that many small charter schools were low-achieving, reformers continued to pitch small schools as a commonsense solution.

As Gates entered the picture, the average American high school still had an enrollment of nearly 800 students, and high schools in urban areas were significantly larger. Chicago high schools had an average enrollment of 1,114 students. Average enrollments in New York and Los Angeles were 1,235 and 1,584, respectively. And that was after nearly a decade of small schools efforts. Less than ten years earlier, those rates had been even higher.[78] Still, while many small school experiments had been launched, they were serving only a fraction of students. As one group of research-ers noted, "although often begun by reformers concerned with the racial achievement gap and other equity issues, small schools usually only serve a small percentage of young people in a district," frequently serving "families with the wherewithal to seek out options."[79]

Vander Ark and others at the Gates Foundation saw in small schools a way of promoting educational opportunity for all students—a way of giving "disadvantaged students the kind of quality school that is available to middle class and affluent families."[80] The idea of going to scale with small schools was neither new nor exclusive to Gates. In 1996, for instance, Deborah Meier had observed that "what we small school fanatics are work-ing for is schools that do for all kids what we now do for a few."[81] But Gates had the resources to make that vision a reality. Leaders there talked not just about remaking particular schools, or even particular districts, but about transforming all the nation's roughly twenty-five hundred urban high schools.[82]

In the coming years, the Gates Foundation provided the small schools effort with the financial backing necessary to make it a national move-ment. Equally important, Gates provided the leadership needed to solidify a coalition spanning the ideological spectrum. Speaking the language of both social efficiency and social justice, of business-oriented reform as well as progressive education, leaders at the foundation built a national reform alliance around large-scale small schools efforts.[83]

SMALL GOES BIG

Though the Gates Foundation stood at the center of the small schools movement, it could not have had the impact it did without the support of other small schools advocates. In addition to continuing support from the Annenberg Foundation and the Carnegie Corporation, major funding for small schools ventures came from new sources like the Michael and Susan Dell Foundation and the Eli and Edythe Broad Foundation. But just as important as the funding stream that became available for the creation of small schools was the political support from an expanding group of busi-ness leaders, policy makers, community leaders, and nonprofit intermedi-ary groups that worked to build broad support for the small schools vision. Consequently, the Gates Foundation and its allies turned small schools into a national phenomenon.

The first major step forward in the Gates-era small schools movement came in 2000 when the Gates Foundation, along with the Carnegie Corporation and the Open Society Institute, announced a $30 million grant to create more small high schools in New York through the New Century High Schools Consortium. While the size of the grant was only slightly larger than that received by the city through the Annenberg Challenge, the rationale was different.

Annenberg had aimed to provide greater individual attention to students with a focus on community projects or vocational preparation. These new funders, however, argued that small schools would promote equity; they simply needed to be reproduced at scale. In voicing support for small schools, then-president of the Carnegie Corporation Vartan Gregorian referenced "promising models" that had been shown to improve student achievement.[84] Patty Stonesifer, then-president and cochair of the Gates Foundation, justified her support by arguing that "small-school designs have a proven track record of helping all students achieve . . . and this partnership will help bring these innovations to scale by supporting both new small high schools and the redesign of large high schools."[85] And although neither specified which schools served as models, both indicated a strong desire to provide all children with the elements of top-flight education, particularly through smaller schools.

Small schools advocates quickly began to promote their efforts to parents and community organizations. New Visions for Public Schools, a partner in the city's New Century High Schools Consortium along with the Department of Education, the United Federation of Teachers, and the Council of Supervisors and Administrators, reached out to more than eight hundred community-based organizations, universities, and cultural institutions to foster support for small schools. They also distributed the New Visions Small Schools Guide to more than nine hundred thousand people through the *New York Post* and *El Diario*, as well as to families of middle school children. Not surprisingly, this marketing effort intensified "the demand for student placements at small high schools."[86] Parents, students, and teachers, according to a later evaluation of the program, had come to believe that a small school plant provided a "huge advantage," though they could not always specify why they felt that way.[87]

Small schools advocates also worked diligently to engage city and community leaders in support for small schools. New Visions, for instance, coordinated city and community leader visits to schools and convened a number of meetings and breakfasts with them. They also mounted aggressive public relations efforts, reaching out to reporters and editorial staff from the *New York Times*, advertising in union newsletters, running newspaper inserts about small schools, and engaging different constituencies such as faith leaders and the coalition of immigrant organizations.[88]

More importantly, the city gained a strong advocate for small schools in entrepreneurial schools chief Joel Klein. In 2002, newly elected mayor Michael Bloomberg, who would later call small schools "a crucial part of [the city's] strategy to close the achievement gap," centralized authority over the schools by abolishing the city's thirty-two community school boards.[89] Exercising his mayoral jurisdiction, Bloomberg appointed former CEO and assistant U.S. attorney general Klein as school chancellor. By the end of the year, Klein announced his "flagship school improvement strategy" to close at least twenty failing schools and open two hundred small high schools by 2010.[90] According to the plan, 14 percent of New York City's high school students would attend small schools by 2010; as New Visions put it, the district was "moving toward scale."[91] Klein's leadership was instrumental, though in no small part because it coincided with a successful grassroots effort at developing support for small schools.

Besides marketing efforts, other aspects of the small schools movement continued to appeal to those interested in education reform. In keeping with market principles, for instance, grant money would not go directly to the public schools. Instead, it would be channeled through New Visions for Public Schools, which would manage grants and redistribute funds. This, in turn, would ostensibly foster competition among districts within the city system while also making funds available to charter school efforts.[92] As Eva Moskowitz, chairwoman of the New York City Council Education Committee, put it: "any way we can create competition from within or without will speed up the reform process."[93]

The degree to which the effort actually promoted competition was questionable, given the fact that New Visions was receiving so much grant money that supply easily met demand. In 2001 the Gates Foundation gave New Visions another $10 million, which it followed in 2003 with $29 million more. In 2006 the Annenberg Foundation gave $20 million to New Visions over eight years to strengthen and sustain New York's portfolio of small schools. With this tremendous outpouring of financial support, small schools in New York grew at a nearly exponential rate. Along with 225 community partners, the New Century Schools project created eighty-three small high schools over the course of five years, increasing the number of public high schools in New York to roughly four hundred. Small, in short, had gone big.

The story was much the same in Chicago, which like New York had experimented for over a decade with small schools and was beginning to ramp up its small schools efforts. With major grant support, and with the leadership of an entrepreneurial superintendent, the reform quickly spread across the district.

In 2001, Mayor Richard M. Daley appointed Arne Duncan—later to be tapped as President Barack Obama's secretary of education—as chief executive officer of the Chicago Public Schools (CPS). Himself the founder of a small school, Duncan was an outspoken advocate of the cause and quickly created the Office of Small Schools in August of that year. Supporting this effort, the Gates Foundation granted CPS $12 million, which local foundations matched with $6 million, to support the conversion of five high schools into twenty autonomous small schools. Gates also gave $7.6 million to create twelve new freestanding small high schools.[94]

In the last decade of the twentieth century, Chicago educators created 130 small public elementary and secondary schools, mostly in the form of schools-within-schools. In the early twenty-first century, the district aimed to complete the transformation. CPS's Renaissance 2010 plan, strongly influenced by the Commercial Club of Chicago, an organization of the city's top corporate, financial, and political elites, called for the creation of one hundred new small public schools in six years in minority and low-income neighborhoods.[95] But, to the chagrin of many small schools advocates, money would not go directly to communities or to the district. Instead, Renaissance 2010 would seek to go to scale by contracting out at least two-thirds of the new schools to private groups other than the district—a move that leaders like Duncan hoped would produce greater efficiency. "Hailed as a 'reform model' for other large urban districts," the plan loomed, as William Ayers noted, "as part of a new national wave of fierce market fundamentalism."[96]

Los Angeles, unlike New York and Chicago, had been slow to adopt small schools. By the dawn of the new century, however, L.A. was pushing small schools reforms even more aggressively than its large district counterparts. Mandated by top-down fiat, the entire district would go small.

Appointed superintendent of LAUSD in 2000, former Colorado governor Roy Romer was instrumental in L.A.'s move to small schools. Early in

Romer's tenure, UNITE-LA—an affiliate of the Los Angeles Area Chamber of Commerce—sponsored trips for district leaders to visit small schools in cities like New York and Chicago.[97] Soon, Romer began promoting small schools. Citing his visits to small schools in other cities, Romer made the argument that "our schools are too large. . . . We need to give students a more personalized educational experience."[98] Further, he contended inaccurately, "all of the literature in the country says smaller is better."[99]

The concerns of business-minded groups like the Chamber of Commerce clearly were social efficiency and economic productivity. Other advocates of small schools, however, were concerned with social justice. Equity advocates had long criticized L.A. public schools for failing to adequately serve low-income and minority students, and any LAUSD superintendent would need to make visible efforts toward addressing those grievances.[100] Yet, for these advocates, social justice was not a wholly separate concern from that of workforce preparation. One PTA head, for instance, made the case that the comprehensive school had been appropriate when "K–12's mission was to train a workforce of factory workers" in an age when community colleges and four-year colleges "were icing on the cake."[101] But times had changed, and groups like the Los Angeles Small Schools Center and the Los Angeles Parents Union mobilized support for a reform they believed would more equitably serve L.A. students.[102] Small schools, they believed, could kill two birds with one stone.

Framed as a solution for both social justice and social efficiency concerns, small schools quickly became district policy. In 2005, Romer, through District Bulletin 1600, mandated that all secondary schools in L.A. Unified begin converting to small learning communities in two to three years. According to the language of Bulletin 1600, district policy required "the design of new . . . school configurations and the redesign of existing secondary school configurations into smaller learning communities of approximately 350–500 students."[103] Acknowledging that the accelerated timetable was extreme, Romer observed that slow "bottom-up" change was not an option. "I can't wait that long," he argued. "If you take what's happening in this city I've got to risk the change being very, very rapid."[104]

Faced with major problems and under pressure to take action, the nation's largest school districts went big with small schools. Promising to promote educational excellence for all, small schools appealed to both the right and the left. Further, such efforts seemed to be well-proven, not only in the cases of private schools and in the heavily promoted cases of public charter schools like Central Park East in New York and Best Practice High School in Chicago, but also in selective harvesting of the scholarly research. In 2002, for instance, the National Conference of State Legislatures claimed that "research overwhelmingly supports" small schools—a commonly echoed claim. Somewhat less enthusiastically, however, the report also noted that student achievement was only "possibly higher" in small schools than large ones. Yet somehow the skepticism of the latter claim did not disrupt the certainty of the former.[105]

Finally, there was money for small schools efforts. Foundation assistance "is flexible money," noted Chicago schools CEO Arne Duncan. "When you're just trying to literally balance the budget, that doesn't give you room to think differently, think big."[106] So think big they did. But in thinking big about small schools, districts would also have to think differently about the definition of small.

A REFORM ADAPTED

Despite the enthusiasm about smallness as a transformative characteristic and despite the funding that accompanied that enthusiasm, there were obstacles to producing small schools at scale. If small schools were as effective as their promoters claimed, it would be difficult for districts to justify converting some schools but not others, providing some students with needed facilities while continuing to send others through failing large comprehensive high schools. Even though districts rapidly pursued the construction of new facilities, districtwide conversion in cities like New York, Chicago, and Los Angeles would potentially take decades. Further, while grant money was relatively abundant, construction of new schools at a citywide scale would far outstrip any district's budget. Thus, against the warnings of small schools supporters like Deborah Meier who argued that "a small school must be a school—not a school-within-a-school (whatever that is) or a 'mini-school' or a house or a family," most conversion efforts created semi-autonomous units within existing buildings.[107]

In order to overhaul their facilities swiftly, large urban districts made necessary compromises. Consequently, much of the small schools work in urban districts has been creating small learning communities—independent units in the style of schools-within-schools. Of the ninety small schools recently created in Chicago, for instance, thirty-six are freestanding, while fifty-four are schools-within-schools.[108] Publicizing the benefits of small learning communities, CPS CEO Arne Duncan observed in 2002 that "small schools and community schools create environments where there's a sense of belonging, where teachers work together, where students look out for one another." But, he added, "since we cannot afford to build new buildings, we have to work with the facilities we have to support these ideas and make them work."[109] As one CPS publication put it, "challenged by ever tightening budgetary constraints . . . creative districts have had to find other solutions. Sharing large buildings among small schools and community groups has become the recurring answer."[110]

The schools-within-schools strategy was also made necessary by the managerial challenges inherent in a massive public school system. As Shelley Weston, former assistant superintendent for the Office of School Redesign in Los Angeles, noted: "If we go from eighty-some schools being accredited to five hundred schools being accredited, the cost factor would be extensive." Equally problematic, though, would be the level of assistance required to support all those schools. "And," she added, "I don't know if that's something that we have."[111] As David Ferrero of the Gates Foundation dryly remarked, "you can't shut down every school and start a new one."[112]

Creating small learning communities within large high schools was also appealing insofar as it was compatible with bureaucratic systems—an ironic twist given the antibureaucratic nature of much small schools support. Federal funding for small schools efforts could be administered most efficiently through a one-size-fits-all model, and creating schools-within-schools could be conducted in a similar manner in any large high school across the nation. Creating freestanding small schools, by contrast, would require securing sites, selecting designs, finding leaders and staff members, and recruiting students—messy and place-specific work.

In 2000, Congress created its major small schools initiative: the Smaller Learning Communities Grant Program (SLC). A subsection of the Elementary and Secondary Education Act, the SLC program, its creators wrote, would "ensure all students graduate with the knowledge and skills necessary to make successful transitions to college and careers, and to be good citizens."[113] For a one-year planning grant, a local educational agency could apply for $25,000 to 50,000 per project, and three-year implementation grants to create schools-within-schools were available for up to $4 million. Over the next decade, the Department of Education would award more than $500 million to create hundreds of schools-within-schools. Los Angeles public schools received forty-four Smaller Learning Communities grants from the federal government between 2000 and 2007. New York City and Chicago public schools received thirty-five and sixteen grants, respectively, during the same period.[114]

Whatever the promise of small schools, providing them on a scale large enough to serve millions of urban students required significant adjustments to the original model. One report noted that small learning communities "often bear little resemblance to autonomous small schools, in large part because they are layered onto the existing organizational structure of large comprehensive high schools."[115] As one principal complained: "You're running a small-schools concept that was a bastardized form of what it was supposed to be."[116] Those adjustments were not without consequence.

One unintended consequence of the schools-within-schools approach, at least in many cases, was increased stratification of students by race, academic ability, and socioeconomic status. Typically, while some schools-within-schools were "full of brains," others were "dumping grounds" for weak students.[117] In short, the tracking system from the comprehensive high school had, in many cases, merely been transposed; schools were no more heterogeneous after downsizing than they had been before.

Converting large high schools to small learning communities also raised questions about what would happen to an existing school's curricular and extracurricular offerings, how students and teachers would be divided among their new schools-within-schools, and what would distinguish a converted school from its previous incarnation. Further complicating these inherent hurdles to school-within-school conversion efforts was the hasty speed at which districts moved, often outstripping the capacity of district personnel and leaving stakeholders unclear about the purpose of the transformation.

MIXED RESULTS

Some small schools experienced major turnarounds. Others did not. In New York City, for instance, some New Visions schools had graduation rates in the 80 to 90 percent range by 2006. Some, however, still graduated only half of their students.[118] Even within single schools, results were uneven, as schools might experience increased graduation rates but only marginal gains in academic achievement.[119] In short, though smallness often promoted positive changes in aspects of the school like its culture and climate, small schools were also plagued by shortcomings.

One major challenge was translating changes in school size into changes in classroom teaching and learning. One recent report on Gates-funded small schools, for instance, found mixed results for affecting achievement, most discouragingly for math.[120] Another report, on the foundation's work in Chicago, found that instruction in small schools was "generally quite similar" to instruction in larger schools, that program coherence was not statistically different, and that standardized test scores did not improve. The report did find that small schools may have created a "more supportive context" for schooling—a finding sustained by studies concluding that small schools often succeed in "creating a culture for learning."[121] But the direct impact on learning was uncertain and often disappointing.[122] Creating an environment more conducive to good teaching was simply not enough.[123]

Changing the internal practices of a school has been even more difficult for school-within-school conversions than for freestanding schools. One report to the U.S. Department of Education noted that whatever their successes, schools receiving SLC grants have been "less likely to report classroom level changes."[124] In another study supported by the Department of Education, school-within-school promoters First Things First and Talent Development found that large school "conversions have struggled in the face of seemingly less control over key variables such as staffing, student motivation and preparation, funding, scheduling, curriculum and facilities." While the report noted that successful conversions have been documented, the smaller learning communities effort "has produced high schools that have started down the path to small learning communities only to turn back." And though only some schools consciously rejected conversion to schools-within-schools, many efforts simply ran out of momentum and reverted.[125]

One notable example of the problematic nature of school-within-school conversion efforts was Locke High School in Los Angeles. Locke, a popular site for school reform efforts in Los Angeles, used Department of Education funds to reorganize into small learning communities after having already experimented with the model. But when the Smaller Learning Communities grant came through, "many veterans saw the small learning communities as a new iteration of the old . . . yet another half-baked idea handed down from above."[126] Nevertheless, the school pursued the grant and, after winning funds, was deconstructed into schools-within-schools. But the new small schools, often missing key staff members, were "much less proactive—and much more disorganized."[127] Despite an additional gift of

$7.8 million from the Gates Foundation, as one author observed, "Locke's small schools [became] even less functional."[128] Rather than revert Locke back to a big-school model, the district washed its hands of the project and handed the school over to charter management organization Green Dot Public Schools.

The Locke High experience was not entirely unique in Los Angeles. While most school conversions in the city have not been as dramatic, many have struggled to improve achievement scores or graduation rates. As Shelley Weston, former assistant superintendent for the Office of School Redesign, noted, "we find that students are staying in school longer. . . . [It] doesn't mean they're graduating, but they're staying."[129] And yet, even in light of mixed results and despite the challenges of converting schools like Locke, L.A. Unified has continued to pursue small schools and small learning communities.

Federal support also continued throughout the first decade of the twenty-first century in the face of mixed results. While the Department of Education found a number of positive outcomes in the SLC program, they were largely within career and technical education programs.[130] According to one study, between one-third and one-half of schools receiving Department of Education SLC grants have created career academies.[131] On a positive note, career and technical education, according to a sizable body of research, serves non-college-bound students quite well. However, this runs exactly counter to what small schools were heralded as being useful for—creating a college-preparatory experience for all students.

Outside of Career and Technical Education (CTE), the results of such efforts have been largely disappointing. According to a 2007 edition of the *Federal Register*, "structural" and "personalization strategies" like the creation of small schools, "by themselves, do not appear to improve student academic achievement and readiness for postsecondary education and careers."[132] Student learning, the piece noted, seemed only to improve "in those schools that also have made considerable changes in curriculum and instruction." Conversely, "some large comprehensive high schools that have not implemented SLCs have significantly increased student achievement in reading or mathematics and narrowed achievement gaps by implementing more rigorous courses, providing extra support to struggling students, and systematically using data to improve instruction."[133] Despite these findings, the Small Learning Communities program continued to issue tens of millions of dollars in grants each year, enticing more schools and districts to downsize.

THE CHALLENGE OF CHANGE

Supporters of small schools have been extremely successful in enacting their vision on America's high schools. They have been less successful, however, in delivering the sort of achievement results that justified the remaking of so many schools. So what went wrong?

First, small schools reformers relied on common-sense comparisons between struggling schools and schools that worked, and these comparisons overlooked particular aspects of successful schools. While many small charter-school efforts had succeeded with public school teachers and students, for instance, they were still working with distinct populations of adults and young people who had self-selected into those environments. What reformers like Tom Vander Ark failed to realize was that the successful schools they visited were not only small; they also happened to be run by exceptional teachers and leaders. With large numbers of a district's high schools converting to small schools, whether freestanding or schools-within-schools, that selection effect disappeared. Small schools at scale worked with the same students, teachers, and administrators that had attended and staffed large schools. In fact, moving rapidly toward a small schools model unintentionally created an even higher demand for capable principals in districts plagued by poor leadership.

Another reason for the mixed results of small schools reforms, particularly in the case of small learning community efforts, is that many simply implemented formal changes without changing practices. As Richard Elmore writes, the comprehensive high school, rather than affecting teaching and learning, "was a largely empty structural vessel into which educators and communities could pour whatever content and pedagogy they wished."[134] And the same was frequently true with small schools, which often reproduced the structure of successful independent, parochial, and charter schools without capturing what made those schools work. According to one report, the pitfall in small schools efforts has been "in trying to reduce a terrifically complicated process—with intricate mechanical, interpersonal and systemic factors to be reckoned with—into a lockstep, overly prescribed formula."[135] The result has been that schools have, despite the best efforts of many faculties and staffs, succumbed to institutional inertia and resisted reform.[136]

The movement also suffered from a divide between theory and practice. The idea of giving underserved students the same kind of education as their more privileged peers is hard to take a stand against. What it ignores, however, is the reality that public schools serve an incredibly broad range of individuals and have consequently sought "to do many different things for many different kinds of students."[137] Whatever their inherent natural abilities, students in urban public schools, on the whole, face different realities than students in suburban and private schools. In light of this, small schools have been criticized for not meeting the complex and often nonacademic needs of students.[138] And parents and teachers, for their part, have expressed greater interest in pursuing other kinds of school reform efforts.[139]

The nature of the small schools movement was also deeply shaped by the urgency of going to scale. If all students needed a top-flight education, some argued, systemwide solutions needed to be found—solutions that would transform schools without sacrificing a generation in the process. That, however, meant finding simple answers and pushing them aggressively, which both private foundations and the federal government did. One researcher, for instance, found that educators in Gates-funded schools viewed the organization as "arrogant in the way it operated, coming into cities with a whole lot of money and a half of an idea." When pushing reform without deep knowledge of local context and capacity, he concluded, "the results can get ugly."[140]

Local leaders, desperate for reforms that might boost student achievement, appear to have been no more critical in their evaluations of small schools than were federal- and foundation-based funders. As a *Phi Delta Kappan* study found, one district's adoption of small schools reforms was "a result of the strongly held philosophical views of some influential members of the central staff," of selective reading of research, and of working backward to find "theories and 'evidence'" that would justify their chosen approaches.[141] Thus, while there was some research supporting size as an element of school quality, the movement to dismantle large high schools was equally shaped by other forces, not the least of which was the availability of funding.

Three decades into the small schools movement and only a few years past the pinnacle of spending for the creation of new small schools, once-fervent advocates have shifted their allegiances. While the Department of Education continues to issue SLC grants, the Gates Foundation has moved away from supporting small schools and has begun pursuing other reforms. As the foundation acknowledged, "many of the results were disappointing," particularly concerning hoped-for gains in achievement or increased college-going rates. And, though Gates continued to support small high schools, the foundation moved to put most of its efforts into, as one official noted, "filling schools with effective teachers and putting good tools in their hands."[142] The movement had lost its champion.

Whatever its setbacks, the small schools movement maintains supporters. True believers, of course, continue to make the case that size is an essential factor in the fate of a school, determining an entire slate of achievement outcomes. But perhaps more important is the general notion about school size that has emerged among modern reform advocates: that small is good. For most, this is not a tenet of impassioned faith; rather, it is simply something that makes sense. Not because of the empirical data, which no doubt will continue to reveal a more complex picture, but because as reform paradigms shifted, so did notions about school size. The idea of small schools was a sensation because it was a perfect fit for the excellence for all era—an era shaped by new assumptions about the challenges facing schools and the places to look for solutions.

3

THE RIGHT TEACHERS

Teach For America

GETTING THE RIGHT TEACHERS in the classroom has been a major part of the school reform agenda for as long as policy makers have sought systemic change in education. As school quality depends in large part on teacher quality, school reformers across the twentieth century worked to establish criteria to identify suitable teachers for the nation's schools. And yet, despite this continuity of purpose, the teacher question has been answered quite differently in different eras. Thus, while school reformers during the Cold War era, for instance, hastened to draw content experts into top high schools in order to more rigorously prepare future leaders, social justice advocates in the following decades sought to bring culturally sensitive teachers from diverse backgrounds into low-income urban schools. In short, the evolving nature of teacher recruitment efforts, rather than reflecting a closer approximation of the ideal teacher, instead indicated ever-changing priorities shaped by shifting perceptions of social problems.[1]

In the era of excellence for all, school reformers began to promote a new vision of teacher quality. All students, they contended, regardless of background, needed access to the kind of teachers traditionally found in top private schools and sometimes found in cutting-edge charter schools. Social justice and social efficiency aims both demanded that underserved students begin attending college at the same rates as their more privileged peers. In light of this, it made sense to look at the college-preparatory experiences of those privileged students, particularly at the kind of teachers they had. Consequently, many reformers sought to identify and recruit college students who were both service oriented and highly skilled. Marked by their high grade-point averages and prestigious alma maters, whether or not they had received professional training, these were the future teachers who reformers believed would make a difference in the nation's poorest schools.

Nowhere has this approach to the teacher question manifested itself more clearly than in the work of Teach For America (TFA). Founded in 1989 as a two-year service commitment modeled on the Peace Corps, TFA currently has more than eight thousand participants placed in more than one thousand low-income urban and rural schools across the country.[2] Those teachers, the organization points out, come from the nation's most elite schools—roughly 10 percent of the graduating classes of Harvard, Princeton, and Yale, as well as top liberal arts colleges like Williams and Amherst—where they collectively maintained an A-minus average.[3] By enlisting them in temporary teaching assignments, the organization aims to end the educational inequity that separates low-income students from their more privileged peers.

Although TFA produces only a fraction of the nation's teachers, it receives a disproportionate share of public attention, and its roughly $200 million annual budget dwarfs that of other teacher recruitment efforts. Commentators like Thomas Friedman and David Brooks of the *New York Times* have praised the program as a force for school reform, foundation heads and corporate donors extol its entrepreneurialism and efficiency, and presidents from both parties have been strong backers.[4] Thus, while TFA is not representative of teacher preparation and recruitment efforts as a whole, it is an exemplary case of the excellence for all approach to school reform, and particularly to the teacher question. Well suited for the late twentieth and early twenty-first centuries, the organization has been successful in a number of ways, especially in terms of growth and recognition. Yet, despite a much-lauded core philosophy, the success of TFA in bridging the achievement gap—even on a small scale—remains unclear, raising questions about the organization as well as about the excellence for all movement as a whole.

This chapter is an attempt to understand the TFA phenomenon and its particular approach to fixing the nation's schools. Why, it asks, did leaders in education, government, and the nonprofit sector throw their support behind this particular organization? What made TFA unique?

Equally, though, this chapter is focused on what TFA's popularity, as well as its impact on public education, reveals about school reform in the excellence for all era. Situating the history of TFA within the broader history of teacher credentialing and alternative licensure, it seeks to understand the ways in which reformers of the era approached the teacher question.

THE BIRTH OF TEACHER CREDENTIALING

In the early nineteenth century, little training was required of teachers. The primary concern in hiring teachers tended to be with moral character rather than content mastery. However, as the process of licensing teachers shifted from ecclesiastical to civil control, criteria began to include content knowledge and pedagogy.[5] Though some common-school teachers were college graduates or college students earning money on the side, many more were those with little academic training, often graduates of the very schools in which they were teaching.[6] Much of the work was seasonal, limited to summer terms in rural areas, and the profession was marked by high levels of turnover. Consequently, by the 1840s "reports of the ignorance of common-school teachers were widespread" and reformers were pushing for more thorough certification procedures.[7] And, while local communities were generally content with their teachers, reform advocates commonly excoriated locally certified teachers who lacked basic skills.[8]

Those who would reform the teaching profession sought to increase pay and training, but they particularly sought to institute more rigorous examinations. As scholar David Angus has written, "the vast majority of U.S. teachers in the second half of the nineteenth century received their first, and perhaps only, certificate to teach from local officials on the basis of their performance on an exam."[9] Consequently, states tried to assert greater control over the certification process by making tests longer and more detailed. By the end of the nineteenth century, most states were issuing statewide certificates.

The first "normal school" for training teachers was established in Lexington, Massachusetts, in 1839, and two more were established in the following year.[10] Over the course of the next half-century, 127 state-sponsored normal schools, often offering the equivalent of a high school education, were created.[11] The reformers who established these schools were frustrated at low passing rates of exams, concerned with uniformity, and attracted to the pursuit of system building. Expanding a network of normal schools across America became a high priority among reformers and was supported by teachers interested in professionalizing their occupation.[12] In 1830, for example, the American Institute of Instruction was formed in Boston and began to depict education as a science, requiring careful preparation of the individual teacher.[13]

The results of the effort to promote normal schools were considerable.

By the beginning of the twentieth century, twenty-eight states certified teachers on the basis of graduation from a normal school or college without the need for testing.[14] In Massachusetts, for instance, 40 percent of public school teachers had attended a normal school.[15] Still, a majority of teachers did not attend these institutions. Further, only three states by this time had assumed sole authority for establishing teacher qualifications and issuing licenses, while most states issued only guidelines.[16]

At the dawn of the twentieth century, reformers began to push for teacher licensure through state government. This had the effect of establishing minimum competency requirements, ensuring uniformity across the state, and counteracting the patronage system that still characterized most teacher hiring practices. As scholar Christopher Lucas writes, "uniform, impartial procedures governing teacher hiring and retention were a high priority."[17] Professional educators, anxious to "demonstrate that good teaching did indeed require a kind of specialized knowledge that could be transmitted through training programs," urged states to accept professional training as grounds for certification.[18]

Many states took that leap. In 1919 Vermont dropped its examination in favor of certificates issued for professional training, and within two decades twenty-seven other states had dropped examinations.[19] While professional educators did not eliminate exams entirely, they did succeed in expanding professional schooling requirements. By 1930, thirty-one states required at least a high school education and some professional training.

Normal schools had long conducted much of the teacher training in the United States, and, as early as 1900, roughly a quarter of higher education institutions were offering formal professional work in education for their students.[20] But normal schools were fast transitioning into teachers colleges awarding bachelor's degrees—eighty-eight did so between 1910 and 1930—and then from teachers colleges into general-purpose colleges. Consequently, much of teacher education by the beginning of World War II was consolidated in college departments of education or university education schools.[21] Professionalization efforts were also increasing. In the late 1930s, for instance, the General Education Board granted $1.1 million to create a Commission on Teacher Education, which in turn recommended expanding the normal school curriculum to four years from two.[22] Thus, working together, reformers, teachers, and professors of education created certification requirements dictating the number of course-hours in education classes.

In 1946 the National Education Association created the National Commission on Teacher Education and Professional Standards (TEPS), which recommended teacher credentialing both as a method of quality control and as a means of controlling entry into the profession. By the 1950s, "the certification of individual applicants was granted on the basis of their completion of an approved program, designed by the institution, and the recommendation of that institution."[23] The certification movement aimed to ensure that teachers would not simply know something about subject matter but would also know about the art of teaching. This was important for those hoping to professionalize the occupation and was seen as a way of improving teacher quality in an era of tremendous growth in high school attendance.

After a century of work, those concerned with teacher quality had successfully built networks of teacher training institutions and created statewide certification standards. Such efforts, they believed, would make the process of teacher selection fairer and less haphazard, while professionalizing the teaching occupation. As Ted Sizer observed, certification laws "came out of *extraordinary* abuse by a system in which some mayor's half-drunk, illiterate uncle was hired to teach twelfth-grade English."[24] Nevertheless, such "oppressive" regulations would become an object of scorn among future school reformers.

A SOCIALLY EFFICIENT ALTERNATIVE

The teacher licensure movement had its share of critics. With the rise of the undergraduate education major designed to certify would-be teachers, disciplinary expertise among American high school teachers, some argued, had steadily eroded. Critics of the bureaucratization of school staffing argued as early as the 1950s that a shift toward credentialing through schools of education gave inadequate attention to content knowledge, focusing instead on whether individuals possessed much-maligned course credits in pedagogy.[25] In the words of Arthur Bestor, "the question that is asked is not whether a man or woman is a good teacher, but whether he or she has course credits in pedagogy. Experience in teaching—gained, let us say, in a private school— will not satisfy the requirement."[26]

Such criticisms found an audience with a particular group of reformers who looked at American schools in the context of the nascent Cold War and saw a need for change. Given rising fears about national competitiveness, these reformers, like those at the Ford Foundation who decided to fund alternative certification programs like the master of arts in teaching (MAT), were increasingly concerned about the education of the so-called best and brightest. They argued that students trained in content areas at the nation's best schools would make the best teachers and that realizing this social efficiency aim was essential for maintaining American dominance. The belief that the space race would be won or lost in the nation's classrooms only served to raise additional questions about instructional quality.[27]

While teacher certification ensured a baseline of training, it did little to identify content-area expertise. In fact, some argued that certification indicated that, problematically, a teacher had spent more time in pedagogy classes than in core academic classes. In the Cold War context, this took on new importance. In an outline of a 1951 keynote address, Ralph W. Mc-Donald, executive secretary of the National Commission on Teacher Education and Professional Standards, listed what to him was the fundamental reality of the day: "Defense against communist aggression requires that American education be strengthened."[28] Pedagogy experts, in other words, were not going to put a man on the moon.

The aim of increasing teacher quality would be complicated by the fact that many public schools still struggled to fill all teaching positions with college graduates.[29] As a result, even if reformers had not been focused on high-achieving students at top schools—the nation's future leaders—they would still have to concentrate resources where they would be most useful. In a keynote address delivered before the 1954 Regional TEPS Conference on "Competent Teachers for America's Schools," T. M. Stinnett observed that "providing some children with master teachers and some with intern teachers would be acceptable."[30] Such a strategy, MAT founder James Conant noted, would be effective in public schools. While the public high school graduate "does better than the private school boy in Harvard College," he noted, "only the top quarter of the class of many high schools apply for admission to Harvard whereas all the graduates of a private preparatory school are potential college students."[31] Thus, MAT, which would bring content experts into the teaching profession, would not have to reach every public school student in order to make a major impact—just those at the top.

While this aim was shaped primarily by a focused concern on challenging the so-called best and brightest, it was also influenced by perceptions of what could be accomplished in schools attended by lower-income and lower-achieving students. A 1953 issue of *Time* magazine described the New York City public schools attempting "with genuine compassion and real hope to educate them and to fit them for useful, decent, even happy lives." But, the piece noted, "the classroom struggle for the minds and hearts of New York's young is as complex, as baffling and painful as the struggle for gain and survival which goes on in the perpendicular jungles of masonry outside." The article concluded that, despite the idealism of some, "harsh reality has often forced [the New York schools] to modify the classical educational concepts in order to give its raw levees of children some simple understanding of the language, of the country and its ideals, and of their duties as citizens."[32] In short, many still believed that students from different backgrounds required different kinds of educational experiences and that differentiating the curriculum was both pragmatic and fair.

Although incarnations of the MAT program differed from campus to campus, they shared a similar structure. Participating colleges and universities aimed to recruit superior students for fifth-year programs in which they would take both "academic" and education courses. Most programs required practice teaching, which was usually part-time and lasted between one and two semesters. Participants generally identified this "internship" as the most important part of their experience. After this training, MAT teachers generally were placed in high-performing secondary schools. Pleased with the program design, the Ford Foundation in 1959 announced grants of nearly $10 million (roughly $70 million in 2008 dollars) in support of teacher education programs, the majority of which were MAT programs at top universities and liberal arts colleges.

As MAT programs grew, though, some critics began to argue that they failed to meet the particular needs of less-privileged students. MAT graduates rarely worked in low-income schools, teaching primarily in suburban schools in which the majority of students were high achieving, white, and middle to upper class.[33] As Wendy Kopp would note in her original plan for Teach For America, whereas the MAT program was "successful in recruiting individuals of high academic ability who did not major in education," it was hindered by its inability to solve the "acute shortages" that plagued underserved areas.[34] Further, even if MAT graduates had wanted to work in low-income minority schools, a number of studies found that academically oriented teacher education reform efforts like the MAT program failed to prepare them for such work.[35]

Notably, reaching the underserved was never the primary intention of the MAT program, which was designed to connect content experts with high-achieving college-bound students. As the concerns generated by the Cold War ebbed and as social justice became a more prominent aim in education reform, the MAT program gave way to a different sort of alternate credentialing effort.

THE SOCIAL JUSTICE ALTERNATIVE

Before the 1960s, most experiments in teacher preparation were led by private foundations. The creation of the Teacher Corps, however, marked the entrance of the federal government into the act—an experiment that would last fifteen years and on which over a half billion federal dollars would be spent, making it the largest effort in teacher education reform to date.[36]

In the 1960s, the civil rights movement initiated a national discussion about teacher quality in underserved communities. Public schools, some argued, had failed to respond to the special needs and rights of racial minorities and low-income children. In response to such criticisms, policy makers and educators began to dedicate time and resources to create greater equality of opportunity and to keep students in school.[37]

In support of such efforts, President Lyndon Johnson pushed through Congress the Elementary and Secondary Education Act. The ESEA, however, lacked provisions for improving the quality of teachers in low-income schools.[38] Ensuing debates on addressing that oversight centered on whether to focus on recruiting experienced teachers or teacher interns. In part because recruiting experienced teachers to low-income schools would mean removing them from their current schools, Congress agreed on a model that emphasized interns.[39] With the details worked out, the Teacher Corps was created as a part of the Higher Education Act of 1965.

The concerns that shaped the creation of the Teacher Corps were characteristic of an era dominated by President Johnson's Great Society programs.[40] In 1966, the U.S. Office of Education, under Title XI of the National Defense Education Act, created the National Institute for Advanced Study in Teaching Disadvantaged Youth. Among other things, the institute's steering committee advocated preparing teachers to understand race- and class-based differences, to empower underserved students, and to work toward the goal of social equity.[41] A year later, in a study funded by the Department of Health, Education and Welfare, scholar Joseph Lohman made the case that future teachers needed to learn "more about the children themselves, especially those children whose values and ways of life vary from that of our society's mainstream."[42] And in 1972 the Office of Education established the Study Commission on Undergraduate Education and the Education of Teachers, which eventually called for giving teachers experiences in "culturally pluralistic atmospheres," helping them recognize "community-articulated needs" and develop insights "needed to make education serve the interests and survival needs of a child's class, culture and person."[43]

The Teacher Corps program, like other manifestations of the concern with equity and social justice, was created out of a different mold than that of the MAT program. As Johnson put it, the Teacher Corps would "enlist thousands of dedicated teachers to work alongside of local teachers in the city slums and in areas of local poverty."[44] Concerned with the "special needs" of "poverty area schools," volunteers viewed themselves as "innovators" and "activists" rather than "conventional educators."[45] Teacher Corps personnel also differed from conventional teachers in their racial backgrounds as well. Selecting Corps members for their "suitability," the program recruited minority teachers at significantly greater rates than American schools on the whole and eventually produced a group that that included as many African Americans, Latinos, and Native Americans as it did whites.[46]

Further, unlike MAT participants, Teacher Corps members were not necessarily content experts from the nation's best schools embarking on careers in teaching. While many of the earliest volunteers had been middle-class students from prestigious colleges, the program began to place an increasing emphasis on nonacademic criteria, underscoring what social scientist Kenneth Clark described as "the problems of identifying with children of different backgrounds—especially for persons from the white middle class."[47] A 1974 recommendation for teacher training based on lessons learned from the Baltimore Teacher Training Project, for instance, noted that "the guiding policy concept should be compensatory support; the direct opposite of the emphasis on 'quality' or 'excellence' which are fine sounding terms but which cover a perpetuation of an elitist approach."[48]

Teacher Corps programs tended to be headed by a program director, usually a faculty member at the sponsoring college of education, and funds were jointly controlled by the college and the participating school district.[49] Beyond that, however, there was little uniformity, and specific goals changed from project to project. Not all participants, for instance, taught in public schools. A 1969 legislative amendment, for example, allowed Teacher Corps members to serve juvenile delinquents, youth offenders, and adult criminal offenders, and a 1970 amendment allowed volunteers to serve as tutors and instructional assistants in schools.[50] Those who did teach in schools, as teacher-interns, could be assigned and transferred within the system by the local education agency, which also had the power to determine the subject matter to be taught and whether or not corps members continued on an assignment.[51] In 1974 there were ninety-four projects operating in 158 school districts, and with the cooperation of ninety-three institutions of higher education. Projects reached 125,000 children and cost roughly $40 million each year.[52]

Although programs varied greatly, a number of studies found that the corps was, overall, successful in meeting its goals. Corps members were effective at such things as developing ethnically relevant curricula, using community resources, and improving children's self-concept.[53] A General Accounting Office study found that corps members generally remained in the field of education, and most interns took teaching positions in schools serving low-income students.[54] One year out of the Teacher Corps, 76 percent of "first cycle" graduates were still in teaching, 72 percent in low-income schools.[55]

But there were also shortcomings to the Teacher Corps, as some critics readily noted. One study found that interns made ineffective change agents and that the demands on interns and their time were extreme.[56] Perhaps more seriously, another study found that interns were somewhat more competent in the classroom than other education students, but not overwhelmingly so. Further, "the interns who were the most self-consciously personable, warm, and compassionate in their relationships with students also appeared to be the most hostile to scholarship; they not only discounted the importance of cognitive achievement in their own pupils but often regarded university course work as meaningless and irrelevant for themselves."[57] Meeting some goals, it seems, was being done to the exclusion of others.

By 1980, cultural sensitivity and compassion began to give way to the priority of academic rigor in discussions about how to reform urban public schools. While some reformers would continue to push for community schools and ethnically appropriate education, the ultimate goal of social justice was transforming as perceptions of American social problems changed.[58] Rather than providing a community education to the underserved, the aim of many equity advocates was more and more to provide them with an elite-level education. A rising class of educational entrepreneurs happened to have a similar vision.

A NEW ERA

Criticism of America's system of preparing and certifying teachers continued unabated through the 1970s and 1980s.[59] By the early 1980s, however, reformers began to sharpen their criticisms with warnings about the demands of a rapidly changing economy. "As far back as the early seventies," wrote Robert Alley in 1989, "most futurists agreed that a fundamental change away from the industrial society was underway . . . [leading to] an information or communications based society."[60] The 1980s were seeing that futurist argument become a present reality—a reality that would require more rigorous educational experiences for all students, not just those perceived as most likely to take leadership positions.

Yet the teaching force, many argued, was inadequate. While some teachers were "up to the task of imparting highly complex knowledge and powerful new tools for effective analytical reasoning," others were not.[61] Particularly troubling to reformers was the fact that the weakest teachers, or at least those without strong content backgrounds, tended to be concentrated in low-income areas. While midcentury efforts at improving teacher content expertise for the perceived best and brightest had been successful, they had not reached the majority of public school students. In 1983, the *A Nation at Risk* report advocated the creation of incentives to attract "outstanding students" into teaching, having found half of newly employed mathematics, science, and English teachers unqualified to teach those subjects, with the majority of those unqualified working in underserved schools.[62] Reformers like Diane Ravitch argued that "teachers who do not have a strong education themselves are not well prepared to inspire a love of learning in their students," and she made the case that addressing this issue was a matter of equity.[63]

Leaders at education schools and state departments of education sought to bolster the academic preparation of future teachers. Some schools, for instance, strengthened their admissions requirements, and roughly twenty states set minimum grade point averages for admission to teacher training programs. Some states reduced the number of education credits required for teacher licensure. And some, like Texas, instituted *ceilings* on pedagogy course hours for education majors as a way to encourage students to take courses in subject matter areas.[64] Similarly, the Carnegie Task Force on Teaching as a Profession advocated requiring a bachelor's degree in the arts and sciences as a prerequisite for entering into a graduate program in teaching—much as the MAT program had done.[65] Yet some reformers saw the process of certification and credentialing as a fundamental problem, arguing that only by dismantling the certification system could the profession begin to draw in content-area experts.

Advocates of deregulation argued that while increasing teacher pay and professionalism would encourage strong candidates to consider a career in education, a more important first step was capturing the qualified potential teachers driven away by certification requirements. In making this case, they frequently used examples from successful private and parochial schools that did not give preference to certified teachers. "Almost no private schools require teaching certificates," Phil Kiesling argued in 1985; "instead, the emphasis is on whether instructors know their subjects and can teach them well. . . . Compare this with public schools, where only people with proper credentials can teach."[66] Similarly, a pair of researchers working with data from the Schools and Staffing Survey of 1987–1988 observed that "private schools employ a disproportionate share of the graduates of the nation's more selective colleges and universities," with teachers in the private sector "more likely than their public school counterparts to hold an undergraduate degree in an academic subject, as opposed to education."[67]

The state of New Jersey had implemented an experimental alternative certification program in 1985 as a way to broaden the state's pool of teachers. The Provisional Teacher Program required would-be teachers only to pass a state-sponsored test and participate in a training program during their first year of teaching. To some, the New Jersey program represented a revolutionary departure from the "long-standing education-school monopoly on teacher training."[68] Still, while the program opened the profession, it did not specifically recruit content experts, nor did it promise to channel them into the neediest schools.

There was a clear demand for an answer to the teacher question, but no program on its own seemed to meet the needs of a new era. As the authors of one study observed, "none of the traditional solutions is likely to address the basic problem of attracting highly competent people in such a dramatic manner as to alleviate the problem to any significant degree."[69] Aspects of the MAT program, which promoted content training, were attractive and road ready, as were aspects of the Teacher Corps, which focused on the underserved. Also entering policy conversations was the idea of alternate credentialing, replete with references to the practices of top private schools that did not require training for their teachers and that managed to be highly selective.[70]

Recruiting top students from top colleges to teach in the nation's struggling schools would require a creative approach, even if certification requirements were loosened. One idea floated among those concerned with promoting excellence for all was the notion of framing teaching as a form of temporary national service.[71] In a roundtable discussion in the mid-1980s, Ernest Boyer, former U.S. commissioner of education, argued that in order to improve the quality of teacher personnel, states might have to revert to short-term commitments from teachers. "Outstanding young people might agree, after they've gotten a Federal scholarship, that they will devote three years to teaching science or math, such as they might serve in the Peace Corps," he argued. "I'd rather see good people teaching for short periods than third- and fourth-rate people there for a lifetime."[72]

Other thinkers believed that such a recruiting effort would require a major commitment to mission and rhetoric. As Ted Sizer argued, "talented people—the best of the prospective students in teacher education, will join the teaching ranks as they see a chance for reform and an opportunity to be part of it. The excitement of a crusade for reform could be an elixir."[73]

These ideas about how to solve the perceived teacher quality problem—many of them half-formed—were a garage full of parts. Alternative credentialing, the notion of funneling top graduates into needy schools, the use of limited terms of service, and the development of a national reform movement were all responses to the same challenge: promoting excellence for all. It was a favorable environment for an engineer with a unifying vision of reform.

ONE DAY, ALL CHILDREN . . .

Teach For America was neither alone nor even first in answering the call to recruit teachers in the excellence for all era. With time, however, it would become the most visible, as well as the only truly national response.

In 1983, eight states reported having an alternative to traditional teacher licensing. By 2010, forty-eight states and the District of Columbia had some type of alternative route to teacher education and certification, resulting in the licensure of roughly sixty thousand new teachers a year.[74] But while programs like the New York Teaching Fellows adopted an approach similar to TFA, TFA is an exemplar of a new approach to reform for a new era. And though TFA produces only a fraction of the nation's teachers each year, it has continued to expand, reaching seven hundred thousand students per year by 2010.

In 1988, Wendy Kopp wrote her Princeton University senior thesis outlining a program for introducing elite college graduates into underserved urban and rural public schools for a two-year period of service. As Kopp told the *New York Times* in 1989, "the idea just popped into my mind. . . . I realized that top students might go into teaching if we could find a way to recruit them. It seemed so simple. One problem with the education reform movement is that people don't talk to college students."[75] The new teacher corps would help underserved students realize their "potential to learn," while also preparing them to "contribute to [the] country."[76]

By the late 1990s, the conditions were perfect for an organization like Teach For America to launch. By addressing concerns about social efficiency and national strength, as well as about equity and access, Kopp was able to frame TFA, from its inception, as a big-tent reform movement. The organization would promote excellence for all, and in so doing serve both the nation and the less privileged. Equally important, TFA promised a rising-tide sort of equity that would not come at the expense of more privileged groups. Thus, as the first director of the organization's New York office put it, TFA was able to pitch itself as "a big solution for the national problem."[77] TFA's message quickly attracted corporate funders working in the world of education reform, and Kopp secured grants from Union Carbide, Morgan Stanley, and Mobil Corporation. In the fall of 1989, TFA launched recruiting efforts at dozens of campuses, asking disciplinary majors at elite colleges and universities to commit two years to teaching in traditionally underserved urban and rural schools.

In terms of equity and social justice, the organization's public message was clear. "One day," the TFA "vision statement" reads, "all children in this nation will have the opportunity to attain an excellent education." The message had strong resonance—as Wendy Kopp explained in 2001, securing "educational opportunity for all Americans" is her generation's "civil rights issue"—and TFA leveraged it intentionally.[78] Mark McClinchie, a 1996 Houston corps member, recalled that he and others like him "joined to pursue social justice opportunities rather than contribute to social injustice."[79] Another corps member described the impact that a TFA recruiting poster made on her: "It was a black-and-white photograph of an African American man in a loose tie standing in front of a chalkboard facing excited students of color. There was no explanation, just a phone number. I wanted in. I wanted to be standing in front of a chalkboard, dazzling the students before me with new information. . . . I wanted to . . . give them something they would not have had without me."[80] By making the case that the organization would prove the "feasibility" of "educational equality," Kopp and her staff tapped into powerful wells of sentiment.[81]

TFA's message about promoting national political and economic aims was equally clear. The organization's early recruiting letters, for instance, noted that "our nation faces a number of internal threats that call for the help of our brightest young minds." Implicitly referencing the decline of American manufacturing and the increasing importance of a college education for maintaining economic competitiveness, they asserted that "one thing on which business and government leaders from different industries and political parties agree is that the state of the educational system is threatening America's future."[82] As the organization's first recruiter at Harvard University noted, TFA's effort to "make America stronger" was "clearly patriotic."[83]

Thus, at a time when it was becoming clear that social justice and social efficiency aims could not be pursued in exclusion of each other, TFA carefully worked to include both. Sometimes particular aspects of its mission were emphasized over others, but from the very beginning the TFA message was squarely in line with the emerging vision of excellence for all. In one of the clearest examples of this, an early recruiting letter distributed at Yale simultaneously addressed two separate audiences: "People of color, recall that perhaps the single greatest key to achieving full equality lies in achieving high levels of education. Liberal arts majors, remember that America is headed towards dangerously low levels of literacy, at precisely the time that they need to be high."[84] Whatever the artfulness of its wording, the letter reflected a clear understanding of broader reform currents.

The TFA message was designed to appeal to potential participants, without whom there could be no program. But Wendy Kopp also carefully crafted the organization's image with major donors and grant makers in mind. Alden Dunham, former senior program officer for educational programs at the Carnegie Corporation, recalled being struck in his 1989 meeting with Kopp by how well she had responded to "the national conversation" about education reform. As he saw it: "Kopp had come forward with a powerful idea at the right time."[85] This perception was not a matter of chance. Kopp noted in her original plan for TFA that the concerns of business leaders about the decline of the American workforce presented an opportunity to secure corporate financial backing, and grants from companies like Union Carbide and Morgan Stanley bore out her claim.[86] She was also well aware of philanthropic support for projects focused on the promotion of equity, and by emphasizing that aspect of TFA's mission she found a number of friends with deep pockets. As Carnegie Corporation president Vartan Gregorian explained: "insofar as organizations like Teach For America help to expand and open doors to educational opportunities for many of our citizens who still do not enjoy the socioeconomic and cultural benefits of American society, we are deeply grateful for their efforts."[87]

Finally, TFA's approach was attractive to the federal government, which over two decades poured tens of millions of dollars into the program through the Corporation for National Service, as well as through other grants.[88] Yet federal support has not been limited to a budgetary line item. Rather, support for TFA has been highly visible, perhaps most clearly through congressional recognition of "National Teach For America Week." In justifying the resolution, the U.S. Senate highlighted TFA as an organization buffering America's position in the world, as well as—noting that "6,000 corps members have aided 1,000,000 low-income students at urban and rural sites"—an organization working toward the aims of equity and social justice.[89]

SMART KIDS IN POOR SCHOOLS

In designing the TFA model, Wendy Kopp, knowingly or otherwise, borrowed key elements from both the MAT and the Teacher Corps models, drawing together social efficiency and social justice aims. Like the MAT program, TFA would focus on recruiting top students from prestigious colleges into teaching; like the Teacher Corps, though, it would aim to place teachers in low-income communities. In short, the vision was to draw on elite college graduates and recruit them into low-performing urban and rural schools. "If there was a certain beauty to the plan," one author concluded, "it was its simplicity . . . smart kids [recent college graduates] in poor schools."[90]

The TFA model was also influenced by work in one other domain: America's private schools. While public schools were characterized by complicated recruitment and hiring practices, private schools had long pursued an approach that was simpler and, some argued, more effective. As one Haverford College graduate observed, "the majority of my friends who want to teach will do so in private schools [which] don't require their teachers to be certified, and . . . [which] conduct aggressive on-campus recruiting sessions to find would-be teachers." It is, she concluded, "almost too easy to find a job at a private or independent school."[91] Wendy Kopp's vision was to change that.

The first lesson that private schools seemed to teach was that lowering barriers would promote the entrance of top talent into the teaching profession. As TFA Chicago's first executive director observed, "private schools, especially before alternative certification, were able to choose from a larger talent pool than public schools were . . . and that was a disadvantage for public schools."[92] And as TFA New York's first executive director put it, "the bureaucracy is massive" in urban public schools. "Private schools don't suffer from [that]. It's a major deterrent."[93]

Schools with high concentrations of low-income and minority students, of course, represented different kinds of environments than well-resourced private schools. As Kevin Hall, TFA's regional director in Los Angeles from 1991 to 1993, observed: "teaching in a classroom at Locke High School is a lot different than teaching in a classroom at [private] Harvard Westlake." Yet Hall also acknowledged that the comparison with private schools is a "very good analogue" and "there is some thinking on TFA's part about that."[94]

But top private schools did not simply lower barriers to entrance; they also tended to recruit graduates of prestigious high schools and colleges. The practices of private schools implied that smart people, regardless of training, made good teachers, and that message had a strong resonance with a particular audience. As Arthur Powell noted in 1996, roughly 10 percent of independent-school faculties—and a significantly higher percentage of the faculties at elite independent schools—are drawn from schools like Stanford, Yale, and Amherst. How, Powell and others wondered, could that not matter? "In short," he concluded, "there is a substantial educational fit between the college origins of prep school faculties and prep school academic missions. The fit does not guarantee good teaching, but it is hard to see how very good academic teaching can consistently occur in its absence."[95]

In light of this, Kopp sought from the organization's inception to make TFA exclusive, even if it meant limiting its scale. "I'd like people to someday talk about TFA," she commented in 1996, "the way they talk about the Rhodes scholarship."[96] Advancing this aim, the organization, from its origins, has promoted its corps members' prestigious alma maters, their high grade-point averages, and their SAT scores. Though TFA corps members have little training and often lack experience in the urban context, TFA advertises that its current national corps has an average GPA of 3.6 and an average SAT score of 1333.[97]

This approach had a strong common-sense appeal, particularly among reform-minded leaders attracted to the idea of placing the smartest college graduates into the neediest classrooms. In discussing his early support for TFA, Ross Perot emphasized in an interview with Larry King that the typical corps member "went to a private school . . . to one of our country's more elite schools."[98] Clearly, he believed, that was a game-changing difference. Speaking in an interview in 1990 about the popularity of TFA, Wendy Kopp observed: "I think what sells this to people is the fact that it's so simple and obvious."[99] TFA's approach, Kopp notes, "is not rocket science. It's the most basic, common-sense stuff."[100] Thus, while TFA was only one of many alternative routes into the classroom—Troops to Teachers, Transition to Teaching, and a number of regional teacher fellowship programs, among others—it was the purest manifestation of the excellence for all vision.

Even if it did not conjure up visions of private schools, TFA's antibureaucratic, promarket approach was attractive to a new generation of entrepreneurially oriented funders. In an early evaluation of TFA, University of Illinois professor Cameron McCarthy noted that the organization "seemed to rise out of . . . demonstration against the establishment, against the bureaucratic codes of traditional teacher training."[101] When TFA began operations in 1989, remarked Kevin Hall, "there really hadn't been much entrepreneurial work" in K–12 education. "There weren't really lots of . . . organizations that had been started by what we would view as younger, entrepreneurial types," he noted; "that was an interesting thing about Teach For America." Insofar as TFA was "willing to look outside of the conventional public school system, it was pretty early in its time," and that, Hall concluded, was "resonant" with funders.[102]

In New York this translated to support from organizations like the Edwin Gould Foundation. As Timothy Knowles, the first director of TFA's New York office, recalled, Gould donated office space to the organization because "they liked [that] we were young and entrepreneurial."[103] In Chicago, though the particular circumstances were different, the underlying theme was the same. Already established in places like New York and Los Angeles, TFA came late to Chicago. Still, bringing TFA to the Windy City was a major priority of the Chicago Public Education Fund—a venture capital fund created in 2000. In TFA they saw an opportunity to promote reform through a business model and leaped at the opportunity to fund a startup, help it grow, and then exit.[104] Of course, the TFA message also resonated with the so-called new philanthropists who emerged as a force in the late 1990s. Organizations like the Michael and Susan Dell Foundation, by issuing grants in the magnitude of $10 million, made in-kind gifts like the donation of office space look trivial by comparison.[105]

Entrepreneurially oriented figures in government and in public school systems also found themselves drawn to TFA and its antibureaucratic approach. Abigail Smith, vice president for research and public policy at TFA, noted that "the Bush administration [was] very supportive of Teach for America . . . because, we like to think, it's a good program, but also because there are no regulations." And, she added, "social justice [proponents] also support it. So we can reach in both directions."[106] At the district level, former New York City schools chancellor Joel Klein, who by 2006 was tapping TFA for nearly 10 percent of the city's new hires, praised TFA teachers for being "much less excuse-bound and more entrepreneurial and creative" than traditionally trained teachers. "I've got 1,000 [TFA corps members] affecting 70,000 or 80,000 kids," Klein added, "and I keep ramping it up."[107]

While many of the parallels between TFA and private schooling are implicit rather than explicit, the organization and its supporters have drawn direct comparisons between TFA and elite private schools for the purpose of justifying practice. In a letter to the *Christian Science Monitor* in 1990, for instance, a supporter responded to an op-ed critical of the organization, noting that TFA is in good company in pursuing noncredentialed teachers with subject-area expertise. "The best schools and colleges . . . [look for those who] know their subject and are willing to be with kids," the author argued. "These schools usually do not hire prospective teachers who have been trained and certified by the standard system."[108] Twenty years later, reformers would continue drawing such comparisons, with policy analyst Stafford Palmieri defending alternative licensing by noting that "the overwhelming majority of private schools . . . don't even require certification."[109] Wendy Kopp, in defending TFA against its critics, frequently counters the argument "that the only path to the classroom is through campus-based teacher education programs and notes that many successful private schools employ noncertified teachers."[110] Further, in making recommendations for future educational change, Kopp has revealed a preference for the private school model, as well as for market forces, arguing that "by providing parents with vouchers that allow them to place their child in a parochial or private school or in the public school of their choice, we could create market pressure that would force schools to improve themselves."[111]

Other aspects of TFA's approach have marked private schools, ostensibly the nation's best schools, as a model for the organization in its pursuit of excellence for all. As part of professional development, for instance, recent Los Angeles corps members were encouraged to observe teachers at "an 'excellent' L.A. school—such as the renowned Harvard-Westlake and the Marlborough School"—both highly selective private schools.[112] One TFA teacher visited Marlborough and returned to her classroom with lessons she had gathered from her school visit. She "was going to rearrange the desks in her classroom so that the space was circular and more conducive to discussion."[113] Others, no doubt, took different lessons from similar assignments.

It would be simplistic to say that TFA's organizational model was based on that of elite private schools. And yet, TFA has succeeded in attracting funders and recruiting corps members because of the parallels it established between its work and the work of such schools. At a time when antibureaucratic and promarket backlash was peaking, TFA promised to transform underserved schools by engaging in practices similar to those of high-status college-preparatory academies. And, at a time when all students ostensibly required top-notch academic training, TFA promised to replicate successful practices in order to get the right people into the classroom. Thus, both funders and participants—in both cases, frequently graduates of elite schools—were drawn to the program, as well as to the idea of taking elite education to scale.

A TWO-YEAR MISSION

Perhaps more than any other educational organization, TFA has effectively drawn on the support of reformers and private philanthropists taking a market-oriented approach to social change. In part, that success has been based on the fact that TFA, like private schools, takes an antibureaucratic, entrepreneurial approach to promoting excellence for all. To some degree, the organization has also succeeded because of a preference among funders for the private school model. Yet important aspects of TFA's model differ from that of private schools, and none more so than the two-year teaching commitment of TFA corps members.

Whereas private school teachers work in comfortable environments, TFA corps members would be asked to work in the most troubled schools. Consequently, in order to get the "best and brightest" into low-income urban public schools, the organization made a key tradeoff: time.[114] As Kopp put it in her thesis, "rather than fighting a losing battle" against higher-paying and higher-status opportunities, TFA would opt "not to compete." Instead, it would request "that individuals take a break from their fast-paced lives to serve the nation. *That* the best and brightest will be willing to do."[115] TFA, according to its leadership, has seen it infeasible to ask for more than a two-year commitment to placement sites. "People were opting not to go to law school or medical school . . . and instead pursue teaching," a former site director noted. If Wendy Kopp had "tried to pitch Teach For America for the rest of your life it wouldn't have worked."[116] While some TFA corps members stay in the profession after their terms of service, 60 to 70 percent of corps members leave teaching after two years, and many do not complete their stints.[117]

TFA has always encouraged corps members to stay in teaching, yet the organization's recruiting message places little emphasis on that goal. A TFA recruiting brochure, for instance, publicizes that corps members gain from their two-year placements "the skills, perspective, and experience" that will help them pursue "personal and professional goals, regardless of your career path."[118] Consequently, TFA corps members, though they may be committed to service, are also résumé builders attracted to the program's exclusivity and bounded time commitment. Asked about the fierce competition for acceptance to the program, one corps member responded: "I'd compare it with being accepted to an Ivy League grad school."[119] Such prestige no doubt helps TFA in its recruitment process, but it also places very real limits on what it can hope to achieve in terms of retention. As one TFA alumnus observed, the organization "presents itself one way when they recruit. They say this is a two-year Americorps program." If TFA really wants people "to make long-term commitments," he added, "then they need to repackage themselves as a long-term deal." In questioning whether the organization could ever ask for more than two years, he asked: "is it logical to think that the top college grads will commit long-term to teaching in high-need areas?"[120] The answer, at least currently, is no.

School districts and principals over the years have continued to seek out TFA corps members, indicating something unquestionably positive about the organization and its recruits. From the outset in New York City, according to its first site director, superintendents agreed to take on corps members because they "knew that they would otherwise be hiring substitutes or have class sizes that were too big."[121] Had corps members not staffed classrooms, one writer noted in 1993, "other teachers would have stood in their places. But they would not have been as well educated."[122] Los Angeles Unified School District superintendent Sylvia Rousseau brought TFA in because "the district was desperate for math and science teachers," and she reckoned that a TFA recruit would be better than a long-term substitute or what she called a "dying-on-the-vine" teacher.[123] Although those are low standards of comparison, principals report that corps members work hard, they are intelligent, and they are well organized. And they are filling a desperate need. According to one L.A. principal, "if you took all the TFA teachers out of Locke, we would have forty percent roving subs and mass chaos. We would not be able to survive."[124]

In a 2008 interview, Kopp argued that "we have the potential to end educational inequity."[125] TFA has operationalized this broad goal by using the concept of "significant gains" in academic performance. In elementary school, a significant gain is defined as a 1.5-grade-level jump each year; in high school, it means each teacher producing a class average of 80 percent mastery. Yet ambitious as those targets are, they fall short of Kopp's rhetoric about ensuring "that children in the poorest communities in America have the same average achievement rates as more privileged children."[126] That would require great teaching, and great teaching, it seems, requires time to learn, even if that learning takes place on the job.

Because corps members commit for such a short period of time, TFA cannot afford to spend a significant period training them. Additionally, as Richard Ingersoll suggests, schools with the highest turnover are the least well equipped to support new teachers.[127] Consequently, many of TFA's academically talented corps members realize their potential as teachers much later than they might otherwise have. As Larry Cuban has written, because of TFA's truncated schedule, "specifying how novices should teach is of less importance than individual teachers getting a grip on classroom discipline and their students doing well on state and district tests." As Gary Rubinstein, a 1991 Houston corps member, remembered, "that's how I made it through my first year. Scream. Teach for two minutes. Repeat as needed."[128] Consequently, according to Cuban, "traditional practices of controlling classroom behavior and habitual teacher-directed patterns of classroom instruction [continue to] trump other pedagogies."[129] Ironically, such reliance on traditional practices runs distinctly counter to TFA's entrepreneurial rhetoric of institutional transformation and radical change.

TFA teachers are a consensus favorite over long-term substitutes or unqualified teachers. Yet the results produced by corps members, while frequently positive, are mixed. Some studies have found students of TFA teachers to outperform other students, particularly in math.[130] Others, however, have found that the students of TFA teachers score lower than those of traditionally certified teachers, particularly in measures of reading.[131]

Regardless of the results, however, most studies compare TFA teachers only against other novices, though some have compared them with more experienced teachers. However, if excellence for all is the aim, the true standard of comparison is not novices or even experienced teachers.[132] Rather, it is master teachers in top schools. As former TFA corps member Jonathan Schorr writes, "a tough class requires a teacher with skills that come with experience and practice." Underserved students at low-performing schools, he adds, "need more than an enthusiastic college graduate's good intentions and good ideas. . . . [They need] a top-notch veteran, a master of the craft of teaching."[133] Of course, many scholars would consider it completely unfair to make such a comparison between novices and masters of their craft. TFA representatives, however, argue that they "believe that low-income kids deserve to have the same opportunities as kids in high-income schools."[134] Consequently, whether TFA is moving achievement toward that of students in high-income schools is exactly the sort of analysis it invites.

TFA's mission of seeking educational equity is compromised not only by its two-year commitment but also by factors inherent to TFA's particular excellence for all approach. One manifestation of this is the fact that while TFA teachers have academic and leadership backgrounds similar to those of suburban and private school teachers, they are often placed in schools that do not have much need for content experts. TFA teachers, one author notes, are often put "in the most difficult placements—in special education classes, bilingual classes, and limited-English classes."[135] Outside of their areas of expertise, their content mastery becomes nearly irrelevant. "I was a literature major at Yale," one corps member recalled. "I knew how to deconstruct texts. I had no idea how to help someone learn to read."[136] Sherry Wagner, a 1998 Washington, D.C., corps member, noted that "Teach For America doesn't want corps members to think that the realities and the circumstances matter, but they do. It does matter that I taught nine students who were in foster care."[137] Another corps member recalled her experience teaching in Los Angeles: "Sometimes my inexperience was relatively harmless, resulting in botched lessons or an inability to get everything done that I needed to do. Other times my newness had more dangerous consequences—I bungled home visits, didn't contact Child Protective Services when I should have, and sometimes even failed to keep my students safe."[138]

Further complicating TFA's organizational goal is the fact that corps members tend to come from different socioeconomic backgrounds than their students. As Serapha Reed, a 1995 New York corps member, noted: "In the literature of TFA, the organization writes about being a diverse corps wanting to be even more diverse. Yet, with all the statistics kept on demographics, none are kept on the economic status of the families that corps members come from and it is never addressed as a concern. It is not enough to recruit people of color, if the majority come from suburban, middle-high income families and go to the most elite schools."[139]

Committed to TFA's mission, corps members are willing to place themselves in challenging and unfamiliar situations, and are often confident that they will succeed. University of Illinois professor Cameron McCarthy observed in 1996 that TFA participants "entered the profession certainly with a degree of idealism, but also with this confidence that because of their high GPAs from reputable universities they would innately be able to deliver within the classroom."[140] Still, many corps members feel unprepared for their placements.[141] And many who believe they are prepared end up changing their minds.

The two-year commitment does a great deal to reduce any anxiety corps members might feel about their placements, which are by nature short term. Still, the experience of cultural dislocation can be a major impediment to the already difficult work of teaching in a low-performing school. Shelley Weston, assistant superintendent for secondary instruction in Los Angeles, observed that teaching in L.A.'s neediest schools can be "hard for someone who's lived in the suburbs all their life . . . [and] sometimes they can get overwhelmed by it all." Further, she added, "if 35 percent of your population is in foster homes, there's not necessarily the parent support that you need."[142] Often, by the time corps members have acculturated, their terms of service are up.

Many TFA participants, of course, are deeply familiar with the kinds of schools and communities they are placed in. Others work to avoid being seen as missionaries or "white knights." As one corps member advised, we "must keep in mind that we are not in these schools to save anybody. I never said that I was a part of a movement to save people. I was in New Orleans because there was a classroom that might be empty without me."[143] Despite its romantic rhetoric, TFA is not without its realists.

But while realism keeps some corps members from losing their resolve, it can also have the opposite effect in an organization that depends on participants feeling a sense of mission. TFA corps members are predominantly placed in low-income urban schools with lower-achieving students—schools where teachers, particularly those early in their careers, are far more likely to leave the profession.[144] "The frustrations that plague an inner-city teacher," two early TFA corps members wrote, "drive motivated and talented individuals to either mediocrity or other professions.

We cannot imagine a more important job, and yet to maintain such high demands upon ourselves would result in burnout." The authors suggested that teachers be trained to serve in the roles of "parent, organizer, researcher, counselor, and community activist"—a description of training reminiscent of the bygone Teacher Corps.[145]

TFA's defenders respond to criticisms of the organization and its work by arguing that placing corps members at a school site is better than whatever alternatives a school might have faced. "The truth is," one TFA booster argued, "up to half of all the country's 3.5 million teachers bail within five years. Low pay, low status and low satisfaction undoubtedly drive many out."[146] Anina Robb, a 1996 New York corps member, defended TFA in spite of high rates of turnover by noting that "there are other things that young people can show children besides content area knowledge that are important aspects of educating our students. The sad reality is that other people aren't jumping in to fill these positions."[147] Nevertheless, none of this indicates that TFA is fulfilling its organizational promises and solving the problems of urban public schools or providing opportunities equal to those received by suburban and private school students.

A MISSION TRANSFORMED

By the dawn of the twenty-first century, TFA's mission began to change in response to, and in anticipation of, criticism. Such shifts were not new to TFA. In her original plan for the organization, Wendy Kopp had argued that her new teacher corps would "not be telling the nation that its inexperienced members were preferable to, or as qualified as, experienced teachers."[148] Yet as the organization grew and as it justified its growth, it did begin to heavily promote supportive findings, like those of a study by Mathematica Policy Research that found TFA teachers more effective than traditionally certified teachers.[149]

But opponents of the TFA model began to mount new criticisms of the organization, focused primarily on TFA's brief service commitment. Placing recent college graduates for two-year terms into the neediest classrooms, critics argued, was a patch at best and a public disservice at worst, and it fell well short of excellence for all.

TFA was putting the same kind of teachers into underserved schools who were usually only found in the nation's best schools, but it failed to retain them the way that suburban or private schools so frequently do. In the case of another alternative pathway into the profession—the MAT program—participants who left teaching taught for an average of five years be-fore leaving. And those who were still teaching at the time of a 1986 study had been in the classroom for an average of over 13 years.[150] TFA teachers, on the other hand, generally leave just as they are beginning to establish competency in the classroom.[151] Whatever potential TFA corps members have as teachers, it is rarely realized in full.

In the case of Los Angeles's Locke High School, TFA quickly became the primary source for new teachers because of the principal's faith in the quality of TFA corps members. In 2005, TFA supplied 20 percent of the teachers on staff. However, by the end of that year, nearly a dozen TFA teachers had resigned and eight others left before finishing their two-year commitments.[152] This disappointment caused the principal to lament: "you invest in them, get them to a level of skill, and then they leave. I have to look for stability at the school. Last year I hired all TFAers for my vacancies. This year, I'm going to be looking for a significant number of non-TFA teachers."[153] Other principals in the city have had comparable experiences. "All in all, it has been a very positive relationship and the teachers are readily selected by principals," said Deborah Ignagni, assistant chief human re-sources officer for the Los Angeles Unified School District. But, she noted, "if the principals could change one thing, it would be to retain the teachers longer so that the students would continue to benefit and the school com-munity would have continuity."[154]

In Chicago, the story was similar. Although data from TFA showed that 43 percent of its teachers who started in Chicago Public Schools in 2001 remained on the job in 2004, Toni Hill, director of CPS's Routes to Teaching office, cautioned that the district might have to "re-evaluate" its partnership if retention did not improve.[155] "These people are really good—well-trained, highly motivated—so they leave to pursue advanced degrees or positions in other fields," noted Principal James Breashears of Robeson High in Englewood, who lost five of six TFA teachers in two years. "That's the downside, that they have so many possibilities. It's hard to keep them."[156]

TFA has tried to combat criticism of this sort by publicizing high degrees of persistence in the field of education among corps members. According to TFA, 60 percent of corps alumni are still working full time in education, though not necessarily in the classroom.[157] However, according to an in-dependent study, 69 percent of TFA teachers had left the classroom by the end of their second year of teaching, and 88 percent had left the profession by the end of their third year.[158] According to another set of researchers, 73 percent of corps members in one sample had left by year three and 85 percent had left by year four, compared to 50 percent of other nontraditional entrants and 37 percent of those receiving traditional training who had left by the fourth year.[159] Many corps members stay in education—going to graduate schools of education, entering into policy work, opening charter schools—but generally not in the teaching profession. Consequently, the degree to which TFA directly improves education in underserved communities remains in question.

A decade into its work, TFA's message began to change subtly. Acknowledging retention issues, the organization began to promote itself as being equally committed to leadership development as it was to recruiting top college students into teaching. "The program was never intended to solve the teacher shortage problem or even to fix public education simply by preparing bright college students to teach for two years," argued TFA advocate Julie Mikuta in 2008. "Instead," she contended, "TFA intends to transform public education by exposing these talented people to the challenges of public education and engaging them in figuring out solutions." Thus, she concluded, TFA's impact will only be seen in the future, once "alumni take on more visible and influential roles."[160]

Despite this belief in the organization's ability to develop future leaders in education, that was not the original intent. Kopp's original plan mentioned nothing about leaders.[161] In speculating about where corps members would head after two years, a TFA representative noted in 1990: "Of course, Teach For America hopes that after two years people will be interested in trying to get certification and continuing on."[162] That is no longer a common TFA message. More prominently cited by the organization, TFA alum Megan Hopkins argues, are "its successes in generating a 'force of leaders,' some of whom stay in the classroom." Because the majority of corps members leave to pursue related endeavors, the question, at least according to Hopkins, is whether TFA is "flourishing as a leadership development program rather than a teacher preparation program."[163]

Why did this shift take place? From its earliest stages, TFA has framed itself for funders, taking care to promote the legitimacy of its model even if volunteers did not stay in the teaching profession. Consequently, in the mid-1990s Wendy Kopp developed an additional goal for the program: to help those "expected to become leaders in their chosen occupations . . . become knowledgeable about education and experienced in teaching, whether or not they remain in education after their two years of service."[164] Only in the coming years, however, would that goal gain the same prominence as the organization's goal of improving teacher quality. "Since the beginning," one author noted, "TFA had been on the defensive about the short-term nature of the teaching commitment, particularly when talking to school districts and funders. By emphasizing the longer-term goal of the mission, TFA was able to neutralize some of the well-founded concerns around the issue of teacher churning in underperforming schools."[165] According to former TFA New York director Timothy Knowles, such a shift was "a very logical response to that criticism."[166]

Still, according to Marion Hodges-Biglan, the first executive director of TFA's Chicago office, as late as 2000 the organization was making its case by emphasizing that it had great people who wanted to go to the west and south sides of the city to teach. At that time, Hodges-Biglan noted, "we weren't pitching the long-term impact" of TFA corps members becoming future leaders, "though," she added, "we do that now." In TFA's first few years in Chicago, Hodges-Biglan recalled, the message was that "we're doing this because we believe that low-income kids deserve to have the same opportunities as kids in high-income schools."[167]

TFA's strategic shift, as author Donna Foote details it, took place in 2001 with the introduction of Melissa Golden as the organization's "brand czar."[168] According to Foote, Golden

> helped to reposition the brand by making sure that potential recruits and supporters understood that there were two parts to the TFA mission, and that both were equally important. In the short term, TFA teachers would make an immediate, catalytic impact in lower-income classrooms; longer term, they would join a burgeoning army of teacher leaders who, transformed by their teaching experience, would force systemic change to ensure educational equity, whether or not they stayed in the classroom beyond their two-year commitment.[169]

Once the organization had clearly articulated its new theory of change, "it moved quickly to bring uniformity to the look and feel of the brand."[170]

By the time TFA began a $60 million expansion effort in 2005, it was articulating its purpose in a new way. The mission of the organization, according to a press release announcing $30 million in grants, was billed as building "the movement to eliminate educational inequality by enlisting the country's most promising future leaders in the effort."[171] According to supporter Don Fisher, founder of Gap, Inc., and a major funder of TFA and KIPP charter schools, "Teach For America's growth and success is critical to the growth of other education reform efforts including the charter school and small schools effort." Its success was vital not because of the teachers it would produce, but because it would "create reform leaders for the coming decades."[172]

Despite this shift in branding, TFA has remained a favorite of reformers in pursuit of excellence for all, and particularly those seeking an answer to the teacher question. A 2002 U.S. Department of Education press release explained a $1 million grant to TFA by making the case that students in the nation's "poorest schools" would be taught, just as their more privileged peers, by "outstanding recent college graduates of all academic majors."[173] As backer Eli Broad reasoned in 2005, TFA's "infusion of high-quality teachers" into underserved schools would "improve the education of all children and narrow achievement gaps."[174] Thus, it seems, the vision of Ivy League–educated teachers working in low-performing urban schools has been so powerful that reformers have willingly suspended disbelief about its challenges.

THE NEXT BIG THING

Born during the excellence for all era, TFA quickly gained the backing of a new wave of entrepreneurial reformers whose support thrust it onto the national stage. The constituent parts of TFA's model were not, contrary to some popular belief, new. However, unlike its predecessors, the organization sought to advance both social efficiency and social justice aims, promoting academic rigor in the classrooms of the least privileged without affecting the work of schools serving the more advantaged. To the pleasure of school reformers, TFA operated independently of bureaucratic school systems and recruited into teaching the same sort of people who could be found teaching at the nation's best schools.

TFA rapidly became the "next big thing" in education because it offered an appropriate prescription in an era dominated by market-oriented reformers and the aim of excellence for all. Consequently, a look at the organization's challenges and various adaptations reveals as much about the notion of excellence for all and the entrepreneurial approach to education reform as it does about TFA. Despite its many successes, TFA has made a number of necessary compromises, none more important than time. The organization recruits subject-matter specialists from top colleges—the same kind of talent often found teaching in the nation's best schools—and places them in underserved schools. But keeping those young teachers in the neediest schools is, for a variety of reasons, too challenging to mandate service of more than two years. In short, while the premise of TFA makes sense to a wide cross section of school reformers, it has had major difficulties in realizing its lofty aim and raises questions about the broader goal of excellence for all. As former corps member David Wakelyn observed: "cycling bodies in and out of the same positions every two years is not a solution."[175]

Still, low rates of teacher retention and their consequences did not erode support for TFA or undermine the vision of ensuring educational equity. It did not empty TFA's coffers, usher in a new next big thing, or bring the excellence for all era to a close. Instead, the organization and its supporters began to publicize TFA in a new way. While improving teacher quality was a part of the mission, they argued, the real impact of TFA would come from giving tomorrow's leaders firsthand experience in low-income schools. Consequently, it has continued to receive outsized attention and funding relative to other teacher recruitment efforts. Thus, while TFA may be so visible because it is the answer to the nation's teacher problems, it seems likelier that it simply drew together the right ideas for the context of a particular time period. Its success may better reflect the sociopolitical climate of the past two decades than the program's ability to improve the teaching profession.

A look at the wider history of alternative credentialing efforts reveals how teacher reform efforts succeed because they promise to address ever-changing social problems. Reformers concerned with inconsistent teacher competency, as well as the problems of patronage systems, pursued bureaucratic solutions to the teacher question in the early twentieth century. By midcentury, however, minimum standards, like certification requirements dictating a number of course-hours in education classes, were perceived as a problem rather than a solution. Reformers concerned more with national competitiveness than with uniformity sought to open alternative routes into the profession as a way of channeling content experts into the classroom. In the 1960s and 1970s, reformers concerned with equity and social justice also pursued alternative pathways into the classroom. But unlike those who had sought to promote rigor, these reformers were less concerned with teachers' content backgrounds than they were with their capacity for understanding and meeting the unique needs of low-income and minority children. Toward the end of the decade, concerns would shift again, and savvy reformers would pitch their work as uniquely situated to respond to new concerns.

Like their predecessors working to improve the preparation of the nation's teaching corps, advocates of TFA have argued that new times call for new solutions. Times change, priorities shift, and policy, in the hands of responsive leaders, adapts for a new context. But the major swings in teacher licensing reform efforts have responded more to context than to any evolving knowledge about how to develop qualified teachers and keep them in the nation's public schools. Each movement, rather than building on the last, instead displaces it, promising to solve new problems with new programs and designs.

The best teacher licensing reform efforts do begin to address those problems, even those as intractable as educational inequity. But in approaching change in this manner, old debates go unresolved and the teaching profession is left vulnerable to the next attack, the next problem, and the next crisis. Primed to turn against efforts that come up short, reformers are ready to make the case for the next big thing.

Reformers in the excellence for all era, however, continued to smile on Teach For America. To paraphrase Alden Dunham, it was the right idea at the right time.

4

THE RIGHT CURRICULUM
Expanding Advanced Placement

THE 1980S USHERED IN A NEW ERA of concern over the quality of the school curriculum. At a time when economic competitiveness demanded greater educational achievement, standardized test scores revealed that American students were continuing to fall behind their international counterparts.[1] And, in the post–civil rights era when promoting equality was an increasingly prominent goal in education, national test scores revealed dramatically lower scores for black and Latino students than for whites.[2]

But while many American schools struggled to help their students reach levels of proficiency, some were among the best in the world. Such schools not only promoted high achievement but also sent their graduates off to first-rate colleges. And though curricula varied across top schools, they did have something in common: the Advanced Placement Program (AP)—a series of courses and exams across a variety of subject areas designed to promote rigor and achievement among top high school students.

AP was conceived of shortly after the Second World War as a way of engaging and challenging the academically able and awarding them advanced standing in college. School administrators and reformers concerned with these high-achieving students and, for that matter, with national security after the launching of Sputnik, argued for increased academic rigor and tracking students by ability. Consequently, with assistance from the College Board, which administered AP, the best American high schools quickly adopted it as a way of promoting giftedness. Within two decades, the program became a signal of a top school.

The design of the program was simple. High schools with the means to do so would offer ostensibly college-level versions of school subjects, tracking their best students into AP classes. At the end of the academic year, participating students would sit for a standardized exam, which would then be graded between "1," indicating below-average understanding, and "5," indicating exemplary comprehension. Those grades would then determine whether students received college credit, which participating colleges and universities initially agreed to grant for scores of "3"—in theory the equivalent of a "C" in a college-level course—or higher.

AP provided tangible benefits for students. It allowed them to earn college credit and, as a curricular status symbol, it gave them an edge in an increasingly competitive college admissions process. Consequently, it was not long until advocates for underserved students labeled the program elitist, and they were right. In 1954 only 532 students took AP tests. By 1988, though, that number was up to 292,164. But while the program did expand dramatically over that period of time, it still remained a rarity in urban public education, growing mostly in suburban and private schools.

In the last decades of the twentieth century, however, a hybrid of the Cold War–era social efficiency arguments and civil rights–era social justice arguments began to emerge. Supporters of AP began to argue that bringing the program into urban public schools would promote both equity and excellence, aiding underserved students while increasing national achievement and attainment rates. Further, it would expand access without interfering with the work of suburban and private schools. Consequently, AP exploded. One million students participated in the program in 2002; by 2008, that figure had grown to 1.6 million.

By the dawn of the twenty-first century, able and ambitious students across the nation had acquired access to Advanced Placement courses and exams. This had the effect of strengthening the curricular offerings of many schools, but, more importantly, it gave a leg up in the college admissions race to throngs of young people adorning their high school transcripts with AP courses each year. "Like cellphones, lattes and other once-elite products," noted one commentator, Advanced Placement courses "have become ubiquitous."[3] The expansion of AP seemed a triumph for advocates of excellence for all.

Yet the expansion of the program was not without consequence. As AP lost its uniqueness and moved to a wider range of schools, it less effectively identified the most talented and ambitious students. As a result, colleges began to give the program less recognition in the admissions process. Educators at top high schools had long expressed reservations about the program for its focus on breadth over depth and on preparation for an end-of-year test. But they stuck with it as long as colleges awarded preference to students with AP on their transcripts. As colleges began distancing themselves from AP, a number of high schools began dropping the program from their course rolls. Thus, a half century after AP's inception, many of the elite schools that participated in designing the program had rejected it and, in so doing, began to undermine the AP brand.

This chapter explores the history of the Advanced Placement Program, from its roots in the 1950s as a program for challenging top students at elite schools, through its expansion, and up to the present as it faces threats to its credibility and prestige. Why, it asks, did support for AP change over time? What does that reflect about broader reform trends? And what about the program kept it from realizing the aim of excellence for all that it took on at the end of the century?

ORIGINS

In 1950, John Kemper, the headmaster of Phillips Andover, invited the recently created Alumni Educational Policy Committee to consult with Andover's faculty on revising the school's curriculum. As discussions progressed, "it became more and more evident that the real problems extended far beyond the curriculum of any one preparatory school." As a report of the proceedings noted, "they paralleled problems in other schools and reached into the colleges."[4] Top students, they argued, were simply not being pushed hard enough. And in the context of the Cold War, the consequences were potentially disastrous.

Soon Andover, working with two other elite high schools—Exeter and Lawrenceville—as well as Harvard, Princeton, and Yale, began a project to promote rigor in secondary education. A new division at the Ford Foundation, the Fund for the Advancement of Education (FAE), paid for the work, which squared with the FAE's concern with educating the gifted and talented. Leaders at the FAE liked what they saw.

Addressing the needs of the gifted and talented was of particular concern to reformers in an era characterized by, as the Ford Foundation's Edward J. Meade put it, "the pursuit of excellence." Maintaining the nation's global position, many argued, required that the so-called best and brightest be prepared for the demands of political and scientific leadership. "Ultimately," as one Rockefeller Brothers Fund report put it, "the source of a nation's greatness is in the individuals who constitute the living substance of the nation."[5]

Education was one means of addressing the perceived crisis, yet some found the schools unprepared for the task. In his memoir, scholar Jerome Bruner recalled the passion of Cold War–era reformers "convinced that the trouble with schools was the shoddy stuff they taught."[6] Such reformers believed that "the cure was to narrow the gap between knowledge locked up in the university library or the scholar's mind and the fare being taught in the schools." If "an untrained teacher stood between the knowledge and the student," then it only made sense to "bypass the teacher" through the curriculum.[7] Concern for national strength through education, however, did not extend to "issues of race and poverty in education," which, Bruner noted, "had not come into [reformers'] consciousness."[8]

In this context, the FAE funded the School and College Study of Admission with Advanced Standing to continue looking into the question of rigor in the secondary curriculum. The study was led by twelve colleges and universities—Brown University, Haverford College, MIT, and Swarthmore College among them—and thirteen secondary schools including prestigious public schools like Newton High School and the Bronx High School of Science, as well as private academies like Groton, Andover, and Exeter. Its intention, according to the 1952 *Bulletin of Information* it issued, was "that able school boys and girls . . . proceed farther than at present in the standard studies of a liberal education."[9] Consequently, the group, led by then-president Gordon Chalmers of Kenyon College, aimed to devise a program that would allow high-achieving secondary students from elite schools to take advanced classes and earn college credit while still in high school.

Those who crafted the 1952 report held a number of assumptions about what such a program would look like. The study leaders wanted to "offer an opportunity and a challenge to . . . the strongest and most ambitious boys and girls."[10] But because they believed that such advanced levels of work could "be done only in exceptional secondary schools, public and independent," the opportunity would only be provided to the strongest students in elite schools.[11] This was not surprising, given that most of the participating high schools would later be listed by James Conant as America's best. But it did shape the nature of the program they created, which focused on a predominantly prep-school clientele.[12] Study leaders also assumed that students would learn advanced material and take placement tests to push themselves harder, not anticipating the use of such a program to gain status or an edge in college admissions. An ambitious and able student, they wrote, would "be able, by means of extra courses and summer work, to earn his bachelor's degree in three years."[13] Thus, they believed, such a program would make secondary and postsecondary education more challenging while accelerating transitions into graduate school or the workplace.

Because of the nature of its development, only elite schools offered the embryonic Advanced Placement Program and only top students were invited to participate. Given the schools and the students involved with the program, however, AP quickly became a mark of academic prestige. Unintended though it may have been, one of the most influential results of the establishment of AP would be the creation of a branded curricular status symbol.

BUYING INTO AP

In the spring of 1954, 532 students in the eighteen participating schools took 929 Advanced Placement examinations.[14] The following fall, Charles Keller became the first director of the Advanced Placement Program, which was to be administered under the care of the College Board—the same organization that ran the SAT test. The first board-sponsored testing took place the following May.

At least initially, schools and students used the program as intended: gifted students sought greater challenge and, in so doing, earned college credit. The purpose of AP was to give the best students at top high schools, where they already had the luxury of being bound for prestigious colleges and universities, room to excel and an inducement to continue to work hard. As David Dudley, the second director of AP, wrote: "the basic philosophy of the Advanced Placement Program is simply that all students are not created equal."[15] Some parents complained that this approach was antidemocratic. Yet many leaders like R. Sargent Shriver Jr., president of the Chicago board of education, were unmoved. "Is it wrong," Shriver asked, "to try to give each student a chance to progress as rapidly as he can?"[16]

In 1957 the launching of Sputnik heightened anxiety about the ability of the United States to compete intellectually, particularly scientifically, against the Soviet Union. The crisis seemed to call for an expansion of programs like AP. Congress responded swiftly, tripling the budget of the National Science Foundation and passing the National Defense Education Act, which provided millions of federal dollars for the advancement of science, mathematics, and modern languages in elementary and secondary schools.[17] Neither move directly influenced the adoption of AP in schools. But the National Science Foundation increasingly funded curriculum projects and teacher professional development efforts designed to increase rigor in American high schools, creating a context in which a program like AP looked even more appealing.[18]

Two years after the Soviets launched Sputnik into orbit, James Conant published *The American High School Today* in which he called for schools that challenged students according to ability. Too few schools, the former president of Harvard University argued, met the distinct needs of their variously talented students. According to Conant, the solution was simple: schools needed to implement differentiated curricula, adopting programs like AP for advanced students. Otherwise, the best students would simply slide through high school "without enough rigorous academic work."[19] In cities across the nation, Conant and his supporters made the case that serving the gifted and talented was critical for national strength.

AP was a relatively easy sell for other reasons as well. Teachers, for their part, leapt at the opportunity to teach AP courses. Experienced teachers with advanced content knowledge could cover more challenging material at a faster pace in an AP class than they could in heterogeneous classes, even at schools like Exeter. As David Dudley noted, teachers felt "real satisfaction in teaching the very able and the intellectually restless." Further, administrators believed that "the intellectual tone of a school" was lifted by programs like AP that recognized scholastic achievement.[20] And, with school reformers like Conant pushing for tracking students according to perceived ability, educators teaching Advanced Placement classes were on the cutting edge pedagogically.

AP had a separate and unplanned appeal for students. Increased applications for a fixed number of college and university slots during the 1950s produced rising anxiety about "the growing scarcity of 'spaces,' especially in the Ivy League colleges."[21] Whereas once schools like Yale had "treated respectfully the headmasters and directors of studies at the leading Eastern prep schools, from which Yale drew a sizable part of each freshman class in the 1940s," and each senior in those schools "chose one and only one Ivy League school," times were changing.[22] "The years since 1955," Richard Pearson wrote in the *College Board Review* in 1959, "have seen pressures for competitive admission build up considerably at perhaps 100 institutions across the country and, to a lesser extent, at another 100 to 150 colleges."[23] Those pressures would only continue to increase. As a 1963 *Chicago Tribune* story put it, "the full impact of the post-war increase in the birth rate will be felt in the next two years . . . and many high school graduates of exceptional ability already find it impossible to get into the college of their choice."[24]

Consequently, many students and parents saw in AP an opportunity to gain a measure of distinction. Concerned about how to remain competitive in a process that no longer found places at elite colleges and universities for all qualified applicants, AP gave them a way to signal their superiority to colleges. For their part, colleges seemed untroubled by incipient credentialism, and most AP students proved to be quite capable. In 1958, for instance, Northwestern University reported that 50 percent of its AP students who entered as sophomores were in the top quarter of their class, and all but two of the other 50 percent were in the top half.[25]

Yet not everyone was pleased with the influence AP was having on schools. Less than a decade after the first AP classes were offered, Phillips Exeter faculty member and textbook author Henry Bragdon warned that "too much emphasis" was being placed "on the prestige value of the advanced placement courses." Bragdon also observed "a dangerous tendency to regard advanced placement teachers and students as an elite worthy of special praise."[26] The founding AP schools had intended the program to challenge and track the brightest and most capable students. They had not, however, intended it to provide prestige and privilege for those students—a problem that leaders at the College Board, in whose *College Board Review* Bragdon's piece appeared, seem to have recognized.

AP was also, some argued, dramatically increasing the workloads and stress levels of student participants. One Chicago parent, for instance, would later complain that her son was "scheduled up so tightly it's almost impossible to find half an hour to get him to the barber every three weeks . . . he even brings books to the dinner table with him."[27] Others took issue with the narrowly defined vision of rigor promoted by those like Conant. Paul Diederich of the Educational Testing Service argued that "there is simply too much sitting down, listening to talk, talk, talk. We say that these students ought to learn to 'work hard,' and that they would not mind that in the least; it is the sitting down and listening all day in a space half the size of a grave that gets them down. . . . The teachers come out of it as scarred and tired as the students."[28] Was this, Diederich implicitly asked, the best that American educators could do?

Despite these pedagogical concerns, AP grew quickly as schools rushed to adopt it. Somewhat surprisingly, pressure for expansion was most heavily exerted by parents of students at strong, but not elite, schools. While schools like Exeter still maintained a pipeline into the Ivies, AP offered others a chance to prove their parity with students at elite schools and, consequently, to gain better odds of attaining admission at choice colleges and universities. In his 1961 book *Slums and Suburbs*, James Conant wrote that the schools admitting the largest number of students with AP courses on their high school transcripts were MIT, Michigan, Stanford, Northwestern, and "six of the Ivy League institutions."[29] Further, at Harvard "about half" of the entering class had participated in AP, and "nearly ten per cent" had passed enough tests to confer second-year standing. Enrolling in AP, it seemed, was the next best thing to attending an elite prep school. In response to mounting pressure, the New York public schools announced a plan in the early 1960s to better serve the city's gifted students by expanding the AP Program to accommodate ten thousand students—as many students as had participated in the program nationwide two years earlier.[30]

Despite the resistance of school leaders and those at the College Board, the meaning and purpose of AP had begun to change. In 1956, Harold Gores and Leo Barry, superintendent of the Newton Public Schools and principal of Newton High School, respectively, wrote that it would "be necessary that schools and colleges not let the values inherent in the present concept of enriched courses be lost in the merely utilitarian aspects of accelerated study beyond high school."[31] In short, Gores and Barry, who had taken part in the crafting of AP, were concerned that AP continue to promote learning. But preserving the original meaning of the program was a daunting task when AP's greatest appeal seemed to be that it provided an edge in the college admission process. Students increasingly were drawn to AP classes not because they wanted to work alongside other highly motivated students, but because they wanted to acquire the AP credential. "As pressure to get into the prestige colleges has increased," wrote Henry Bragdon, "it has not taken students long to learn that college admissions officers are impressed when they see advanced placement courses on a candidate's record. The very fact of having taken such a course is as good as a 700–800 College Board Achievement Test score."[32] As the dean of one private college in the Midwest stated, "Just the presence of an advanced placement course on the transcript is enough [for admission]."[33]

Already by the late 1960s, though, there was growing equity-based criticism of AP. During the early years of the decade, school districts had promoted the fact that "within one high school there are advanced placement courses for students ready for college work at one end of the scale [and] basic English and mathematics for the slow and the deprived at the other end."[34] By the end of the decade, however, the practice of sorting and tracking students was being called into question. Elitist moves to increase rigor were leaving "regular" and "slow" students behind, providing them a second-class high school education and shutting doors to postsecondary education. Addressing this critique would lead to the program's dramatic expansion and, consequently, create a new problem for leaders at the College Board.

GROWING INEQUITY

Despite the fact that a new batch of schools was adopting it in the late 1960s and early 1970s, AP remained the reserve of "the wealthiest independent schools and the high schools in affluent suburbia."[35] Efforts to promote rigor, largely by tracking students, were frequently justified by the larger aim of national defense. But in the post–civil rights era, increasing emphasis among parents and reformers on educational equity and social justice began to alter perceptions of AP. As activists fought for the rights of low-income and minority populations, some began to argue that AP was intolerably elitist. Others advocated expanding access to the program to those in underserved communities long denied educational equity and a fair shot at earning a college diploma.

One major contextual development was a further spike in college enrollments, which doubled between 1950 and 1980. Consequently, even students at the original AP high schools needed to compete for spots at schools like Harvard, Princeton, and Yale. As John Thelin writes, "by about 1958 the overall rush to go to college, any college, had evolved into a rush to go to a prestigious college . . . [and] institutional reputation came to be set in large part by the number and percentage of applicants a college admissions office rejected." This, in turn, "spawned a cottage industry of manuals offering advice on 'how to get into the college of your choice.'"[36] Regardless of the degree to which AP actually prepared students academically, it was becoming a standard part of a top secondary education and an impressive résumé. And the more AP classes one took, the better.

In response, schools that had not previously adopted AP began to do so, knowing that in order to provide their graduates with access to better colleges and universities they would have to offer the full range of AP courses. As a 1967 *Chicago Tribune* story reported, the most competitive high schools offered "one to four advanced placement courses as evidence [that their students] can handle college-level work."[37] Seeing this trend, many educators asserted that something needed to be done to keep college admission open "to students who have no opportunity to take advanced placement courses."[38]

The late 1960s and early 1970s also marked a shifting context for crafting school reform. "Top-flight American education," noted Eric Rothschild, "had always been elitist and the democratic trends of the sixties called for better education for the many, rather than the best education for the few."[39] In the fashion of Lyndon Johnson's Great Society programs, public education took on "much of the national liberal agenda" as school reformers engaged in "the vigorous pursuit of egalitarian reforms [that] promised to clarify, expand, and protect the claims of the disadvantaged."[40] One example of that effort was the federal Pell Grant, created in a 1972 amendment to the 1964 Higher Education Act, which granted funds to students enrolling as full-time undergraduates. In order to use such government financial support, however, students would first have to be admitted to college.

Even AP's critics acknowledged that the program provided opportunity—for accelerated study, for advanced placement, and for a leg up in college admissions—but noted that it did so only for those who had access to the program. In 1969, only 14 percent of high schools had students taking AP exams, and more than half of the schools that had students taking the exams had fewer than ten doing so. That came as no surprise, given the fact that the program was created at a time when "the nation was intensely concerned about the education of gifted students."[41] Also unsurprising was the fact that, as of 1968, Beverly Hills High School led the nation in the number of students enrolled in Advanced Placement courses, with prestigious Lowell High School of San Francisco placing second.[42] As attention in education policy making shifted to "issues like the quality of education in inner-city schools," however, disparities in access began to raise red flags.[43]

AP students, social justice proponents and equity advocates critically observed, were primarily white. As a 1971 Federal Emergency School Assistance Program report to the Los Angeles–adjacent Pasadena board of education noted, ability grouping blocked "upward social mobility" for "the children of the less affluent—the poor, the children of the black ghettoes and the brown barrios, who make up most of the low-ability classes in our schools."[44] A 1974 *New York Times* article reflected similar concerns bubbling up on the other side of the nation. Some educators, the piece noted, were disturbed by the fact that curricular tracking was segregating students *within* ostensibly desegregated public schools. The prevailing effect, "because of prior social, economic and cultural imbalance," was "for blacks to predominate in the 'slow' classes and whites in the 'bright' classes."[45] Not surprisingly, as historian William R. Hochman concluded, "some people [began to] regard the [AP] program as touched with . . . 'institutional racism.'"[46]

The de facto segregation of AP programs was a clear manifestation of educational inequality. But few education leaders and school reformers saw AP as a lever for promoting equity and justice in underserved communities. Instead, they continued to advocate for more basic needs like properly trained teachers and equalized funding, and against practices like tracking and ability grouping that tended to marginalize low-income and minority students. As one black Chicago student wrote in 1968, simply putting students in AP classes would not make them "geniuses." Whatever the curriculum, "we still need help and guidance," she added.[47]

Soon, however, that would change. Presaging claims that would later become standard, one activist made the case in 1976 that AP could be "an effective instrument for serving gifted but socially disadvantaged students."[48] As more reformers adopted this position—that AP could advance not just social efficiency aims, but social justice aims as well—the program would begin to appear in schools quite unlike those that originally adopted it.

AP IN SURPRISING PLACES

Despite sustained inequities, the AP Program continued to grow and reach more students. By 1976 3,937 schools and 75,651 students took part in the program; by 1985 there were 6,720 schools and 205,650 students participating.[49]

Ironically, it was during this period of increasing expansion that discourse about curricular rigor and effective teaching, which had once justified the growth of AP, began to change. By the 1980s, "uninspired instruction was an important concern of several critics keen on changing teaching methods." Reliance on lectures, worksheets, and questioning for monosyllabic factual answers, they argued, "often left no time for analysis and discussion."[50] In his 1984 book *A Place Called School*, UCLA Graduate School of Education dean John Goodlad argued for a shift toward schools in which educators "involve students in a variety of ways of thinking . . . introduce students to concepts and not just facts . . . [and] provide situations that provoke and evoke curiosity."[51] What most schools needed, he argued, was "not a somewhat lower-level replication of college courses, most of which . . . do little more than teach students to take notes and memorize facts."[52] This vision, representative of the thinking of a growing group of American educators, did not square with AP.

Yet college admissions standards continued to promote the expansion of AP. The University of California system, for instance, which had used AP exam scores for placement purposes since 1961, began to use AP coursework as a factor in admissions in 1982. Asserting that its purpose was to "encourage students to take demanding advanced academic courses," the UC system resolved to view a B in an AP course the same way it would an A in a non-AP course, awarding up to a 5.0 on the 4.0 grade scale.[53] That meant those students with access to AP courses had an even greater advantage in one of the largest and most prestigious systems of higher education in the country.

For their part, high schools continued to promote their Advanced Placement courses, and schools without AP continued to add it. As one private school leader put it, whatever the concerns of pedagogy experts, AP remained a way for a young school "to gain credibility with both parents and colleges."[54] A 1977 *New York Times* story about Scarsdale, New York, public schools, for instance, cited the offering of AP courses in "several subjects" as evidence that the district's schools ranked "with that of the best public schools in the country."[55]

Particularly in the case of much-maligned urban public schools, AP remained an important indicator of curricular rigor. Systemic adoption of AP in Oklahoma City, for example, was used in the early 1980s as part of a plan to "improve the image and credibility of the public schools" in a district that had seen enrollments cut in half over the course of a decade. According to the district's superintendent, the AP program took away the argument that one could "only get good-quality education by moving into the suburbs or by sending . . . kids to private schools."[56] Joseph P. Allen, associate director of admissions at the University of California at Santa Cruz, noted that the UC system had begun encouraging high schools to develop AP offerings. "In California, where curriculum slipped so badly," he observed, "AP is challenging the students again."[57]

While AP courses continued to be concentrated in well-resourced schools, they were also cropping up in unexpected places. In 1984, high-performing high schools in Los Angeles had the greatest number of students taking AP courses. Still, according to an article in the *Los Angeles Times*, there were "some surprises" among high schools with high rates of AP test-taking. First among those was Garfield High School in East Los

Angeles, which boasted the largest number of students passing AP exams in math—"a reflection of teacher Jaime Escalante's success in encouraging and preparing his students, primarily Latinos, to excel."[58] The story of Garfield High was remarkable because Escalante was teaching an Advanced Placement course to low-income students in East L.A. and because he was doing it in one of AP's most challenging subjects: calculus.

The Garfield High story drew further interest because Escalante was also using AP as a lever to help his students gain admission to colleges like Columbia, Princeton, Berkeley, and UCLA.[59] In 1988 *Washington Post* columnist Jay Mathews wrote *Escalante: The Best Teacher in America* and Warner Brothers released *Stand and Deliver*—a film about Escalante and his students that went on to gross $14 million. The story of AP at Garfield High was the kind of case in point that allowed reformers to dream, and seemingly overnight the nation learned the name of the East L.A. teacher promoting equity through excellence. Soon Escalante began speaking in districts like Oklahoma City about how to implement AP programs for low-income and minority students.[60]

Escalante's work with AP at Garfield High gained traction because it was a good story. But of equal importance was the fact that it captured the essence of the excellence for all mission. It appealed not just to equity and social justice advocates, but to more conservative supporters of standards and accountability as well. While the AP Program did not prescribe a curriculum, it did outline what courses should cover and the end-of-year test held students and teachers accountable for achievement. Consequently, it squared with the work that E. D. Hirsch Jr., author of *Cultural Literacy*, was doing through his Core Knowledge Foundation and that future assistant secretary of education Diane Ravitch was doing on the California state history framework.[61] An additional strength of the program, argued Ronald Reagan's former secretary of education William Bennett, was that AP focused on proficiency outcomes rather than simply on inputs and seat time.[62]

Prior to the 1980s, social efficiency–minded proponents of AP had emphasized the importance of challenging the best and brightest, while those more concerned with social justice had criticized the program as a symbol of inequity. In the Escalante era, both sides had begun to see the potential of expanding AP in low-income urban public schools. Consequently, a new crop of reformers began to merge those two historically separate aims, advocating a world-class curriculum for all students—an argument with near-universal appeal. Writing in the *Los Angeles Times*, Ambrose Brodus, senior director for education services of the San Diego Urban League, made the case that "advanced placement must become a reality for all students who strive for it." "Business, industry and our total society," he concluded, "should benefit from these efforts to insure that each and every student is challenged to reach his/her highest academic potential."[63] Later authors would make a similar case, observing that while expanding AP would promote "educational equity for all students," American society as a whole would "benefit from higher enrollments of minority students in AP classes and in all other rigorous courses."[64]

Still, despite stories like that of Garfield High and major expansion of the program, educators struggled to bring an authentic AP experience to disadvantaged students. Expanding AP's reach was simple, but ensuring that students and teachers were up to the challenge was a major obstacle. As one Chicago principal charged, some schools had students in AP classes "who don't belong there," and added that "schools load up on AP programs to look good."[65] Not surprisingly, AP students in 1986 were still "more likely to come from homes where the parents were highly educated and [in] prominent occupations," from "a large rather than small school," and from "a school with a minority enrollment of fifteen to forty-nine percent, rather than fifty percent or more."[66] They were also extremely likely to earn a passing score of 3 or higher, with only 31.3 percent failing.[67] By the end of the following decade, though, "the typical AP student could no longer be so easily categorized."[68]

PROGRAM EXPANSION

AP expanded rapidly in the 1980s and 1990s. In 1986 7,201 schools and 231,378 students took part in the program. By 1994 10,863 schools and 458,945 students would participate—a major increase, though still a small fraction of American high school students. Further, despite the fact that most AP students remained white and middle to upper class, the program began to reach more and more low-income and minority students. Between 1983 and 1988 minority student participation doubled to 19.5 percent of AP test takers, giving "many educators a new glimmer of hope about the minority pipeline to choice college[s]."[69] By 1994 minorities accounted for 26.3 percent of AP test takers, marking an expansion so accelerated that AP was becoming a standard aspect of American secondary education, whether public or private, elite or otherwise.

AP grew as individual schools and districts recognized the usefulness of the program. "At a time when educators across the nation are looking for a way to improve the quality of education and elevate the level of academic achievement," wrote two Boston public schools officials, AP offered students in urban high schools "the challenge of a rigorous college preparatory curriculum."[70] But program expansion was also heavily promoted from outside the public schools. This push to funnel students into AP stemmed from the belief that "taking an AP course signals to college and university admissions officers that a student is prepared for college level work."[71] If low-income and minority students were enrolled in AP courses, the thinking went, they would have a better shot at winning college admission. Higher postsecondary enrollment was an attractive outcome for leaders at foundations, state and local government, and nonprofit organizations, whether they were concerned with national strength or equal opportunity. An increasing number of reform-minded leaders were interested in both outcomes, and, as a result, AP became a key tool in the excellence for all movement's arsenal.

One force driving the expansion of AP in the 1980s and 1990s was state government, which had begun implementing statewide plans to use the program.[72] South Carolina's Education Improvement Act of 1984, for instance, enacted a plan that would create AP programs in all schools in the state by 1987. Led by future Clinton administration secretary of education Richard Riley, South Carolina also set aside funds to pay AP exam fees for students and was joined by Florida and the District of Columbia in this practice.[73] Other states from Alabama to Wisconsin quickly followed suit, creating legislation promoting AP either through student incentive programs or through mandates that high schools offer a minimum number of AP courses.[74] Given this major shift in access, states that did not take action to expand AP offerings soon found themselves the targets of discrimination lawsuits. In *Daniel et al. v. the State of California*, for instance, the Southern California branch of the American Civil Liberties Union filed suit on behalf of students lacking equal access to AP courses. In response to the suit, the state of California initiated grants to increase and support AP programs and also created a plan to make AP courses available online.[75]

The federal government also supported AP's expansion. In part, federal support for AP stemmed from support among conservative leaders for the standards movement.[76] But standards were not solely the terrain of conservatives, and such efforts continued to receive support under the Clinton administration, which facilitated what would become Goals 2000. Direct federal support for AP came in the form of the Advanced Placement Fee Payment Program—a 1992 amendment to the Higher Education Act directing the secretary of education to provide payments to states covering the cost of AP exam fees for low-income students. According to then-secretary of education Rod Paige, the grants were created in the belief that they could "help close the achievement gap between students from disadvantaged backgrounds and their peers."[77] By the year 2000—the year that Secretary of Education Richard Riley and College Board president Gaston Caperton recommended that ten AP classes be offered in every high school—the federal government was annually authorizing $15 million to subsidize exam fees for low-income students and to train teachers to teach AP courses in low-income schools.[78] In 2001 federal support for AP reached a new peak when Congress passed the Access to High Standards Act as a part of No Child Left Behind legislation. In addition to reauthorizing exam fee subsidies, the law created the Advanced Placement Incentive Program, providing roughly $25 million in annual grants for the expansion of AP in schools with high concentrations of low-income students. Dozens of states quickly took advantage of new federal resources, encouraging participation in AP as a lever for raising standards statewide.[79]

Nonprofit groups and philanthropic organizations joined government in creating incentive and support programs for minorities enrolled in AP classes. In 1980, for example, Mary Catherine Swanson founded a program at San Diego's Clairemont High School that later became AVID—Advancement Via Individual Determination. The program, which by the early twentieth century would be implemented at two thousand sites in twenty-six states, assists schools in opening access to AP programs.[80] By helping schools develop plans to increase curricular rigor, by prescribing pre-AP content training for students, and by facilitating infrastructural developments like the creation of "vertical teams" that begin preparing students for AP in middle school, AVID also hoped to increase minority student achievement in AP classes. The College Board soon joined in, creating programs like AP Potential and SpringBoard, designed to prepare students for success in AP courses.

With the support of school districts, state and federal government, nonprofit organizations, and private funders like the Mellon and Josiah Macy foundations, which began supporting the expansion of AP in the 1980s, the program reached record numbers of students.[81] In California, for instance, 5,258 students participated in AP in 1970. Ten years later, that figure had more than tripled, growing to 17,311. Then, between 1980 and 1990, participation tripled again to 55,948.[82] And while many students in the state continued to lack access to AP, by the end of the twentieth century 144 California schools would offer fifteen or more AP courses.[83]

Although the expansion of Advanced Placement was broadly supported by liberals and conservatives in both the public and private sectors, there were deep rifts in the program. One split was between those passing and those failing end-of-year AP exams. Scores of 2 or lower—failing scores—were recorded for 31.3 percent of all exams in 1986. But after a decade of promotion in urban schools, the percentage of failing scores had risen to 40.4 percent, and as that number continued to inch up it raised questions about the consistency of program quality.[84]

Another divide emerged along subject-matter lines, producing significant discrepancies in participation across the different AP classes. In 1999, for instance, over 175,000 students took the AP test in U.S. History, while only 30,000 students took the test in Calculus BC. One explanation for this discrepancy is the difficulty of the respective tests. The history exam—the sort of test that critics pointed to as evidence of the program's middling quality—consists primarily of multiple-choice questions focusing on factual information that students can memorize. The calculus test, by contrast, is less straightforward. While AP Calculus BC is not impervious to criticism, its protected status seems in no small part a product of inaccessibility—a source of frustration for equity advocates.[85]

Finally, there was the fact that although AP participation was on the whole more diverse, there remained a racial participation gap in particular subject areas and, more troubling, a gap in test scores. Among the 30,000 students taking the AP Calculus BC test in 1999, for instance, only 550 were black and only 383 Latino.[86] And, while the average AP exam score for all subjects in 1999 was 3.01, the average scores for Mexican American students and African American students were 2.8 and 2.2, respectively; that gap would continue to increase into the twenty-first century.[87]

Thus, despite the many successes of those who favored expanding the program in urban schools, using Advanced Placement to promote equity was proving to be a challenge of considerable and increasing complexity.

DECLINING PRESTIGE

By the early twenty-first century, AP participation exceeded seven figures, with 1.1 million students taking 1.85 million exams.[88] One unintended but foreseeable consequence of the enormous expansion of AP has been a declining level of prestige associated with the program. The popularity of AP has brought about a great deal of demand for it, and in meeting that demand educators and reformers have weakened the status of program, at least in top high schools.

In part, this is because there can only be a certain number of elite schools, while anyone who performs well can earn high marks on the AP test. Journalist and AP advocate Jay Mathews defines elite high schools, at least among the twenty-five thousand or so public high schools in the country, as "the top 10 percent." Such schools have status based on their relationships with college recruiters who "decide which schools are going to have records of achievement that impress parents and taxpayers."[89] As prestige is a limited commodity, schools that wish to acquire it must scramble to distinguish themselves and their curricula from others. Consequently, expansion of AP has brought about uncertainty regarding its connection to elite education—is AP the mark of a top school or the mark of an average one?

Critics also raised questions about the credibility of AP. In part, these questions can be attributed to a shift in accepted wisdom about quality teaching and challenging curricula. As early as the 1980s, scholars had begun questioning the rigor and relevance of AP on the grounds that the program did not "represent the kind of thinking skills we want our students to have in college."[90] Colleges, too, began questioning the program, arguing that while they had revised their curricula, the AP program had not changed and was becoming "outdated."[91] In 2002 Haverford College professor Jerry Gollub, cochair of a study group convened by the National Research Council, observed that while AP "contributed a great deal to the quality of science education in American high schools," the program was in need of "many urgent improvements."[92] As a student from New York's private Fieldston School wrote, "it is ironic that the top students, who will be trying to take the most specialized courses available in college, are taking the most general courses available in high school, largely because the course titles are preceded by the letters 'AP.'"[93]

The Advanced Placement brand was also weakened by the move among a number of top high schools toward a vision of scholastic programs—envisioned by scholars like Jerome Bruner, Ted Sizer, and John Goodlad—focused on developing modes of thought and provoking curiosity among students. Top schools, whether or not they offered AP, were promoting classes that centered not on a broad curriculum tied to an end-of-year test, but on the development of disciplinary skills among students. In the case of

Choate Rosemary Hall, for instance, the elite Connecticut boarding school created a world history course in which "the development of skills used by historians—critical reading, writing, and oral presentation—is emphasized."[94] At Deerfield Academy, another prestigious boarding school, history courses began to stress the development of reason and logic in students, aiming to, among other things, "give students practical experience as young historians."[95] While the AP history exams, for instance, do have a section that asks test takers to write essays using historical documents, even those fall short of college-level history assignments, which are more likely to culminate in research papers than short essays.

Questions about the quality of AP can also be attributed to an actual watering-down effect of allowing more and more students into AP classes. Once upon a time "a student earning a 5 in an AP class from a public high school in an economically modest district took the same test as a Choate student whose parents face an annual tuition bill of more than $35,000." But the push for equity resulted in an increase of students taking the class but not the exam—by some estimates, up to one-third of all AP enrollees— or taking a class that was markedly different from the AP class taught at, say, Choate.[96] Thus, as early as 1983 some teachers began to make the case that AP had been "watered down . . . to a euphemism."[97] But while that was a problem for some, it was less so for others. One teacher proudly noted in 1992 that she had chosen to ignore differences in student ability, "confident that the rigors of the AP curriculum, my high expectations, and the example of their peers would improve the quality of the work of students new to honors classes."[98] Ten years later, a principal boasted: "I have taken 'elite' status off of AP." The classes, she noted, are open access: "we don't keep anyone out who wants to enter."[99] Perhaps not surprisingly, 39 percent of teachers surveyed in a 2009 study by the Thomas B. Fordham Institute reported that student aptitude and capacity to do AP-level work has gone down.[100]

Consequently, enrollment in AP classes, which was once "a reasonable barometer of academic ability," is no longer as effective a signaling device for colleges and universities as it once was.[101] Researchers Kristin Klopfenstein and M. Kathleen Thomas have found that "after controlling for the balance of a student's high school curriculum, family, and school characteristics, AP students are generally no more likely than non-AP students to return for a second year of college or to have higher first semester grade point averages."[102]

Klopfenstein and Thomas attributed the results, in part, to the rapid expansion of the program, which diluted any effect due to selection. In other words, whereas AP once captured only the most academically skilled students in a school, it is now much more likely to include the full range of abilities.[103] Another explanation offered was that in response to pressure, many schools had simply renamed existing courses "Advanced Placement."[104] While some AP courses like Calculus BC managed to maintain a high degree of prestige, they tended to have lower enrollments, particularly of minority students.[105]

Programmatic expansion also meant that selective colleges and universities were inundated with applications from students with AP on their transcripts, further undermining the signaling power of the program. At Stanford University in 2000, more than half of first-year students entered with at least ten college credits earned through AP or the International Baccalaureate program, a similar program originally developed for students living outside the United States.[106] In 2007 nearly 3,000 applicants to Stanford had participated in the AP Program—500 more than would be chosen for the incoming freshman class—and they sent a total of 7,500 AP scores to the university. Across the San Francisco Bay, the University of California at Berkeley received over 21,000 exam scores from 7,944 AP participants competing for a spot in the 10,000-person incoming class. At Harvard that year, 2,369 AP participants sent in 5,896 test scores, hoping to secure one of only 2,000 places in the freshman class.[107] And while the leading edge of this phenomenon was most clearly seen at selective colleges and universities, AP expansion and the questions it raised were not confined to a small minority of students angling for spots in elite institutions. As of 2006, nearly two-thirds of college freshmen had taken at least one AP course in high school; roughly 15 percent had taken five or more.[108] In short, simply having participated in the AP Program—once a mark of great distinction—no longer separated students from the pack.[109]

Less certain about the quality of the AP Program, selective colleges and universities began changing their policies for awarding course credit to AP exam takers. As early as the mid-1990s, the *New York Times* reported that as the number of students enrolled in AP grew, "more and more colleges and universities are tightening the number of credits they will award to students."[110] According to William Lichten, a former visiting scholar at the Educational Testing Service, the move had become a movement by the early twenty-first century. Even though nearly two-thirds of AP test takers earned a score of 3 or higher on the 1-to-5 scale, he noted, only 49 percent received college credit for their achievements. Harvard, an early proponent of AP, stopped giving course credit for scores below 5, whereas once a score of 3 had qualified.[111] The University of Pennsylvania stopped allowing students to use AP credits to satisfy general undergraduate graduation requirements. And at schools like Stanford, Yale, Cornell, the University of Virginia, and the University of North Carolina, departments became less willing to let students with scores of 4 or 5 skip courses.[112]

According to Terrel Rhodes, speaking on behalf of the Association of American Colleges and Universities, schools had changed their policies because "high school–age students are not mature enough to grasp the subtleties of some material."[113] Yet, for decades the assumption was that if they were enrolled in AP courses, students *were* mature enough to do university-level coursework in high school. The problem, according to some researchers, was not a function of maturity, but of a standardized curriculum that no longer squared with the practices at top colleges and universities, or even at top high schools, at least not in most subject areas. Further, research began to reveal that college students with AP coursework under their belts often failed to outperform their non-AP peers.[114]

The College Board responded by tightening standards, asking schools to include specific elements in their AP syllabi "or to demonstrate how they are meeting colleges' standards without including such elements."[115] Beginning in the 2007–2008 school year, high schools offering AP classes were required to seek authorization from the College Board to use the AP label, with colleges receiving a list of approved high schools. High schools seeking approval must complete two-page "audit" forms listing the required elements their AP courses included, and teachers, for their part, have to attach their syllabi, a sample assignment, and a sample test.[116] The College Board, however, was careful to note that "the audit does not review anything about teachers beyond how they are demonstrating on their syllabi the inclusion of the course requirements or a viable alternative," anticipating reluctance on the part of teachers to be closely monitored by outside authority.[117]

The College Board's attempt to tighten restrictions on what can and cannot be labeled AP may be effective in maintaining the standards of the AP curriculum. That alone, however, may not be enough to control damage to the AP brand or resolve questions about whether or not the AP curriculum can be squared with current best practices in teaching and curriculum development. Nor will it address the fact that as the program has expanded, it has lost its exclusivity. And, while exclusivity is clearly not the College

Board's goal, any significant decline in the status of the AP brand will have consequences for the board's aim of providing a widely accepted rigorous curriculum to students across different high schools.

MOVES FOR CHANGE

Complaints about AP's content and pedagogy were nothing new, particularly among faculty in top high schools. But as long as colleges continued to give preference to students with AP on their transcripts, no school could afford to drop the program. However, as AP expanded, its prestige declined, freeing particular schools to pursue alternatives to the program. Further, dropping AP allowed elite high schools to once again distinguish themselves from the pack—a particularly important move in an era of dramatically expanding college enrollments. As one school leader put it, "a lot of kids are qualified, but get rejected from some big-name schools."[118] In that even more frenzied environment of competition for enrollment at selective schools, top private and suburban schools in the early twenty-first century began to seek a way to provide their students with a mark of distinction.

While many teachers, particularly those at lower-status schools, no doubt felt positively about AP and the chance to teach more challenging material, many faculties at top high schools had long complained about the constraints imposed by the AP curriculum. Even teachers who remained positive about AP noted that "the class to a large degree is 'test-driven.'"[119] Students, one history teacher complained, "must have comprehensive knowledge of the subject, but they also need test taking skills in the multiple choice and essay sections."[120] According to the assistant principal at Scarsdale High School, which has recently dropped AP, "the test unfortunately drives what . . . and how you teach."[121] Such a narrow test-preparation aim, wrote a former AP student, "stifled the development of . . . skills, capacities, and habits of mind."[122] And yet, until quite recently, even high-status schools continued offering AP, and their ambitious students continued enrolling so long as colleges continued to reward those with AP courses on their transcripts.

But perception of AP had begun to change. Soon colleges and universities began reevaluating not only the soundness of awarding course credit for AP test scores, but also the long-standing practice of giving preference in the admissions process to AP students. Again, while some of this was due to questions about the credibility of AP, much was also due to the fact that merely having participated in AP no longer provided the measure of distinction it once did, at least in the program's more accessible courses like AP U.S. History and AP English Literature.[123] Everyone, it seemed, was taking the toughest classes available at their schools; sometimes they were AP classes, sometimes not. "We look at whether the applicant has taken the high school's most demanding courses," reported Harvard director of admissions Marlyn McGrath Lewis in 2002. "Whether the classes are designated as AP or not is irrelevant," she added, noting that "abolishing AP classes won't hurt the kids."[124] This shift in thinking about AP and college admissions represented a major change. And, because so many colleges had used an informal approach in according preference to students with AP on their transcripts, a move away from such practices was swift in coming. Rarely requiring a change in admissions policy, a shift away from AP in the admissions process usually called simply for a change in attitude.[125]

As AP came under fire, leaders at top high schools began discussing the weaknesses of the program more frequently and more seriously. No independent school leader, wrote Patricia Hager of Concord Academy, "can attend an educational meeting without running into conflict and contention about the AP . . . [specifically] whether AP is the best we can do."[126] Concord Academy's faculty members, she added, "are convinced that they can engage students in much deeper learning if they create their own curricula," though she did note that in "chronically underfunded communities, school boards recognize the value" of AP.[127] As a teacher in Los Angeles–adjacent Newport noted, "dropping the AP designation from accelerated courses at independent schools across the country would allow us to pursue curricula that truly inspire what my own school's mission statement calls 'a love of knowledge and the ability to use that knowledge creatively, compassionately, and courageously throughout life.'"[128] Put another way, schools with greater resources at their disposal were positioned to adapt to a rising tide of best-practice literature promoting depth over breadth, the teaching of skills over discrete facts, and the development of passion alongside ability.[129] They also had reputations strong enough to make such moves without fear of backlash.

Schools such as Crossroads School in Los Angeles–adjacent Santa Monica explored the possibility of dropping AP by contacting admissions offices at schools that their graduates most frequently attended. They surveyed two hundred colleges and universities nationwide and were "assured by 90 percent of them that Crossroads students would not be penalized for taking advanced courses that diverged from the AP curriculum."[130] Colleges and universities were similarly supportive of Concord Academy's move to drop the AP program, given that, in doing so, it was "in excellent company with other strong independent schools, such as New York's Fieldston School."[131] Admissions offices understand and high school faculties believe, wrote Concord Academy's Hager, "that master high school teachers can reach talented students more rigorously than the Advanced Placement program suggests." College admissions officials, she added, "enthusiastically support our efforts in their admissions decisions and increasingly in policies that deemphasize the AP test scores."[132]

Seeing that their students would be accorded status in the college admissions process regardless of whether or not they had participated in AP classes, other elite high schools, including New York's independent Dalton and Calhoun schools, took the leap. Many dropped AP entirely. Others, like Exeter and Andover, created "homegrown courses that are more like college work in tone and depth but may still cover AP material so students are positioned for the exam."[133] Such prestigious schools, "which enjoy an enviable reputation among admissions officers at elite colleges," have the privilege not only of having these debates but of making independent decisions.[134] However, not all schools do.

HANGING ON

While the quality of AP has been called into question, a number of advocates have continued to call for its expansion.[135] And, even though elite schools have begun backing away from it, AP has continued to grow each year, with a majority of that growth coming in underserved schools.

In Chicago, citywide participation in AP courses went from 2,583 in 1978 to 8,691 in 2004.[136] But between 2004 and 2008, it more than doubled to 18,065. As Chicago's director of Advanced Placement, Mark Klimesh, noted in 2009, AP courses had been "viewed as a means of increasing rigor in the classroom and therefore improving test scores."[137] Yet, as critics pointed out, enormous expansion of the program was actually accompanied by declining achievement among AP participants. Whereas Chicago students participating in AP courses maintained a mean grade-point average of 2.83 in 2004—a B/B–average—by 2008 that figure had dropped to 2.58—a B–/C+ average. The average score on AP tests declined from 2.43 to 2.08. And, whereas 43 percent of participating students scored a 3 or better in 2004, only 32 percent did in 2008.[138] Given such disappointing results, the district moved to refocus attention on teacher professional development and on increasing administrator knowledge. Still, the district continued its policy of "equal and open enrollment for all students regarding AP."[139]

In Los Angeles, roughly 38,000 of the district's 1.1 million students participated in Advanced Placement courses during the 2004–2005 school year; of those participating students, 30,000 were nonwhite. Of the fifty-eight high schools in the district, fifty-seven offered at least one course in AP English, math, or social science, and fifty-six also offered an AP foreign language course. On average, each school offered fourteen different AP courses.[140] And yet, as in Chicago, critics questioned what such expansion efforts accomplished if they were not accompanied by a fundamental restructuring of the way teachers were recruited and trained and the way students were prepared in the years preceding their participation in AP.

While AP no longer represents the zenith of academic challenge, many schools do still benefit from the program and many continue to adopt it. Best-practice literature may promote developing modes of thinking and provoking curiosity, but the past two decades have ushered in an era of standards and high-stakes testing for American public schools, which particularly affects high schools in low-income and minority communities. Because these schools stand to lose funding if they fail to adequately prepare students to perform on tests of basic skills, the concept of advanced challenge can often be lost in the fray. In that context, the AP curriculum represents a welcome addition.

Additionally, while AP may no longer carry much distinction on transcripts from elite high schools like Andover and Exeter, it does carry weight on transcripts of students at poorly funded public high schools. When course quality is questionable, AP provides a baseline of substance and rigor. The AP history tests, for example, may be loaded with multiple-choice questions for which students need only recall bits of information, but it also asks them to analyze documents and write short essays. The process of preparing for that can be among the most substantial critical reading and writing work done in some schools.[141] Whatever the damage to its prestige, many students in AP classes get the basic skills and the basic challenge they need—a positive outcome, though one quite distinct from the original purpose of Advanced Placement.

Public school reformers in underserved districts have also continued to push AP for students interested in pursuing postsecondary education. In one community, for instance, the superintendent of schools has made AP open-enrollment and aims to push participation in the district toward 100 percent: "Who is most likely to reap long-term benefits from AP classes?" he asked. His response: "those most likely to struggle in college, the very ones often relegated to second-class status in their high schools."[142] While AP may not be cutting-edge, it still provides an important advantage for some students in the college admissions process, particularly when applying to lower-status colleges and universities. Consequently, the presence of AP classes in the curriculum can be enough to keep able students in otherwise low-performing public schools. As Jan Davis, director of high school programs in the L.A. Unified School District, noted, "some schools, if they offer AP, often get back their local populations."[143]

Teachers at underserved schools also have reasons to hang on to AP. For many of them, attending AP Summer Institutes and participating in the annual scoring of AP tests represents their most thorough professional development opportunity of the year. Working with other teachers from the same subject area gives often-isolated teachers the chance to share teaching techniques, discipline knowledge, and curricular materials. To the extent that the AP brand still carries weight with students, labeling a course "AP" can make it easier for teachers to arouse motivation. To the extent that AP still carries weight with colleges, the label can give teachers a sense of purpose, providing evidence that they are not providing a second-rate education for their students.

Even though they are aware of elite schools dropping the program, many strong public and private high schools still embrace AP for the status it can provide them. According to Barbara Caldwell, associate head of school at Moorestown Friends School, schools that have moved away from AP "already have near-perfect reputations with elite colleges." Independent schools like Moorestown, which is highly competitive regionally but not nationally, still "have to present the most rigorous face possible, including outside benchmarking, to elite colleges in order to give kids the best chance possible of admittance."[144] Despite some faculty resistance, Moorestown is sticking with AP for now. However, four of its competitors have recently dropped the program.[145]

The most prestigious high schools, meanwhile, have the freedom to do what they want—something as true today as it was in 1950 when they created what was to become the AP Program. The result has been a new, though still nascent, form of educational inequity in which some students are more challenged, experience more freedom, and are more favored by colleges than others. According to one student, being unburdened of AP classes "means that you get to learn for the sake of learning."[146] Ironically, learning only for the sake of learning and without the promise of college credit or the challenge of a year-end examination was precisely the condition that sparked interest in the concept of advanced placement half a century earlier.

While AP still serves a purpose at many schools, one must wonder how useful it would continue to be—particularly in the pursuit of excellence for all—if all elite secondary schools dropped it. The discrepancy that such a move would once again create between the curricula of urban public schools and those of top private and suburban schools would certainly be a blow to equity. But because AP has traditionally been valued for its *prestige* rather than its quality, some fear that expansion of the program may succeed only in diluting the value of the AP brand without improving curricular strength. As one author from the once enthusiastically pro-AP Thomas B. Fordham Institute noted, "'AP for all' can quickly become 'truly rigorous courses for none.'"[147]

THE STATUS LADDER

The Advanced Placement Program was designed for high-achieving students at high-status schools as part of an effort to create an academic elite. In the era of the Cold War, administrators at the most prestigious high schools supported AP as part of their duty to challenge the best and brightest and, in so doing, create better leaders. The program gained traction with teachers who had the privilege of teaching groups of talented and motivated students. And, in an era of increasingly competitive college admission, students flocked to AP as a way to distinguish themselves from their peers. Shortly thereafter, schools beyond the original adopters began to institute AP as a way to strengthen their curricula and adjust to what was widely perceived as pedagogically appropriate. By the early 1960s, having AP in the curriculum indicated that a high school was serious about achievement and highly competitive in college admissions.

Having long criticized the program as elitist, equity and social justice advocates soon began to see the potential benefit of expanding the program. In an effort to bring equity to underserved schools, reformers, with the cooperation of the College Board, pushed for the expansion of AP. "We believe you can't have excellence if there's no equity," insisted former College Board president Gaston Caperton. "If there are only a few people who have the opportunity to take AP courses, that's not equity."[148] Parents concerned with providing their children with access to opportunity demanded that public schools adopt the program, and educators were, in many cases, highly responsive. AP quickly branched out of private and suburban public schools, taking root in schools serving high-percentage minority and low-income populations. By 2002, 31 percent of AP students identified themselves as "minorities," compared to 12 percent in 1979 and virtually none at the outset of the program.

As AP was opening up to more and more students, times were changing, and no more consequentially for the program than in perceptions of best pedagogical practice. Further, as the AP circle grew wider and wider, it less effectively signaled elite education to colleges. This decline in status, along with changing ideas about effective teaching in a variety of subject areas, created a new context for dialogue about the program within top schools where faculty and staff had long expressed discontent with AP's prescribed curriculum and uneven balance of breadth and depth. Free to rethink their association with the program, some of the highest-status schools began to move away from AP.

Despite the move away from the program by elite schools, AP will likely continue to persist in most American high schools for some time, particularly in resource-deficient schools still struggling to establish AP courses. At the same time, elite schools likely will continue moving away from AP, finding new ways to distinguish themselves and their students in what Richard Atkinson has called the "educational arms race."[149] As they do, they may fatally undermine the credibility of the AP label. What gave AP weight, after all, was the fact that it was endorsed by the nation's highest-status high schools and was the same no matter what a school's population looked like. Without such recognition, the value of having AP on a high school transcript may continue to decline, forcing students to rely on the widely varying reputations of their schools. Worse yet, it may lose its power to motivate teachers and students, becoming just another packaged curriculum.

Advanced Placement, like many other school reforms designed to promote excellence for all, has failed to level the playing field. However, as one scholar has noted, these "inequities . . . aren't the fault of the AP."[150] In fact, one might argue that AP did succeed, if only for a short time, in promoting both excellence and equity. But as high status is accorded to a distinct few who manage to differentiate themselves from others, those with the greatest resources merely redefined excellence. In a position to move quickly to align themselves with status-bearing standards, they downgraded AP in the curriculum or dropped it entirely.

Those with fewer resources, of course, are not precluded from seeking to align themselves with high-status programs. But as less-well-resourced schools slowly turn their ships, the well-off are free to change course once more, leaving the masses behind yet again. AP spread rapidly as a result of the competitive nature of American education. In the coming decades, it may fail for the same reason.

CONCLUSION

IN 1991, EDUCATION WRITER Thomas Toch observed that public schools had reached a pivotal point in their history. They were, as he wrote, "poised to take the American experiment in free universal education to a new level, one where all students have not only an equal right to walk through the schoolhouse door but also equal intellectual opportunities."[1] Rather than aiming to provide a different kind of educational experience for the underserved, as had often been the practice in American schooling, reformers in the last decades of the twentieth century began to pursue a new goal—providing all children with the sort of education that would enable them to succeed in college and beyond.

This vision, insofar as it aimed to serve all children equally, was the product of wider agitation among progressive camps for equity, access, and social justice. In the wake of the civil rights movement and the Great Society, excellence for all reformers recognized that addressing the needs of the underserved was both a moral imperative and a political necessity. Insofar as excellence for all reformers were also concerned with returns to the nation-state—to say nothing of the free-market philosophies inherent in their efforts—the movement was equally shaped by attitudes traditionally associated with social and economic conservatism. But beyond merely reconciling traditionally opposing aims, the vision of excellence for all promised to rescue the nation from the multiple threats produced by a changing economy increasingly more dependent on knowledge than labor. "Today's fears," wrote James Fallows in the *Atlantic*, "combine relative decline—what will happen when China has all the jobs? and all the money?—with domestic concerns about a polarized society of haves and have-nots that has lost its connective core."[2]

Whatever the opportunities for bridging ideological divides, consensus came neither easily nor immediately. The fractures that characterized the policy-making context of the second half of the twentieth century were significant. Those seeking to preserve their relative advantage, those fighting for access, those adamantly opposed to what they viewed as an overzealous central government, and those split over the question of race, to name just a few, did not see eye to eye. But openings to create common ground for policy making continued to emerge and savvy reformers continued to seize those opportunities. As they did, they created a movement with a king-sized appeal—an appeal powerful enough to generate momentum behind highly ambitious efforts to solve big national problems by transforming the public schools.

Not all reform efforts, of course, matched the grand rhetoric of excellence for all. Yet the core vision was coherent and inclusive and exerted a broad influence across the world of education. Eventually, it emerged as a battle cry among reformers in foundations, think tanks, nonprofit organizations, the federal government, state departments of education, and school districts themselves. Anything short of excellence for all, they began to argue, would contradict either the American pursuit of international preeminence or the realization of its democratic ideals.

Union leaders and entrepreneurs, bureaucrats and billionaires, liberals and conservatives, the privileged and the underserved could all support the aim of excellence for all and the reform efforts that were initiated in its pursuit. The vision did not, of course, emerge into the world fully formed. It grew by fits and starts, and was marked by disagreements and setbacks. But what evolved, and what maintained consistent support, was the dream of finding the right levers to transform struggling public schools into top-notch urban academies and taking those models to scale.

In one sense, the results were remarkable. The pursuit of educational excellence for all generated billions of dollars in financial support and the political will to push through major efforts across the nation, particularly in the urban high schools that so captivated reformers. But despite the redesign of hundreds of high schools, there was one significant problem: they did not succeed in bringing top-flight education to the traditionally underserved.

By the early twenty-first century, tens of thousands of students from low-income and minority communities attended small schools, were enrolled in Advanced Placement courses, and were taught by teachers with degrees from top colleges and universities. Other reforms, reflecting the vision of excellence for all with various degrees of clarity, made their mark as well. And yet, urban public schools and their students continued to lag behind their elite counterparts. In the Chicago Public Schools, for instance, which Secretary of Education William Bennett had called "the worst in the nation" in 1987, student performance improved only modestly, if at all.[3] As of the fall of 2006, 69 percent of CPS graduates entering local community colleges were unprepared for college-level reading, 79 percent were unprepared for college-level writing, and 95 percent were unprepared for college-level math.[4] Even with the explicit goal of promoting excellence for all, it seems, reform-minded leaders struggled to establish a significant degree of parity between the two worlds.

MAKING SENSE OF CHALLENGES

Why, with such broad support and such abundant resources at their disposal, have reformers so far achieved mostly disheartening results in their pursuit of excellence for all students? Why has this new approach, ostensibly grounded in proven practices, failed to eliminate the nation's achievement gap?

While their approach was in many ways a revelation, excellence for all reformers failed to realize their ambitions because of all that did *not* change in the fundamentally complicated work of educational improvement. Schools are institutions of notoriously slippery substance—affected by a wide range of factors, marked by organizational complexity, and noted as sites in which it is nearly impossible to conduct experiments.[5] Yet the entrepreneurial reformers pursuing excellence for all believed that solutions to the school problem existed and that they could be identified through the application of common sense and basic market principles.

Each of the reform efforts explored in this study—the small schools movement, Teach For America, and the expansion of the Advanced Placement Program—was driven by a commonly held belief that improving schools is less difficult than bureaucrats would have the public think. Creating more intimate learning environments, recruiting smart college graduates into teaching, and increasing curricular rigor all seemed like good levers to pull in pursuit of educational excellence. In fact, so much was this the case that supporters of these efforts often eschewed education research or used it selectively in working backward to justify their top-down efforts to remake urban high schools. Still, though such ideas resonated deeply with philanthropists, policy makers, and school leaders, they often encountered unforeseen challenges and unanticipated consequences. As researchers Barker and Gump noted presciently nearly half a century ago in their study of school size, "common-sense theories about schools are not adequate bases for policy decisions." The educational process, they added, "is a subtle and delicate one"—something as true in the twenty-first century as in the 1960s.[6]

The work of self-styled educational entrepreneurs was also complicated by other factors. Much of their thinking about improving urban public schools, for instance, was shaped by perceptions of what was working in successful schools. Excellence for all reformers, generally drawn to market-based solutions, frequently cited the work of America's top schools, either as inspiration for change efforts or as a means of justifying their favored projects. Such schools, well rewarded by the market, ostensibly offered lessons to reformers willing to look outside of the public education establishment for solutions, and in an era of educational entrepreneurship, many were.[7]

But determining what makes successful schools work is a challenging task, and that task becomes even more challenging when, as has so often been the case in the excellence for all era, those model schools are private. In addition to an entire system of interrelated factors that can make schools successful, private schools have the luxury of hand-picking their students, they exact fees and make demands of parents, and they are characterized by a high degree of self-selection.[8] Even nonprivate charter schools introduce a host of other complicating issues like unrepresentative student bodies and atypical parent involvement that make it difficult to pin down which positive effects can be attributed to schooling. In the case of the small schools movement, for instance, reformers cited dozens of successful schools as evidence that size mattered. But successful models abound, even in the form of large schools. "This school was big," noted a student from Los Angeles upon visiting an affluent Orange County school. Unaware of the irony that schools in his neighborhood were rapidly downsizing in an effort to boost achievement, he praised the Orange County school's large size and noted that it was "like a university." That size, he added, meant that "they had everything that is needed to get a good education."[9] But good schools come in all shapes and sizes, and what makes some of them successful is nearly impossible to reproduce on a large scale.

All this is not to say that schooling plays a negligible role in the educational development of more privileged children. Still, determining which aspects of an educational program are effective and which merely do no harm is a difficult task. But even if a particular educational aspect is rightly identified as effective, excellence for all advocates still face the challenge of implementing it in dysfunctional schools and among populations with lower social and cultural capital, all while attempting to achieve equal results. As Charles M. Payne writes, reform has consistently been "undermined by low levels of social capital, especially in our bottom-tier schools."[10] And, as Nel Noddings has reflected: "'All children can learn?' Maybe—if they are not sick, suffering toothache, squinting to see the chalkboard, abused at home, breathing air contaminated with lead, worried about a parent in prison, or serving as a caretaker for younger children."[11] In short, educational practices are always intertwined with the particular social conditions of the community being served. But whether or not reformers choose to recognize that fact is another matter.

Still another challenge to the pursuit of excellence for all is the fact that education is a positional good.[12] While some of the fruits of education are absolute—students either know how to read or do not, for instance—its usefulness in promoting social mobility is, to a great extent, relative. The best schools give their students an edge that other schools do not provide and thus by definition depend on inequality for their status. Providing an elite-level education for all students, including the underserved, is a daunting task. But it is further complicated by the competitive nature of American education, which rewards some students with a more valuable set of credentials than others. Top schools, highly responsive to their status-conscious constituents, do not rest on their laurels. As the case of the effort to expand the Advanced Placement Program reveals, such schools, far from welcoming the prospect of excellence for all, are constantly working to distinguish themselves from others, and in so doing are constantly redefining excellence.

Like many other major school reform efforts, the excellence for all era was characterized by—and complicated by—grand ambitions that manifested in top-down and outside-in efforts at system building. The educational entrepreneurs who led the excellence for all era not only believed that they had answers for the nation's urban schooling problem, but also had the inclination and the means to take their preferred models to scale. Such plans, as products of faith in the righteousness of their design, tended to call for decisive action and abbreviated timelines. Compounded with the eagerness of school leaders and politicians to appear proactive in the pursuit of excellence for all—to "'save a generation of kids' or 'eliminate the achievement gap'"—the result was a headlong leap into each particular reform effort.[13]

In the rush to scale, however, reformers tended to take a relatively rigid approach to creating educational change, producing a whole new batch of

complications and unintended consequences. Ironically, such prescriptive-
ness presented an inherent contradiction in entrepreneurial work that was
promoted by its advocates as highly pluralistic and diverse. Even more problematically, as Larry Cuban writes, "the current orthodoxy of a 'good' school
ignores the history of many 'good' schools that has marked American public
and private education for almost two centuries."[14] In effect, educational
entrepreneurs railed against the search among earlier reformers for a "one
best system" while themselves pursuing the idea of a "one best school."[15]

Entrepreneurial school reformers did get some of it right. In many
schools, small facility size really mattered in fostering relationships, AP
really motivated students, and TFA corps members really made an impact
in the classroom. But those successful schools so often referenced as models
by reformers were also unique in other ways. Each school was its own distinct ecosystem, modeling best practices but also tailor-made for the context in which it operated.

Reformers were not always naïve about what made such schools special, seeing only particular trees rather than the forest as a whole. Rather,
recognizing that successful schools could not be perfectly replicated, they
sought to find high-leverage reforms that might make a significant impact
on struggling schools. And, in cases where particular reforms needed to
be adapted for the sake of scale, they made necessary compromises, aware
that such moves would not be without consequences. In the case of Teach
For America, for instance, founder Wendy Kopp recognized that only a
tiny fraction of Princeton graduates would enter the teaching profession
as a career. In order to funnel top college graduates into urban schools, she
adapted her model to ask only two years from corps members—a major
compromise, but one that was necessary if the program was to be truly
national in scope. Thus, while grand plans were in many ways the manifestation of orthodoxy, they often also required a willingness to settle for less
than ideal results.

Perhaps the greatest challenge that the excellence for all movement faced
was a product of the fact that its leaders sought, in classic American fashion,
to solve social problems through the schools. Rather than directly pursuing
racial equity, creating a universal health care program, or more aggressively
redistributing income, Americans have traditionally turned to education,
and the reformers of the excellence for all era were no exception. In part,
this is a practical response, as schools represent the nation's most fully developed network of sociopolitical institutions. As such, they present the
easiest way for enacting far-reaching change.[16] In equal measure, citizens of

liberal democracies, and particularly the American liberal democracy, are ideologically inclined to see the actions of individuals as primary in shaping the social landscape. If individuals are responsible for the successes and failures of the society, then attempting to shape their capacities and motives makes a great deal of sense. Thus, as Peter Schrag has written, the result has been that "our schools are forced to serve as a fallback social-service system for millions of American children."[17] But though the schools may represent convenient targets for social reformers, they are clearly limited in what they can accomplish.

THE FUTURE OF EXCELLENCE FOR ALL

Each of the three reforms explored in this study is the product of a unique historical period, directly responding to the perceived problems of the late twentieth and early twenty-first centuries. Despite the many disappointments of excellence for all reforms and any inherent challenges to the movement as a whole, the broader vision remains intact. The conditions that created the movement, after all, remain the same. American faith in the power of education to solve social problems, whatever the evidence against it, continues to persist. Particular contextual factors—economic globalization, widespread acceptance of the importance of civil rights, expanding enrollments in higher education, and reluctance to pursue heavy-handed policy efforts like school desegregation, among them—all continue to shape the way education reformers approach their work. And competing aims in schooling have been so successfully fused together that they will be difficult to justify as separate pursuits. Excellence for all, in short, will continue to persist as the highest ideal in American education reform.

For their part, the ambitious reformers who have spearheaded excellence for all efforts are not likely to resign themselves to defeat. The Gates Foundation has moved on from its small schools experiment, major advocates of expanding the AP program have begun to question the effectiveness of that effort, and some supporters of Teach For America have begun to acknowledge the limitations of the TFA model. Yet while educational entrepreneurs recognize their missteps, they have tended to see them as learning experiences. After all, the excellence for all era in the United States has brought about a paradigmatic shift. Beyond merely being a distinct period for historical categorization, it has transformed the way Americans define educational success. Consequently, setbacks alone are hardly enough to disrupt a mode of thought that has increasingly shaped the way a generation approaches school reform. Not surprisingly, ambitious and entre-preneurially minded reformers, with ample resources at their disposal and with willing partners in urban school districts, have continued to pursue systemic transformation.

The shape of reforms in the excellence for all era will, of course, continue to evolve. Educational entrepreneurs will discover new levers for change, and they will pull them with varying degrees of aggressiveness. But the core vision of excellence for all, in its relatively mature form, has produced some-thing close to consensus among an entire generation of reformers. The aim of school reform, as well as the means of achieving it, has become an object of agreement requiring only the willingness to act. "The idea is very simple," Barack Obama observed in 2010.

> If we can make sure that we have the very best teachers in the class-room, if we can reward excellence instead of mediocrity and the status quo, if we can make sure that we're tracking progress in real, serious ways and we're willing to make investments in what goes on in the classroom and not the school bureaucracy, and reward innovation, then schools can improve. There are models out there . . . and the key is how do we duplicate those?[18]

Not surprisingly, Obama's signature educational initiative—the Depart-ment of Education's Race to the Top fund—sought to identify successful practices and incentivize states to adopt them. Far from being an idiosyn-cratic federal effort, Race to the Top generated powerful support among states, among the public, and among a dozen major private foundations that pledged a half billion dollars in order to maximize its impact. Unified in their pursuit of excellence for all, the nation's most influential reform-ers will continue to search for scalable solutions to the nation's perceived schooling problem, looking for lessons about what works. To paraphrase Secretary of Education Arne Duncan, the age of "tinkering" is over; this is the age of excellence for all students.[19]

Looked at one way, that mission is quixotic. America is not Garrison Keillor's fictitious Lake Wobegon—a place where all the children are above average. Even if all schools did an equal job, educational outcomes would differ as a result of the different places students start. And, even if efforts like universal preschool and early interventions like Geoffrey Canada's Har-lem Children's Zone began to level out those initial starting points, there will always be a cross section of parents angling to ensure an advantage for their children. As long as educational credentials matter, as long as top schools limit the number of students they admit, and as long as parents have the right to choose where to send their children, educational inequity will persist. If excellence is measured by the status schools confer, it will not be achieved by all. Reform efforts designed to produce this outcome will continue to fail and, consequently, will deeply damage the legitimacy of the schools implicated in that failure.

But there is another way of thinking about excellence in American education, centered on helping students meet reasonable levels of proficiency. While perhaps somewhat modest rhetorically, such a goal is both challenging and bold. And despite the relentless and unyielding work inherent in such an effort, tireless and thoughtful educators have proven time after time that schools can help all students learn.

Reformers in the excellence for all era have tried to identify particular aspects of successful schools in order to replicate them at scale. Frequently, the results of their efforts were disheartening. But failure to systematically transform the nation's high schools does not alter the fact that reformers' so-called models of excellence were based on schools that had, in fact, managed to work. Many of those model schools were private schools populated by students of privilege. Many, however, were public schools serving low-income students in urban neighborhoods. Thus, although the formula for good schools may remain unclear, and may not exist at all, the lesson that urban schools can work is an important one and should not fail to inspire optimism.

Much to the disappointment of scale-obsessed educational entrepreneurs, schools still appear to improve slowly. As the history of these three reform efforts shows, there are no easy solutions to the school question and no quick fixes. Deborah Meier located her school in a small building. But she also recruited strong teachers, worked to build a culture of professionalism and commitment, and connected the school with the wider community. Jaime Escalante helped Latino students in East L.A. pass the Advanced Placement calculus test, but he did more than just implement the AP curriculum. He related to students, challenged and cajoled them, and refused to give up on them. And, like TFA corps members, many great teachers have degrees from top colleges. But many great teachers do not, and many top college graduates find that teaching is the wrong profession for them. If the magic bullet had been the size of the school, or the curriculum, or the Ivy League degree, the results would have been easily reproduced. The story would end there, with a mission accomplished.

But the end of the excellence for all story is not yet written.

Perhaps its adherents will, despite the obstacles, ultimately prevail. Or perhaps they will strike a balance between idealism and realism that will retain the passion of the movement without making it unsustainable. Or perhaps those seeking excellence for all will continue tilting at windmills until their ranks are thinned of all but a willful few.

Whatever its future may be, the aim of excellence for all continues to bestride the narrow world of education reform like a Colossus. Whatever its flaws, it will not fade quietly into history; it will shape it.

NOTES

INTRODUCTION

1. National Commission on Excellence in Education, *A Nation at Risk: The Imperative of Educational Reform* (Washington, DC: U.S. Government Printing Office, 1983).

2. Barack Obama, Press Conference, September 10, 2010, Office of the Press Secretary, accessed January 6, 2011, *www.whitehouse.gov/the-press-office/2010/09/10/press-conference-president-obama*.

3. Federal News Service, "President-elect Obama nominates Arne Duncan," transcript, December 16, 2008, accessed January 6, 2011, *blogs.suntimes.com/sweet/2008/12/presidentelect_obama_nominates.html*.

4. Barack Obama, "Remarks of President Barack Obama—As Prepared for Delivery, Address to Joint Session of Congress," February 24, 2009, accessed January 6, 2011, *www.whitehouse.gov/the_press_office/remarks-of-president-barack-obama-address-to-joint-session-of-congress/*.

5. U.S. Department of Education, "Homepage," accessed January 6, 2011, *www.ed.gov*.

6. College Board, "Homepage," accessed March 7, 2010, *www.collegeboard.com*.

7. Teach For America, "What We Do," accessed January 6, 2011, *www.teachforamerica.org/mission/index.htm*; The Bill and Melinda Gates Foundation, "Foundation Fact Sheet," accessed January 6, 2011, *www.gatesfoundation.org/about/Pages/foundation-fact-sheet.aspx*.

8. Chester E. Finn Jr. and Kelly Amis, *Making It Count* (Washington, DC: Thomas B. Fordham Foundation, 2001), 5.

9. Frederick M. Hess and Andrew J. Rotherham, "Can NCLB Survive the Competitiveness Competition?," *AEI Outlooks and On the Issues*, June 12, 2007.

10. Orlando F. Furno and J. S. Kidd, *New Teachers for the Inner City* (Washington, DC: Capitol Publications, 1974), 142.

11. David Ferrero, personal communication, February 16, 2006.

12. "The RS 100 Agents of Change," *Rolling Stone*, March 18, 2009,

accessed March 7, 2010, *www.rollingstone.com/news/story/26754176/ the_rs_100_agents_of_change/2*.

13. Arne Duncan, Address to the Education Stakeholders Forum, U.S. Department of Education, Barnard Auditorium, Washington, DC, September 24, 2009; "Spellings: 'No Child Left Behind' Is a 'Toxic Brand,'" *Morning Edition*, National Public Radio, March 17, 2010.

14. "Highlights of the 2010 Phi Delta Kappa/Gallup Poll," *Phi Delta Kappan* 92 (September 2010).

15. See, for instance, Jay Mathews, *Escalante: The Best Teacher in America* (New York: Holt, 1988).

16. Enrollment and poverty figures are from the National Center for Education Statistics, "Enrollment, Poverty, and Federal Funds for the 100 Largest School Districts, by Enrollment Size: 2003–04 and Fiscal Year 2006," accessed January 6, 2011, *nces.ed.gov/programs/digest/d06/tables/dt06_089 .asp*.

17. Diane Ravitch and Joseph P. Viteritti, introduction to *City Schools: Lessons from New York*, ed. Diane Ravitch and Joseph P. Viteritti (Baltimore: Johns Hopkins University Press, 2000), 2.

18. The U.S. Department of Education did not announce a competition for new awards in fiscal year 2010. While it did continue to honor grants made in previous years, the future of the program is unclear.

19. Teach For America, "Our Regions, Chicago," accessed March 7, 2010, *www.teachforamerica.org/about/regions/chicago.htm*.

20. Maureen Kelleher, "CPS a Leader in AP Growth," *Catalyst Chicago*, June 2004, accessed January 6, 2011, *www.catalyst-chicago.org/news/index .php?item=1277&cat=23*.

21. Teach For America, "Our Regions, Los Angeles," accessed March 7, 2010, *www.teachforamerica.org/about/regions/los_angeles.htm*.

CHAPTER 1

1. For a more thorough discussion of policy elites and their characteristics, see David Tyack and Larry Cuban, *Tinkering toward Utopia* (Cambridge, MA: Harvard University Press, 1995).

2. David B. Tyack, *The One Best System: A History of American Urban Education* (Cambridge, MA: Harvard University Press, 1974).

3. Diane Ravitch, *Left Back: A Century of Battles over School Reform* (New York: Simon and Schuster, 2000), 15.

4. For more on the administrative progressives, see Tyack, *The One Best System*.

5. Boston Schools, "School Documents," no. 7 (1908), quoted in Jeannie Oakes, *Keeping Track: How Schools Structure Inequality* (New Haven, CT: Yale University Press, 1985), 34.

6. Department of the Interior Bureau of Education, *Cardinal Principles of*

Secondary Education: A Report of the Commission on the Reorganization of Secondary Education, Appointed by the National Education Association, Bulletin no. 35 (1918).

7.   See, for instance, Walter H. Drost, *David Snedden and Education for Social Efficiency* (Madison: University of Wisconsin Press, 1967).

8.   Stephen Jay Gould, *The Mismeasure of Man* (New York: Norton, 1981), 157.

9.   Educational Policies Commission, *Education for All American Youth* (Washington, DC: National Education Association, 1944), 15.

10. Merle Curti, *The Social Ideas of American Educators* (Paterson, NJ: Littlefield Adams, 1965).

11. Sputnik 1, launched by the Soviet Union on October 4, 1957, was the world's first artificial Earth-orbiting satellite. For more, see Matthew Brzezinski, *Red Moon Rising: Sputnik and the Hidden Rivalries That Ignited the Space Age* (New York: Holt, 2008).

12. "What Price Life Adjustment," *Time*, December 2, 1957, accessed January 6, 2011, *www.time.com/time/printout/0,8816,825347,00.html*.

13. U.S. Office of Education, *Life Adjustment Education for Every Youth* (1951), quoted in Lawrence A. Cremin, *The Transformation of the School: Progressivism in American Education* (New York: Vintage Books, 1964), 335.

14. James Conant, *The American High School Today: A First Report to Interested Citizens* (New York: McGraw-Hill, 1959).

15. John Gardner, *Excellence: Can We Be Equal and Excellent Too?* (New York: Harper and Bros., 1961), 75.

16. Annie Reynolds, "The Education of Spanish Children in Five Southwestern States," U.S. Department of Interior Bulletin no. 11 (1933), in *Education and the Mexican-American*, ed. Carlos E. Cortes (New York: Anno Press, 1974), 13.

17. Sam Tanenhaus, "The Roar of the Liberal," *New York Times*, August 30, 2009, WK1.

18. Charles W. Hobart, "Underachievement among Minority Group Students: An Analysis and a Proposal," *Phylon* 24, no. 2 (1963): 184.

19. Chester E. Finn Jr., *Troublemaker: A Personal History of School Reform since Sputnik* (Princeton, NJ: Princeton University Press, 2008), 70.

20. Title I of the ESEA was titled "Improving the Academic Achievement of the Disadvantaged."

21. For examples of work on gender bias, see, for instance, Nancy Frazier and Myra Sadker, *Sexism in School and Society* (New York: Harper and Row, 1973); Terry Saario, Carol Nagy Jacklin, and Carol Tittle, "Sex-Role Stereotyping in the Public Schools," *Harvard Educational Review* 43 (1973): 386–418; Janice Pottker and Andrew Fishel, eds., *Sex Bias in the Schools: The*

Research Evidence (Rutherford, NJ: Fairleigh Dickinson University Press, 1977).

22. David Tyack and Elisabeth Hansot, *Learning Together: A History of Coeducation in American Public Schools* (New York: Russell Sage Foundation, 1990), 244; Amendments to the ESEA dealing with special education were adopted in 1965, 1966, 1968, 1970, and 1974.

23. See, for instance, Arnold Rose, *The Roots of Prejudice* (Paris: United Nations Educational, Scientific and Cultural Organization, 1951), and Arnold Rose, *America Divided: Minority Group Relations in the United States* (New York: Knopf, 1949).

24. See, among others, James T. Patterson, *Brown v. Board of Education: A Civil Rights Milestone and Its Troubled Legacy* (Oxford: Oxford University Press, 2001); Tyack and Hansot, *Learning Together*, 246–47.

25. For a discussion of inclusion and opposition to it, see *Report Card to the Nation on Inclusion in Education of Students with Mental Retardation* (Arlington, TX: The ARC, 1992); John Goodlad and Thomas Lovitt, eds., *Integrating General and Special Education* (New York: Macmillan, 1993); Thomas Skrtic, *Behind Special Education* (Denver: Love Publishing, 1991).

26. The "Great Society" refers to a string of social reforms enacted during the administration of President Lyndon B. Johnson. It includes the Civil Rights Acts of 1964 and 1968, the Voting Rights Act, the Elementary and Secondary Education Act, the creation of Medicare and Medicaid, and the slate of projects that constituted Johnson's "War on Poverty." Diane Ravitch and John E. Chubb, "The Future of No Child Left Behind," *Education Next* 9, no. 3 (Summer 2009), accessed January 6, 2011, *educationnext.org/the-future-of-no-child-left-behind/*.

27. David Labaree, *How to Succeed in School without Really Learning: The Credentials Race in American Education* (New Haven, CT: Yale University Press, 1997), 24.

28. Edward J. Meade, *A Foundation Goes to School* (New York: Ford Foundation, 1972), 5.

29. Ibid., 26.

30. Gardner, *Excellence*, 82.

31. According to Ugo Pagano, "It is possible to consume a positional good only if it is unequally consumed." Ugo Pagano, "Is Power an Economic Good?," in *The Politics and Economics of Power*, ed. Samuel Bowles, Maurizio Franzini, and Ugo Pagano (London: Routledge, 1999), 64.

32. Don J. Hager, "Social and Psychological Factors in Integration," *Journal of Educational Sociology* 31, no. 2 (October 1957): 59.

33. Patterson, *Brown v. Board of Education*, 172.

34. Arnold M. Rose, *De Facto School Segregation* (New York: National Conference of Christians and Jews, 1964), 21.

35. Richard Nixon, *RN: The Memoirs of Richard Nixon* (New York: Grosset and Dunlap, 1978), 444–45.

36. Douglas S. Reed, "Court-Ordered School Finance Equalization: Judicial Activism and Democratic Opposition," in *Developments in School Finance*, ed. William J. Fowler (Darby, PA: Diane Publishing, 1997), 103.

37. Johnson's War on Poverty, initiated in his 1964 State of the Union address, included programs like VISTA, the Job Corps, Head Start, Legal Services, the Community Action Program, Medicare, and Medicaid.

38. Lisa McGirr, *Suburban Warriors: The Origins of the New American Right* (Princeton, NJ: Princeton University Press, 2001), 10.

39. Ibid., 10.

40. See, for instance, Michael Katz, *Class, Bureaucracy, and Schools: The Illusion of Educational Change* (New York: Praeger, 1971).

41. Marcia Chambers, "U.S. Inquiry into Bias Is Opposed at Prestigious New York Schools," *New York Times*, November 7, 1977, 1.

42. Roslyn Public Schools, *Progress Report on the School-within-a-School Program* (Roslyn, NY: Roslyn Public Schools, January 21, 1974), 1.

43. Jonathan Kozol, *Free Schools* (Boston: Houghton Mifflin, 1972), 16.

44. Maurie Hillson, "The Reorganization of the School: Bringing about a Remission in the Problems Faced by Minority Children," *Phylon* 28, no. 3 (1967): 230.

45. For more, see John Bremer and Michael Von Moschzisker, *The School without Walls: Philadelphia's Parkway Program* (New York: Holt, Rinehart, and Winston, 1971); Terrence Deal and Robert Nolan, eds., *Alternative Schools: Ideologies, Realities, Guidelines* (Chicago: Nelson Hall, 1978); Edward Ignas and Raymond Corsini, eds., *Alternative Educational Systems* (Itasca, IL: F. E. Peacock, 1979).

46. Sol Stern, "The Ed Schools Latest—and Worst—Humbug," *City Journal*, Summer 2006, accessed January 6, 2011, *www.city-journal.org/html/16_3_ ed_school.html*.

47. See David Labaree, "Public Goods, Private Goods: The American Struggle over Educational Goals," *American Educational Research Journal* 34, no. 1 (Spring 1997): 39–81; David K. Brown, *Degrees of Control: A Sociology of Educational Expansion and Occupational Credentialism* (New York: Teachers College Press, 1995); Randall Collins, *The Credential Society: An Historical Sociology of Education and Stratification* (New York: Academic, 1979).

48. See, for example, Andree Brooks, "Enrollment Is Booming at Private Schools," *New York Times*, March 25, 1979, CN1.

49. Floyd M. Hammack, "Does the Comprehensive High School Have a

Future?," in *The Comprehensive High School Today*, ed. Floyd M. Hammack (New York: Teachers College Press, 2004), 131.

50. Meade, *A Foundation Goes to School*, 43.

51. Haynes Johnson, *Sleepwalking through History: America in the Reagan Years* (New York: Norton, 1991), 13.

52. Quoted in Lawrence J. McAndrews, *The Era of Education: The Presidents and the Schools, 1965–2001* (Urbana: University of Illinois Press, 2006), 119.

53. See, for example, David Kearns and Denis Doyle, *Winning the Brain Race: A Bold Plan to Make Our Schools Competitive* (San Francisco: ICS Press, 1988).

54. Madeleine B. Hemmings, *American Education: An Economic Issue*, Human Resources Report (Washington, DC: Chamber of Commerce of the United States, 1982), 3–4.

55. Tom Vander Ark, "Fixing the Factory," *Daily Oregonian*, February 8, 2004; Joyce Baldwin, "Meeting the Challenge of Urban Schools," *Carnegie Reporter* 1, no. 2 (Spring 2001).

56. See, for example, Harold Hodgkinson, "Reform Versus Reality," *Phi Delta Kappan* 73, no. 1, (September 1991): 15–16; for a more recent reflection on this kind of thinking, see Henry M. Levin, "The Economic Payoff to Investing in Educational Justice," *Educational Researcher* 38, no. 1 (January/February 2009).

57. Philip G. Altbach, "The Great Education 'Crisis,'" in *Excellence in Education: Perspectives on Policy and Practice*, ed. Philip G. Altbach, Gail P. Kelly, and Lois Weis (Buffalo: Prometheus Books, 1985), 14.

58. Theodore R. Sizer, *Horace's Compromise: The Dilemma of the American High School* (New York: Houghton Mifflin, 1984), 135.

59. See *University of California v. Bakke* and *Gratz v. Bollinger*.

60. Steven Teles, "The Eternal Return of Compassionate Conservatism," *National Affairs*, no. 1 (Fall 2009): 3.

61. Michael Horowitz, "The Public Interest Law Movement: An Analysis with Special Reference to the Role and Practices of Conservative Public Interest Law Firms" (prepared for the Scaife Foundation, 1980), 85–86.

62. Johnson, *Sleepwalking through History*, 392.

63. Ibid., 115.

64. Pedro Noguera, "More Democracy Not Less: Confronting the Challenge of Privatization in Public Education," *Journal of Negro Education* 63, no. 2 (1994): 237–50; John Chubb and Terry Moe, *Politics, Markets, and America's Schools* (Washington: Brookings Institution, 1990).

65. Peter Cookson, *School Choice: The Struggle for the Soul of American Education* (New Haven, CT: Yale University Press, 1994), 6.

66. Carnegie Forum on Education and the Economy, *A Nation Prepared: Teachers for the 21st Century* (New York: Carnegie Corporation, 1986), 92.

67. Chester E. Finn Jr., "The Excellence Backlash: Sources of Resistance to Educational Reform," *American Spectator*, September 1987, 13.

68. John E. Chubb, "Lessons in School Reform from the Edison Project," in *New Schools for a New Century*, ed. Diane Ravitch and Joseph P. Viteritti (New Haven, CT: Yale University Press, 1997), 102.

69. National Commission on Excellence in Education, *A Nation at Risk*.

70. Ernest L. Boyer, *High School: A Report on Secondary Education in America* (New York: Harper and Row, 1983); Business-Higher Education Forum, *America's Competitive Challenge: The Need for a National Response* (Washington, DC: Business-Higher Education Forum, 1983); College Board Educational Equity Project, *Academic Preparation for College: What Students Need to Know and Be Able to Do* (New York: College Board, 1983); Commission on International Education, *What We Don't Know Can Hurt Us: The Shortfall in International Competence* (Washington, DC: American Council on Education, 1983); Education Commission of the States Task Force on Education for Growth, *Action for Excellence* (Denver: Education Commission of the States, 1983); John I. Goodlad, *A Place Called School: Prospects for the Future* (New York: McGraw-Hill, 1983); National Science Foundation, *Educating Americans for the 21st Century: A Plan of Action for Improving Mathematics, Science, and Technology Education for All American Elementary and Secondary Students So That Their Achievement Is the Best in the World by 1995* (Washington, DC: National Science Foundation, 1983); Sizer, *Horace's Compromise*; Twentieth Century Fund, *Making the Grade: Report of the Twentieth Century Fund Task Force on Federal Elementary and Secondary Education Policy* (New York: Twentieth Century Fund, 1983).

71. Finn, *Troublemaker*, 99.

72. David Boaz, "Educational Schizophrenia," in Assessing the Reagan Years, ed. David Boaz (Washington, DC: Cato Institute, 1988), 301.

73. Thomas Toch, *In the Name of Excellence: The Struggle to Reform the Nation's Schools, Why It's Failing, and What Should Be Done* (New York: Oxford University Press, 1991), 25.

74. Matthew Feldman, "Excellence in Education for Everyone," *New York Times*, May 19, 1985, NJ24.

75. Frederick M. Hess, "The Supply Side of School Reform," in *The Future of Educational Entrepreneurship: Possibilities for School Reform* (Cambridge, MA: Harvard Education Press, 2008), 9.

76. See, for instance, Katherine Fulton and Andrew Blau, *Looking Out for the Future: Executive Summary*, Global Business Network (Emeryville) and Monitor Institute (Cambridge, MA: Monitor Company Group, 2005).

77. Albert Shanker, "Teachers and Reform," in *Excellence in Education: Perspectives on Policy and Practice*, ed. Philip G. Altbach, Gail P. Kelly, and Lois Weis (Buffalo: Prometheus Books, 1985), 204.

78. Boyer, *High School*, xii.
79. Michelle Fine, preface to *Chartering Urban School Reform: Reflections on Public High Schools in the Midst of Change*, ed. Michelle Fine (New York: Teachers College Press, 1994), 3.
80. Albert J. Menendez, "Voters versus Vouchers: An Analysis of Referendum Data," *Phi Delta Kappan* 81 (1999).
81. George H. W. Bush, "Remarks by the President in Ceremony for G.I. Bill Opportunity Scholarships for Children," White House press release, 1992.
82. Peter Frumkin, "Inside Venture Philanthropy," in *Seven Studies in Educational Philanthropy* (Washington, DC: Thomas Fordham Foundation, 2001).
83. "Highlights of the 2010 Phi Delta Kappa/Gallup Poll."
84. See, for instance, the support of those like former Clinton administration secretary of labor Robert Reich, Senator Joseph Lieberman, former U.S. congressman Floyd Flake, and Milwaukee mayor John Norquist.
85. "Charter School Law," Government Innovators Network, Harvard Kennedy School, accessed January 6, 2011, *www.innovations.harvard.edu/awards.html?id=3848*.
86. See the NEA's position on vouchers in National Education Association, *Vouchers: What Is at Stake?* (Washington, DC: NEA, 2008), accessed January 6, 2011, *www.nea.org/assets/docs/mf_PB07_Vouchers.pdf*.
87. Paul T. Hill and Mary Beth Celio, "Catholic Schools," in *City Schools: Lessons from New York*, ed. Diane Ravitch and Joseph P. Viteritti (Baltimore: Johns Hopkins University Press, 2000), 260.
88. See, among others, Eric P. Bettinger, "The Effect of Charter Schools on Charter Students and Public Schools" (working paper, Case Western Reserve University, 2004); Martin Carnoy, Rebecca Jacobsen, Lawrence Mischel, and Richard Rothstein, *The Charter School Dust-up: Examining the Evidence on Enrollment and Achievement* (Washington, DC: Economic Policy Institute, 2005); Eric A. Hanushek, "Choice, Charters, and Public School Competition," in *Innovations in Education*, Proceeding of the Federal Reserve Bank of Cleveland Conference, November 17–18, 2005.
89. State Strategies to Support Curriculum and Assessment Content Development at the School and District Level (Denver: Education Commission of the States, 1985).
90. Rex Hagans and Leslie Crohn, *State Curriculum Standards as a School Improvement Strategy* (Portland, OR: Northwest Regional Educational Laboratory, 1986).
91. Robert Reinhold, "School Reform: Years of Tumult, Mixed Results," *New York Times*, August 10, 1987, accessed January 6, 2011, *www.nytimes.com/1987/08/10/us/school-reform-years-of-tumult-mixed-results.html?pagewanted=all*.

92. E. D. Hirsch Jr., *What Your Sixth Grader Needs to Know* (New York: Random House, 2007), 2.

93. Robert B. Schwartz and Marian A. Robinson, "Goals 2000 and the Standards Movement," *Brookings Papers on Education Policy*, 2000, 173–206.

94. Ibid., 173–206.

95. HR 1804—Goals 2000: Educate America Act, Section 2, "Purpose," accessed January 6, 2011, *www2.ed.gov/legislation/GOALS2000/TheAct/sec2.html*.

96. Schwartz and Robinson, "Goals 2000 and the Standards Movement," 173–206.

97. Education Week, "State Grade Tables," *Quality Counts 2000*, accessed January 6, 2011, *www.edcounts.org/archive/sreports/qc00/tables/standacct-t1.htm*.

98. U.S. Department of Education, *Preliminary Overview of Programs and Changes Included in the No Child Left Behind Act of 2001 (2003)*, accessed January 6, 2011, *www.ed.gov/nclb/overview/intro/progsum/sum_pg2.html*.

99. Duncan, Address to the Education Stakeholders Forum.

100. Diane Ravitch, *The Death and Life of the Great American School System* (New York: Basic Books, 2010), 101.

101. Tom DeLay to Rush Limbaugh, as quoted in Frederick M. Hess and Andrew J. Rotherham, "Can NCLB Survive the Competitiveness Competition?," *AEI Outlooks and On the Issues*, June 12, 2007.

102. National Education Association, "No Child Left Behind," accessed January 6, 2011, *www.nea.org/home/NoChildLeftBehindAct.html*.

103. "Joint Organizational Statement on 'No Child Left Behind' Act," accessed January 6, 2011, *www.nea.org/home/19426.htm*.

104. Libby Quaid, "U.S. Schools Chief Wants D.C. Kids to Keep Vouchers," *Associated Press*, March 4, 2009.

105. Frederick M. Hess, "The Case for Educational Entrepreneurship: Hard Truths about Risk, Reform, and Reinvention," *Phi Delta Kappan* 89, no. 1 (2007): 21–30; Diane Ravitch, "Somebody's Children: Educational Opportunity for *All* American Children," in *New Schools for a New Century*, ed. Diane Ravitch and Joseph P. Viteritti (New Haven, CT: Yale University Press, 1997), 254.

106. See, for example, Ronald Edmonds, "Some Schools Work and More Can," *Social Policy* 9, no. 5 (March/April 1979).

107. Stephen K. Miller, "Research on Exemplary Schools: An Historical Perspective," in *Research on Exemplary Schools*, ed. Gilbert R. Austin and Herbert Garber (Orlando: Academic Press, 1985), 21.

108. Arthur Bestor, *Educational Wastelands* (Urbana: University of Illinois Press, 1953), 6.

109. For more examples of this, see J. Myron Atkin, *America's Schools: Public and*

Private (Boston: American Academy of Arts and Sciences, 1981); Leonard L. Baird, *The Elite Schools: A Profile of Prestigious Independent Schools* (Lexingon, MA: Lexington Books, 1977); Anthony S. Bryk, Valerie E. Lee, and Peter B. Holland, *Catholic Schools and the Common Good* (Cambridge, MA: Harvard University Press, 1993); James Coleman, Thomas Hoffer, and Sally Kilgore, *High School Achievement: Public, Catholic, and Private Schools Compared* (New York: Basic Books, 1982); James Coleman and Thomas Hoffer, *Public and Private High Schools: The Impact of Communities* (New York: Basic Books, 1987); Jane Hannaway and Susan Abramowitz, "Public and Private Schools: Are They Really Different," in *Research on Exemplary Schools*, ed. Gilbert R. Austin and Herbert Garber (Orlando: Academic Press, 1985); Paul T. Hill, Gail E. Foster, and Tamar Gendler, "High Schools with Character" (Report R-3944-RC, Rand Corporation, Santa Monica, CA, 1990); Jacqueline Jordan Irvine and Michele Foster, eds., *Growing Up African American in Catholic Schools* (New York: Teachers College Press, 1996); Arthur Powell, *Lessons from Privilege: The American Prep School Tradition* (Cambridge, MA: Harvard University Press, 1996).

110. "Shared Goals Found Hallmark of Exemplary Private Schools," *Education Week*, December 5, 1984.

111. Tom Vander Ark, "America's High School Crisis: Policy Reforms That Will Make a Difference," *Education Week*, April 2, 2003.

112. Tamar Lewin, "Young Students Are New Focus for Big Donors," *New York Times*, August 21, 2005, accessed January 6, 2011, *www.nytimes.com/2005/08/21/education/21giving.html*.

113. Frederick Hess, ed., *With the Best of Intentions: How Philanthropy Is Reshaping K–12 Education* (Cambridge, MA: Harvard Education Press, 2005), 3.

114. Mark E. Fetler and Dale C. Carson, "Identification of Exemplary Schools on a Large Scale," in *Research on Exemplary Schools*, ed. Gilbert R. Austin and Herbert Garber (Orlando: Academic Press, 1985), 95.

115. Stewart C. Purkey and Marshall S. Smith, "Educational Policy and School Effectiveness," in *Research on Exemplary Schools*, ed. Gilbert R. Austin and Herbert Garber (Orlando: Academic Press, 1985), 183.

116. Antony S. Bryk and Louis M. Gomez, "Reinventing a Research and Development Capacity," in *The Future of Educational Entrepreneurship: Possibilities for School Reform*, ed. Frederick M. Hess (Cambridge, MA: Harvard Education Press, 2008), 182.

117. Steven R. Nelson, James C. Leffler, and Barbara A. Hansen, *Toward a Research Agenda for Understanding and Improving the Use of Research Evidence* (Portland, OR: Northwest Regional Education Laboratory, 2009).

118. Diane Ravitch and Joseph P. Viteritti, eds., *New Schools for a New Century* (New Haven, CT: Yale University Press, 1997), 1.

119. David K. Cohen and Michael S. Garet, "Reforming Educational Policy with Applied Social Research," *Harvard Educational Review* 45, no. 1 (February 1979): 39.
120. Hess, "The Case for Educational Entrepreneurship," 21–30.
121. Deane Mariotti, personal communication, March 26, 2009.
122. Bryk and Gomez, "Reinventing a Research and Development Capacity," 181.
123. Philanthropy Roundtable, "K–12 Education," accessed January 6, 2011, *www.philanthropyroundtable.org/content.asp?contentid=441&print=y*.
124. "2009 Annual Letter from Bill Gates," The Bill and Melinda Gates Foundation, accessed January 6, 2011, *www.gatesfoundation.org/annual-letter/Pages/2009-united-states-education.aspx*.

CHAPTER 2

1. Patrice Iatarola, Amy Ellen Schwartz, Leanna Stiefel, and Colin C. Chellman, "Small Schools, Large Districts: Small-School Reform and New York City's Students," *Teachers College Record* 110, no. 9 (2008): 1840, 1850.
2. Conant, *The American High School Today*.
3. Department of the Interior, *Report of the Commissioner of Education for 1916* (Washington, DC: Government Printing Office, 1917), 456–47.
4. Carroll Smalley Page, *Vocational Education* (Washington, DC: Government Printing Office, 1912), 64.
5. David Tyack, *From Village to Urban System: A Political and Social History* (New York: Carnegie Corporation, 1972), 13.
6. Carol M. Larson, "School-size as a Factor in the Adjustment of High School Seniors" in *Bulletin No. 511, Youth Series No. 6* (Pullman: State College of Washington, 1949), 21.
7. Conant, *The American High School Today*, 77.
8. Arnold M. Rose, "School Desegregation: A Sociologist's View," *Law and Society Review* 2, no. 1 (November 1967), 132.
9. Roger G. Barker and Paul V. Gump, *Big School, Small School: High School Size and Student Behavior* (Stanford, CA: Stanford University Press, 1964), 153.
10. Barker and Gump, *Big School, Small School*, 62.
11. Jonathan P. Sher and Rachel B. Tompkins, "Economy, Efficiency, and Equality: The Myths of Rural School and District Consolidation," in *Education in Rural America*, ed. Jonathan P. Sher (Boulder, CO: Westview, 1977).
12. J. B. Edmonson, Joseph Roemer, and Francis L. Bacon, *The Administration of the Modern Secondary School* (New York: Macmillan, 1953), 79.
13. Coleman and Hoffer, *Public and Private High Schools*, 38.

14. For more on white flight, see Thomas Sugrue, *The Origins of the Urban Crisis* (Princeton, NJ: Princeton University Press, 1998); Becky Nicolaides, *My Blue Heaven* (Chicago: University of Chicago Press, 2002). For more on white flight and schools, see Jack Schneider, "Escape from Los Angeles: White Flight from Los Angeles and Its Schools, 1960–1980," *Journal of Urban History* 34, no. 6 (2008).

15. Heather G. Peske and Kati Haycock, *Teaching Inequality: How Poor and Minority Students Are Shortchanged on Teacher Quality* (Washington, DC: Education Trust, 2006); Coleman and Hoffer, *Public and Private High Schools.*

16. Allen Graubard, *Free the Children: Radical Reform and the Free School Movement* (New York: Pantheon, 1972), ix.

17. Kozol, *Free Schools*, 16.

18. Deborah Meier, *The Power of Their Ideas: Lessons for America from a Small School in Harlem* (Boston: Beacon Press, 1995), 129.

19. Ibid., 133, 134.

20. Jeannie Oakes, "Tracking in Secondary Schools: A Contextual Perspective," *Educational Psychologist* 22, no. 2 (1987): 129–53; Anne Wheelock, *Crossing the Tracks: How Untracking Can Save America's Schools* (New York: New Press, 1992).

21. National Commission on Excellence in Education, *A Nation at Risk.*

22. Susan Chira, "Harlem's Witness for the Chancellor," *New York Times*, August 10, 1992, B3.

23. Ann Bradley, "Advocates Seek to Make Small Schools the Rule, Not the Exception," *Education Week*, May 19, 1993, accessed January 6, 2011, *www.edweek.org/ew/articles/1993/05/19/34small.h12.html?print=1.*

24. Toch, *In the Name of Excellence*, 235.

25. Meier, *The Power of Their Ideas*, 16.

26. Michelle Fine, "Not in Our Name," *Rethinking Schools Online* 19, no. 4 (2005), accessed January 6, 2011, *www.rethinkingschools.org/archive/19_04/name194.shtml.*

27. Deborah W. Meier, "The Big Benefits of Smallness," *Educational Leadership* 54 (1996): 12–15.

28. Craig Gordon, "My Small School Journey," *Rethinking Schools Online* 19, no. 4 (2005) accessed January 6, 2011, *www.rethinkingschools.org/archive/19_04/jour194.shtml.*

29. "Editorial: The Small Schools Express," *Rethinking Schools Online* 19, no. 4 (2005), accessed January 6, 2011, *www.rethinkingschools.org/archive/19_04/expr194.shtml.*

30. Meier, *The Power of Their Ideas*, 36.

31. Ibid., 107.

32. Theodore Sizer, *Horace's School: Redesigning the American High School* (Boston: Houghton Mifflin, 1992), 128.

33. Theodore Sizer, *Horace's Hope: What Works for the American High School* (Boston: Houghton Mifflin, 1996), 154–55.

34. Hannaway and Abramowitz, "Public and Private Schools"; Coleman and Hoffer, *Public and Private High Schools*, 38.

35. Rural schools were generally excluded, given the urban nature of the perceived problem.

36. Coleman, Hoffer, and Kilgore, *High School Achievement*.

37. Gerald Grant, "The Character of Education and the Education of Character," *Daedalus: Journal of the American Academy of Arts and Sciences, America's Schools: Public and Private*, 110, no. 3 (1981); Hannaway and Abramowitz, "Public and Private Schools."

38. Thomas Gregory, "Small Is Too Big: Achieving a Critical Anti-Mass in the High School," in *Source Book on School and District Size, Cost, and Quality* (Minneapolis: University of Minnesota, Hubert H. Humphrey Institute of Public Affairs, 1992), 1–31; Michael A. Copland and Elizabeth E. Boatright, "Leading Small: Eight Lessons for Leaders in Transforming Large Comprehensive High Schools," *Phi Delta Kappan* 85, no. 10 (2004): 762–70.

39. Gregory, "Small Is Too Big"; Craig B. Howley, "The Matthew Principle: A West Virginia Replication?," *Education Policy Analysis Archives* 3, no. 18 (1995): 1–25; Dan T. Smith and Alan J. DeYoung, "Big School vs. Small School: Conceptual, Empirical, and Political Perspectives on the Re-emerging Debate," *Journal of Rural and Small Schools* 2, no. 2 (1988): 2–11; Herbert J. Walberg, "On Local Control: Is Bigger Better?," in *Source Book on School and District Size, Cost, and Quality* (Minneapolis: University of Minnesota, Hubert H. Humphrey Institute of Public Affairs, 1992), 118–34.

40. Anthony S. Bryk and Yeow Meng Thum, "The Effects of High School Organization on Dropping Out: An Exploratory Investigation" (unpublished paper, University of Chicago, 1988), 26; Aaron M. Pallas, "School Climate in American High Schools," *Teachers College Record* 89, no. 4 (Summer 1988): 549, 551; Judith Baum, ed., *Making Big Schools Smaller: A Review of the Implementation of the House Plan in New York City's Most Troubled High Schools* (New York: Public Education Association and Bank Street College of Education, 1989), 11.

41. Anthony S. Bryk and Mary Erina Driscoll, "An Empirical Investigation of the School as Community" (unpublished paper, University of Chicago, 1988), 54–63.

42. Mary Anne Raywid, *Taking Stock: The Movement to Create Mini-Schools,*

Schools-within-Schools, and Separate Small Schools (New York: ERIC Clearinghouse on Urban Education, 1996).

43. Mark Fetler, "School Dropout Rates, Academic Performance, Size, and Poverty: Correlates of Educational Reform," *Educational Evaluation and Policy Analysis* 11, no. 2 (1989): 109–16; William Fowler and Herbert Walberg, "School Size, Characteristics, and Outcomes," *Educational Evaluation and Policy Analysis* 13, no. 2 (1991): 189–202.

44. Bryk and Thum, "The Effects of High School Organization on Dropping Out"; Craig B. Howley, "Synthesis of the Effects of School and District Size: What Research Says about Achievement in Small Schools and School Districts," *Journal of Rural and Small Schools* 4, no. 1 (1989): 2–12; Gary Huang and Craig B. Howley, "Mitigating Disadvantage: Effects of Small-Scale Schooling on Students' Achievement in Alaska," *Journal of Research in Rural Education* 9, no. 3 (1993): 137–49.

45. Gregory, "Small Is Too Big"; Smith and DeYoung, "Big School vs. Small School"; Walberg, "On Local Control: Is Bigger Better?"; Caroline Hendrie, "High Schools Nationwide Paring Down," *Education Week*, June 16, 2004; Nina Hurwitz, "Competing for College," *Education Week*, January 25, 2006; Larry Lashway, "School Size: Is Small Better?," *Research Roundup* 15, no. 1 (1999), accessed January 6, 2011, *eric.uoregon.edu/publications/roundup/W98-99.html*.

46. Valerie E. Lee and Julia B. Smith, "High School Size: Which Works Best and for Whom?," *Educational Evaluation and Policy Analysis* 19, no. 3 (1997): 205–27.

47. Kathleen Cotton, *School Size, School Climate, and Student Performance*, School Improvement Research Series (Portland, OR: Northwest Regional Educational Laboratory, 1996), 16.

48. Chicago Public Schools "Small Schools: Research," accessed January 6, 2011, *smallschools.cps.k12.il.us/research.html*.

49. See, for example, Cotton, *School Size, School Climate, and Student Performance*.

50. William Ayers and Michael Klonsky, "Chicago's Renaissance 2010: The Small Schools Movement Meets the Ownership Society," *Phi Delta Kappan* 87, no. 6 (February 2006): 453.

51. Ibid., 453–54.

52. Veronica Anderson, "Smaller Is Better," *Catalyst Chicago*, May 1998, accessed January 6, 2011, *www.catalyst-chicago.org/news/index.php?item=1723&cat=35*.

53. Susan Klonsky and Michael Klonsky, "In Chicago: Countering Anonymity through Small Schools," *Educational Leadership* 57, no. 1 (1999): 38–41.

54. Chicago Public Schools, "Small Schools: History," accessed January 6, 2011, *smallschools.cps.k12.il.us/history.html*.

55. Anderson, "Smaller Is Better."

56. Chicago School Reform Board of Trustees, "Resolution No. 95-0829-RS2," August 29, 1995.

57. Sam Dillon, "30 New High Schools Report First-Year Success," *New York Times*, May 14, 1994.

58. Sam Dillon and Joseph Berger, "New Schools Seeking Small Miracles," *New York Times*, May 22, 1995, accessed January 6, 2011, *query.nytimes.com/gst/fullpage.html?res=990CE1D81E3EF931A15756C0A963958260&sec=&spon=&pagewanted=all*.

59. Ibid.

60. Dillon, "30 New High Schools Report First-Year Success."

61. Mitch Nauffts, "Vincent McGee, former Executive Director, Aaron Diamond Foundation: Spending Out as a Philanthropic Strategy," *Philanthropy News Digest*, January 10, 2007, accessed January 6, 2011, *foundationcenter.org/pnd/newsmakers/nwsmkr_50th.jhtml?id=166500002*.

62. Kathleen Teltsch, "Foundation Grant Sought to Start 50 Small Schools," *New York Times*, July 5, 1994, accessed January 6, 2011, *query.nytimes.com/gst/fullpage.html?res=9C01EFDD1E3CF936A35754C0A962958260&sec=&spon=&pagewanted=all*.

63. Anemona Hartocollis, "The 10 Biggest Little Stories of 1997; Crew's Misstep on Small Schools," *New York Times*, December 26, 1997, accessed January 6, 2011, *www.nytimes.com/1997/12/28/nyregion/the-10-biggest-little-stories-of-1997-crew-s-misstep-on-small-schools.html*.

64. Finn, *Troublemaker*, 193.

65. Meier, "The Big Benefits of Smallness."

66. "Resolution S1295, The National Dropout Prevention Act of 1997," Cong. Rec. S10, 859 (October 20, 1997).

67. U.S. Department of Education, "Four Pillars of NCLB," accessed January 6, 2011, *www.ed.gov/nclb/overview/intro/4pillars.html*.

68. Linda Shaw, "Gates Foundation Turns Attention to Higher Education," *Seattle Times*, November 12, 2008.

69. David Ferrero, personal communication, January 22, 2009. See also Chubb and Moe, *Politics, Markets, and America's Schools*.

70. Ferrero, ibid.

71. Tony Wagner, "The Case for 'New Village' Schools," *Education Week*, December 5, 2001, 42, 56; Ferrero, ibid.

72. Ferrero, ibid.

73. Linda Shaw, "Foundation's Small-Schools Experiment Has Yet to Yield Big Results," *Seattle Times*, November 5, 2006, accessed January 6, 2011, *seattletimes.nwsource.com/html/education/2003348701_gates05m.html*.

74. Powell, *Lessons from Privilege*, 206.

75. Tom Vander Ark, "New Educational Options," *America* 189, no. 13 (2003): 2.

76. Gates Foundation, "2009 Annual Letter from Bill Gates."

77. Vander Ark, "America's High School Crisis," 1.

78. Iatarola et al., "Small Schools, Large Districts," 1840, 1850.

79. James P. Connell, Adena M. Klem, Julie M. Broom, and Mark Kenney, *Going Small and Getting Smarter: Small Learning Communities as Platforms for Effective Professional Development* (Portland, OR: Northwest Regional Educational Laboratory, 2006), 4.

80. Vander Ark, "New Educational Options," 4.

81. Meier, "The Big Benefits of Smallness."

82. Anthony Garofano, Jennifer Sable, and Lee Hoffman, *Characteristics of the 100 Largest Public Elementary and Secondary School Districts in the United States: 2004–05* (Washington, DC: National Center for Education Statistics, 2008).

83. Ferrero, personal communication, January 22, 2009.

84. "Three National Foundations Launch 'New Century High Schools Consortium for New York City' with New York City Public Schools," *Carnegie Corporation of New York*, December 14, 2000, accessed November 10, 2009, *www.carnegie.org/sub/news/schoolsi.html.*

85. "Three National Foundations Launch 'New Century High Schools Consortium.'"

86. New Visions for Public Schools, "New Century High Schools Initiative—Final Report to Carnegie Corporation of New York" (working paper, New York, August 30, 2006), 21.

87. Policy Studies Associates, *Evaluation of the New Century High Schools Initiative: Report on the Third Year* (Washington, DC: Policy Studies Associates, 2006), 50.

88. New Visions for Public Schools, "New Century High Schools Initiative—Final Report," 21–22.

89. Elissa Gootman, "Small Schools in City Program to Grow by 52 in September," *New York Times*, February 2, 2005, accessed January 6, 2011, *www.nytimes.com/2005/02/02/nyregion/02school.html?oref=login.*

90. New Visions for Public Schools, "New Century High Schools Initiative—Final Report," 9.

91. Ibid., 12.

92. Lili Allen and Adria Steinberg, *Big Buildings, Small Schools: Using a Small Schools Strategy for High School Reform* (Boston: Jobs for the Future, 2004).

93. Thomas Toch, "Liberal Reforms: A Conversation with Eva Moskowitz," *Education Sector*, June 13, 2006, accessed January 6, 2011, *www.educationsector.org/analysis/analysis_show.htm?doc_id=376661.*

94. Chicago Public Schools, "Small Schools: History."

95. Pauline Lipman, "'We're Not Blind. Just Follow the Dollar Sign,'" *Rethinking Schools Online* 19, no. 4 (2005), accessed January 6, 2011, *www.rethinkingschools.org/archive/19_04/blin194.shtml*.

96. Ayers and Klonsky, "Chicago's Renaissance 2010," 454.

97. Shelley Weston, personal communication, January 26, 2009.

98. "Romer Advocates for Smaller Schools to Promote Community Building," *New Schools Better Neighborhoods*, Newsletter, Summer 2003, accessed January 6, 2011, *www.nsbn.org/publications/newsletters/summer2003/romer .php*.

99. Ibid.

100. See, for instance, *Crawford et al. v. Board of Education of the City of Los Angeles et al.*; see also Jack Schneider, "Escape from Los Angeles: White Flight from Los Angeles and Its Schools, 1960–1980," *Journal of Urban History* 34, no. 6 (2008): 995–1012.

101. Scott Folsom, "A Parent Looks at Small Learning Communities," *Office of School Redesign Newsletter*, Winter 2007.

102. CES National Web, "Los Angeles Small Schools Center," accessed January 6, 2011, *www.essentialschools.org/affiliates/705*; Los Angeles Parents Union, "About Us," accessed November 10, 2009 *www.parentsunion.org/about_us/ index.php*.

103. Los Angeles Unified School District, "Policies and Procedures Governing the Development and Implementation of Small Learning Communities in Middle Schools and High Schools," *Bulletin 1600*, February 28, 2005, accessed January 6, 2011, *www.lausd.net/SLC_Schools/docs/slc/BUL_1600 .pdf*.

104. "Schools' Dropout Remedy: Get Small," *Los Angeles Times*, March 26, 2005, accessed January 6, 2011, *articles.latimes.com/2005/mar/26/local/ me-dropout26*.

105. National Conference of State Legislatures, "Small Learning Communities," June 2002, accessed November 10, 2009, *www.ncsl.org/programs/employ/slc .htm*.

106. Erik W. Robelen, "Gates Learns to Think Big," *Education Week*, October 11, 2006.

107. Meier, *The Power of Their Ideas*, 115.

108. Chicago Public Schools, "Small Schools Types," accessed January 6, 2011, *smallschools.cps.k12.il.us/types.html*.

109. Schools Sharing Buildings: A Toolkit—Principles and Practice from the Chicago Public Schools (Chicago: Chicago Public Schools, n.d.), 7.

110. Ibid., 4.

111. Weston, personal communication.

112. Ferrero, personal communication, January 22, 2009.

113. Smaller Learning Communities Grant Program, Department of Education, *Federal Register* 65, no. 96, (2000): 31386.

114. U.S. Department of Education, "Awards—Smaller Learning Communities Program," accessed January 6, 2011, *www2.ed.gov/programs/slcp/awards.html.*

115. Connell et al., *Going Small and Getting Smarter*, 3.

116. Valerie E. Lee and Douglas D. Ready, *Schools within Schools: Possibilities and Pitfalls of High School Reform* (New York: Teachers College Press, 2007).

117. Lee and Ready, *Schools within Schools.*

118. New Visions for Public Schools, "New Century High Schools Initiative—Final Report," 4.

119. Floyd Hammack, "Off the Record—Something Old, Something New, Something Borrowed, Something Blue: Observations on the Small Schools Movement," *Teachers College Record* 110, no. 9 (2008); Douglas D. Ready and Valerie E. Lee, "Choice, Equity, and the Schools-within-Schools Reform," *Teachers College Record* 110, no. 9 (2008).

120. American Institutes for Research and SRI International, *Executive Summary: Evaluation of the Bill and Melinda Gates Foundation's High School Grants, 2001–2004 (*Washington, DC: AIR and SRI, 2005).

121. Joseph E. Kahne, Sue Sporte, Marisa de la Torre, and John Q. Easton, *Small Schools on a Larger Scale: The First Three Years of the Chicago High School Redesign Initiative* (Chicago: Consortium on Chicago School Research, 2006). Findings were echoed in Janet Quint, *Meeting Five Challenges of High School Reform: Lessons from Research on Three Reform Models* (New York: MDRC, 2006).

122. Eric W. Robelen, "Gates High Schools Get Mixed Review in Study," *Education Week*, November 16, 2005, accessed January 6, 2011, *www.edweek.org/ew/articles/2005/11/16/12gates.h25.html?ra.*

123. Erik W. Robelen, "Schools-within-Schools Model Seen Yielding Trade-Offs," *Education Week*, September 19, 2007, 10.

124. Lawrence Bernstein, Mary Ann Millsap, Jennifer Schimmenti, and Lindsay Page, *Implementation Study of Smaller Learning Communities*, Report to the U.S. Department of Education (Cambridge, MA: Abt Associates, 2008), 16.

125. James P. Connell, Nettie E. Legters, Adena Klem, and Thomas C. West, *Getting Ready, Willing, and Able: Critical Steps toward Successful Implementation of Small Learning Communities in Large High Schools* (Portland, OR: Northwest Regional Educational Laboratory, 2006), 2.

126. Donna Foote, *Relentless Pursuit: A Year in the Trenches with Teach for America* (New York: Knopf, 2008), 120.

127. Ibid., 329.

128. Ibid., 334.

129. Weston, personal communication.

130. United States Senate, Report 108-384.

131. Bernstein et al., *Implementation Study of Smaller Learning Communities*, 4.

132. "Notices," Federal Register 72, no. 45 (2007): 10502–7, accessed January 6, 2011, *www.ed.gov/legislation/FedRegister/proprule/2007-1/030807b.html*.

133. Ibid.

134. Richard F. Elmore, "Change and Improvement in Educational Reform," in *A Nation Reformed?*, ed. David T. Gordon (Cambridge, MA: Harvard Education Press, 2003), 24.

135. Connell et al., *Getting Ready, Willing, and Able*, 40.

136. Connell et al., *Going Small and Getting Smarter*, 3.

137. Coleman and Hoffer, *Public and Private High Schools*, 40.

138. Parents for Inclusive Education, *Small Schools, Few Choices: How New York City's High School Reform Effort Left Students with Disabilities Behind* (New York: New York Lawyers for the Public Interest, October 2006).

139. Jean Johnson, Ann Duffett, Steve Farkas, and Kathleen Collins, *Sizing Things Up: What Parents, Teachers and Students Think about Large and Small High Schools* (New York: Public Agenda, 2002).

140. Charles Payne, "Still Crazy after All These Years: Race in the Chicago School System" (lecture, College of Education, University of Illinois at Chicago, April 22, 2005).

141. Tom Corcoran, Susan H. Fuhrman, and Carol L. Belcher, "The District Role in Instructional Improvement," *Phi Delta Kappan* 83, no. 1 (September 2001): 78.

142. Shaw, "Gates Foundation Turns Attention to Higher Education."

CHAPTER 3

1. For a more detailed account on the relationship between schools and social problems, see Henry J. Perkinson, *Imperfect Panacea: American Faith in Education, 1865–1976* (New York: Random House, 1977).

2. Teach For America, "Teach For America Fields Largest Teacher Corps in Its 20-Year History," press release, May 24, 2010, accessed January 6, 2011, *www.teachforamerica.org/newsroom/documents/20100524_Teach.For.America .Fields.Largest.Teacher.Corps.In.Its.20.Year.History.htm*; Teach For America, "Teach for America Adds Largest Number of New Teachers and Regions in 20-Year History" press release, May 28, 2009, accessed January 6, 2011, *www.teachforamerica.org/newsroom/documents/20090528_Teach_For_ America_Adds_Largest_Number_of_Teachers_in_History.htm*.

3. Teach For America, "Teach For America Fields Largest Teacher Corps in Its 20-Year History."

4. David Brooks, "Who Will He Choose?," *New York Times*, December 5, 2008; Thomas Friedman, "Swimming without a Suit," *New York Times*, April 22, 2009.

5.   David L. Angus, *Professionalism and the Public Good: A Brief History of Teacher Certification* (Washington, DC: Thomas B. Fordham Foundation, 2001).

6.   Carl Kaestle, *Pillars of the Republic* (New York: Hill and Wang, 1983), 20.

7.   Ibid., 21.

8.   Ibid.

9.   Angus, *Professionalism and the Public Good*, 4.

10.   The term "normal school" refers to the effort to establish norms in teacher practice—a translation of the French *école normale*.

11.   Angus, *Professionalism and the Public Good*, 7.

12.   Kaestle, *Pillars of the Republic*, 129.

13.   Leslie Lenkowsky and Emily Spencer, "The History of Philanthropy for Education Reform," in *Seven Studies in Education Philanthropy* (Washington, DC: Thomas B. Fordham Foundation, 2001).

14.   Angus, *Professionalism and the Public Good*, 4.

15.   David A. Gould, *Policy and Pedagogues: School Reform and Teacher Professionalization in Massachusetts, 1840–1920* (PhD diss., Brandeis University, 1977).

16.   Christopher J. Lucas, *Teacher Education in America: Reform Agendas for the Twenty-First Century* (New York: St. Martin's Press, 1997), 50.

17.   Ibid., 52.

18.   Angus, *Professionalism and the Public Good*, 11.

19.   Ibid., 19.

20.   Lenkowsky and Spencer, "The History of Philanthropy for Education Reform."

21.   Geraldine J. Clifford and James W. Guthrie, *Ed School: A Brief for Professional Education* (Chicago: University of Chicago Press, 1988), 60.

22.   Lenkowsky and Spencer, "The History of Philanthropy for Education Reform."

23.   Angus, *Professionalism and the Public Good*, 23.

24.   John Taylor Gatto, Kristin Kearns Jordan, and Theodore Sizer, "School on a Hill," *Harper's Magazine*, September 2001, 61.

25.   Mortimer Smith, *And Madly Teach* (Chicago: H. Regnery, 1949).

26.   Bestor, *Educational Wastelands*, 131.

27.   Meade, *A Foundation Goes to School*, 40.

28.   Ralph W. McDonald, "The Educational Situation Today," in *Journey to Now, 1946–1961* (Washington, DC: National Education Association, 1961), 45.

29.   John Walton, "An Alternative to the Fifth Year," *Journal of Teacher Education* 5, no. 2 (1954): 118.

30.   T. M. Stinnett, "Security—and Adequacy, Too," in *Journey to Now, 1946–1961* (Washington, DC: National Education Association, 1961), 117.

31. James Conant, *Education and Liberty* (Cambridge, MA: Harvard University Press, 1953), 131.

32. *Time*, October 19, 1953, quoted in T. M. Stinnett, "Security—and Adequacy, Too," 103.

33. Richard J. Coley and Margaret E. Thorpe, *A Look at the MAT Model of Teacher Education and Its Graduates: Lessons for Today* (Princeton, NJ: Educational Testing Service, 1986), ii.

34. Wendy Kopp, "An Argument and Plan for the Creation of the Teacher Corps" (undergraduate thesis, Princeton University, 1989), 42.

35. Coley and Thorpe, *A Look at the MAT Model of Teacher Education*; F. Keppel, "A Field Guide to the Land of Teachers," *Phi Delta Kappan* 67, no. 10 (1986): 18–23; Kenneth M. Zeichner, "Learning from Experience in Graduate Teacher Preparation," in *Research Perspectives on the Graduate Preparation of Teachers*, ed. A. Woolfolk (Englewood Cliffs, NJ: Prentice-Hall, 1988).

36. Robert N. Bush, "Teacher Education Reform: Lessons from the Past Half Century," *Journal of Teacher Education* 38, no. 3 (1987): 15.

37. Wesley J. Little, "Conditions and Forces Influencing Educational Reform," in *Reforming Teacher Education: Issues and New Directions*, ed. Joseph A. Braun Jr. (New York: Garland, 1989), 7.

38. National Advisory Council on Education Professions Development, *Teacher Corps: Past or Prologue? A Report with Recommendations* (Washington, DC: Government Printing Office, 1975), 1.

39. Ibid.

40. The phrase "Great Society" was first used by Lyndon Johnson in a 1964 speech in Ann Arbor, Michigan, when the president told students at the University of Michigan that "we have the opportunity to move not only toward the rich society and the powerful society, but upward to the Great Society." Subsequent legislation included the Civil Rights Acts, the Voting Rights Act, the Economic Opportunity Act, the Higher Education Act, and the Elementary and Secondary Education Act.

41. B. Othanel Smith, Saul Cohen, and Arthur Pearl, *Teachers for the Real World* (Washington, DC: American Association of Colleges for Teacher Education), 1969.

42. Joseph Lohman, *Cultural Patterns in Urban Schools: A Manual for Teachers, Counselors, and Administrators* (Berkeley: University of California Press, 1967), 88.

43. Study Commission on Undergraduate Education and the Education of Teachers, *Teacher Education in the United States: The Responsibility Gap* (Lincoln: University of Nebraska Press, 1976). In a definition of "cultural pluralism" at the end of the report, Antonia Pantoja wrote that "the

educational system of this country fails to educate all its students, especially non-white students. . . . The goal of the school system is the maintenance of the status quo with respect to cultural, racial, sexual, and economic class, superiority-and-inferiority relations."

44. National Advisory Council on Education Professions Development, *Teachers Corps: Past or Prologue?*, 1.

45. Senate Committee on Labor and Public Welfare, Report, March 29, 1974, 99; "National Teacher Corps Task Force: Conference on Recruitment and Selection," agenda, November 18–19, 1965, DHEW, Roll 86 Microfilm, Records from Federal Government Agencies, Lyndon Baines Johnson Library, 1.

46. "National Teacher Corps Descriptive Material, Draft I," January 26, 1966, Cater: Teacher Corps, Box 56, Office Files of the White House Aides, Lyndon Baines Johnson Library; National Advisory Council on Education Professions Development, *Teachers Corps: Past or Prologue?*, 13.

47. Kenneth Clark, *Dark Ghetto: Dilemmas of Social Power* (New York: Harper, 1965), 133–34.

48. Furno and Kidd, *New Teachers for the Inner City*, 142.

49. Roy A. Edelfelt and Ronald Corwin, *Lessons from the Teacher Corps* (Washington, DC: National Education Association, 1974), 20.

50. William Smith, "The American Teacher Corps Programme," in *World Yearbook of Education 1980: Professional Development of Teachers*, ed. Eric Hoyle and Jacquetta Megarry (London: Kogan Page, 1980), 206.

51. National Advisory Council on Education Professions Development, *Teachers Corps: Past or Prologue?*, 7.

52. Ibid., 11.

53. David D. Marsh and Margaret F. Lyons, *A Study of the Effectiveness of Sixth Cycle Teacher Corps Graduates* (Berkeley, CA: Pacific Training and Technical Assistance Corps, 1974).

54. National Advisory Council on Education Professions Development, *Teachers Corps: Past or Prologue?*, 17.

55. House Appropriations Hearings, 91st Congress, March 10, 1970, 675.

56. G. Thomas Fox Jr., *Who Is Being Evaluated? Teacher Corps Evaluations over the Past Ten Years* (unpublished manuscript, 1975).

57. Ronald G. Corwin, *Reform and Organizational Survival* (New York: Wiley, 1973), 84, 374.

58. For example, Peter C. Murrell Jr., *The Community Teacher: A New Framework for Effective Urban Teaching* (New York: Teachers College Press, 2001); M. Foster, *Black Teachers on Teaching* (New York: New Press, 1997); Gloria Ladson-Billings, *The Dreamkeepers: Successful Teachers of African American Children* (San Francisco: Jossey-Bass, 1994); Lisa Delpit, *Other*

People's Children: Cultural Conflict in the Classroom (Toronto: University of Toronto Press, 1996).

59. Peter F. Carbone Jr., "Liberal Education and Teacher Preparation," *Journal of Teacher Education* 31, no. 3 (May–June 1980): 13–17; Richard Mitchell, *The Graves of Academe* (Boston: Little, Brown, 1981); Rita Kramer, *Ed School Follies: The Miseducation of America's Teachers* (New York: Free Press, 1991).

60. Robert Alley, "A Futurist View: Forces Framing the Future of Teacher Education Programs," in *Reforming Teacher Education: Issues and New Directions*, ed. Joseph A. Braun Jr. (New York: Garland, 1989), 118.

61. Gerald A. Dorfman and Paul R. Hanna, "Can Education Be Reformed?," in *Thinking about America: The United States in the 1990s*, ed. Annelise Anderson and Dennis L. Bark (Stanford, CA: Hoover Institution Press, 1988), 387.

62. Pam Grossman, "Teaching: From a Nation at Risk to a Profession at Risk," in *A Nation Reformed?*, ed. David T. Gordon (Cambridge, MA: Harvard Education Press, 2003), 70.

63. Ravitch, *Left Back*, 465.

64. Toch, *In the Name of Excellence*, 158.

65. Carnegie Forum on Education and the Economy, *A Nation Prepared*.

66. Phil Keisling, "Do Private Schools Do It Better and Cheaper?," in *The Great School Debate*, ed. Beatrice Gross and Ronald Gross (New York: Simon and Schuster, 1985), 461.

67. Dale Ballou and Michael Podgursky, "Teacher Recruitment and Retention in Public and Private Schools," *Journal of Policy Analysis and Management* 17, no. 3 (Summer 1998): 394.

68. Toch, *In the Name of Excellence*, 159.

69. Robert K. Wimpelberg and Jean A. King, "Rethinking Teacher Recruitment," *Journal of Teacher Education* 34, no. 1 (1983): 5.

70. See, for example, Baird, *The Elite Schools*.

71. For an example of the continuing relevance of the "service" model, see comments by Ernest Boyer in Terrel H. Bell et al., "Reformers Bite the Bullet," in *The Great School Debate*, ed. Beatrice Gross and Ronald Gross (New York: Simon and Schuster, 1985), 442–43.

72. Bell et al., "Reformers Bite the Bullet," 442–43.

73. Theodore R. Sizer, "High School Reform and the Reform of Teacher Education," *Journal of Teacher Education* 38, no. 1 (1987): 28.

74. National Center for Alternative Certification, "Alternative Teacher Certification: A State by State Analysis," accessed January 6, 2011, *www.teach-now.org/intro.cfm*. Only Alaska and Oregon report that they do not have alternative routes to teacher licensure.

75. Fred M. Hechinger, "About Education," *New York Times*, December 6, 1989, B15.

76. Kopp, "An Argument and Plan," ii.

77. Timothy Knowles, personal communication, December 17, 2008.

78. Wendy Kopp, *One Day, All Children* (New York: Public Affairs, 2001), xi.

79. Molly Ness, *Lessons to Learn: Voices from the Front Lines of Teach For America* (New York: Routledge Falmer, 2004), 21.

80. Sarah Sentilles, *Taught by America: A Story of Struggle and Hope in Compton* (Boston: Beacon Press, 2005), 31.

81. Kopp, *One Day, All Children*, 182.

82. Ibid., 30.

83. Laurel Shaper, "'Teach for America' Seeks Young Graduates," *Christian Science Monitor*, March 14, 1990, 13.

84. Kopp, *One Day, All Children*, 37.

85. Anne Grosso de León, "Teach For America: A Band of Thinkers and Doers," *Carnegie Reporter* 5, no. 1 (Fall 2008).

86. Kopp, "An Argument and Plan," 8.

87. Grosso de León, "Teach For America: A Band of Thinkers and Doers."

88. See, for instance, U.S. Department of Education, "Teach for America Awarded $1 Million to Extend Its Reach," press release, September 25, 2002, accessed January 6, 2011, *www.ed.gov/news/ pressreleases/2002/09/09252002b.html*.

89. "National Teach For America Week," Cong. Rec. S10, 937 (October 24, 2000).

90. Michael Shapiro, *Who Will Teach For America?* (Washington, DC: Farragut, 1993), 3.

91. Elizabeth Greenspan, "A Look at . . . the Desire to Teach," *Washington Post*, November 8, 1998, C3.

92. Marion Hodges-Biglan, personal communication, December 12, 2008.

93. Knowles, personal communication.

94. Kevin Hall, personal communication, January 29, 2009.

95. Powell, *Lessons from Privilege*, 154–55.

96. Rachel Shteir, "Teaching Teachers; Teach for America: Learning the Hard Way," *New York Times*, January 7, 1996.

97. Teach For America, "Teach For America Adds Largest Number of New Teachers and Regions in 20-Year History."

98. "Interview with Ross Perot," *Larry King Live*, CNN, February 20, 2002, accessed January 6, 2011, *transcripts.cnn.com/TRANSCRIPTS/0202/20/ lkl.00.html*.

99. Susan Chira, "Princeton Student's Brainstorm," *New York Times*, June 20, 1990, 1.

100. Jodi Wilgoren, "Wendy Kopp, Leader of Teach for America," *New York Times*, November 12, 2000, A23.

101. Ness, *Lessons to Learn*, 35.

102. Hall, personal communication.
103. Knowles, personal communication.
104. Mariotti, personal communication.
105. "Dells' Foundation Pledges $10M for Education Campaign," *American Business Journal*, October 7, 2005, accessed January 6, 2011, *www.bizjournals.com/austin/stories/2005/10/03/daily48.html*.
106. Anne Grosso de León, "Alternative Paths to Teacher Certification," *Carnegie Reporter* 2, no. 4 (Spring 2005).
107. Patricia Sellers, "Schooling Corporate Giants on Recruiting," *Fortune*, November 27, 2006, accessed January 6, 2011, *money.cnn.com/magazines/fortune/fortune_archive/2006/11/27/8394324/index.htm*.
108. Edwin C. Vare, letter to the editor, "'Teach for America' vs. Traditional Training," *Christian Science Monitor*, September 14, 1990, 20.
109. Finn, *Troublemaker*, 283; Stafford Palmieri, "Ed Schools, Hallowed No More," *Education Gadfly 9*, no. 39 (November 5, 2009).
110. Foote, *Relentless Pursuit*, 35.
111. Kopp, *One Day, All Children*, 176.
112. Foote, *Relentless Pursuit*, 205.
113. Ibid., 143.
114. Kopp uses the phrase the "best and brightest" frequently in her original plan for TFA, defining them at one point as those "nominated by deans of their universities as the top students on campus and . . . selected from a large pool of applicants on the basis of extracurricular activities and essays." See Kopp, "An Argument and Plan," i.
115. Ibid., 45.
116. Knowles, personal communication.
117. Linda Darling-Hammond, Deborah J. Holtzman, Su Jin Gatlin, and Julian V. Heilig, "Does Teacher Preparation Matter? Evidence about Teacher Certification, Teach for America, and Teacher Effectiveness," *Educational Policy Analysis Archives* 13, no. 42 (2005); Donald Boyd, Pam Grossman, Hamilton Lankford, Susannah Loeb, and James Wyckoff, "How Changes in Entry Requirements Alter the Teacher Workforce and Affect Student Achievement," *Education Finance and Policy* 1, no. 2 (2006): 176–216; Debra Williams, "Teach For America on Hot Seat," *Catalyst Chicago*, September 2004, accessed January 6, 2011, *www.catalyst-chicago.org/arch/09-04/0904tfa.htm*.
118. Teach For America, *Teach For Solving Our Nation's Greatest Injustice* (brochure, 2009), 2.
119. Michael Winerip, "A Chosen Few Are Teaching for America," *New York Times*, July 11, 2010, accessed January 6, 2011, *www.nytimes.com/2010/07/12/education/12winerip.html?_r=1*.
120. Ness, *Lessons to Learn*, 12.

121. Knowles, personal communication.
122. Shapiro, *Who Will Teach For America?*, 188.
123. Foote, *Relentless Pursuit*, 26.
124. Ibid., 40.
125. Sam Dillon, "Two School Entrepreneurs Lead the Way on Change," *New York Times*, June 19, 2008, 16.
126. Kopp, *One Day, All Children*, 174.
127. Richard M. Ingersoll, "Teacher Turnover and Teacher Shortages: An Organizational Analysis," *American Education Research Journal* 38, no. 3 (2001): 501.
128. Ness, *Lessons to Learn*, 75.
129. Larry Cuban, "Educational Entrepreneurs Redux," in *Educational Entrepreneurship: Realities, Challenges, Possibilities*, ed. Frederick M. Hess (Cambridge, MA: Harvard Education Press, 2006), 229–39.
130. Paul Decker, Daniel Mayer, and Steven Glazerman, *The Effects of Teach For America on Students: Findings from a National Evaluation* (Princeton, NJ: Mathematica Policy Research, 2004), accessed January 6, 2011, *www.mathematica-mpr.com/publications/pdfs/teach.pdf*; Thomas J. Kane, Jonah E. Rockoff, and Douglas O. Stalger, "What Does Certification Tell Us about Teacher Effectiveness? Evidence from New York City" (working paper 12155, National Bureau of Economic Research, 2006); Margaret Raymond, Stephen Fletcher, and Javier Luque, *Teach For America: An Evaluation of Teacher Differences and Student Outcomes in Houston, Texas* (Stanford, CA: Center for Research on Education Outcomes, 2001).
131. Boyd et al., "How Changes in Entry Requirements Alter the Teacher Workforce and Affect Student Achievement"; Darling-Hammond et al., "Does Teacher Preparation Matter?"; Julian V. Heilig and Su Jin Jez, *Teach For America: A Review of the Evidence* (Boulder, CO: Education and the Public Interest Center; Tempe, AZ: Education Policy Research Unit, 2010), accessed January 6, 2011, *epicpolicy.org/publication/teach-for-america*.
132. Most studies of TFA effectiveness compare corps members against novices. See, for instance, Don Boyd, Pam Grossman, Karen Hammerness, Hamp Lankford, Susanna Loeb, Matt Ronfeldt, and Jim Wyckoff, *Recruiting Effective Math Teachers, How Do Math Immersion Teachers Compare? Evidence from New York City* (Albany, NY: Teacher Policy Research, 2009). Among the few studies comparing TFA recruits with experienced teachers is Zeyu Xu, Jane Hannaway, and Colin Taylor, *Making a Difference? The Effects of Teach for America in High School* (Washington, DC: Urban Institute and CALDER, 2009).
133. Jonathan Schorr, "Where Have They Gone?," *Teacher Magazine*, March 1, 1999.

134. Hodges-Biglan, personal communication.
135. Ness, *Lessons to Learn*, 52.
136. Sentilles, *Taught by America*, 112.
137. Ness, *Lessons to Learn*, 105.
138. Sentilles, *Taught by America*, 6.
139. Ness, *Lessons to Learn*, 19.
140. Ibid., 36.
141. Barbara Torre Veltri, "Teaching or Service: Site-Based Realities of Teach For America Teachers in Poor, Urban Schools," *Education and Urban Society* 40, no. 5 (2008): 520.
142. Weston, personal communication.
143. Ness, *Lessons to Learn*, 70.
144. Eric Hanushek, John F. Kain, and Steven G. Rivkin, "Why Public Schools Lose Teachers," *Journal of Human Resources* 39, no. 2 (2004): 326–54.
145. Michael Lach and Michael Loverude, "Our Abandoned Teachers," *Christian Science Monitor*, August 31, 1992, 19.
146. Donna Foote, "Lessons from Locke," *Newsweek*, August 11, 2008, 47.
147. Ness, *Lessons to Learn*, 213.
148. Kopp, "An Argument and Plan," 50.
149. Decker, Mayer, and Glazerman, *The Effects of Teach For America on Students*.
150. Coley and Thorpe, *A Look at the MAT Model of Teacher Education*, 9.
151. Steven G. Rivkin, Eric A. Hanusheck, and John F. Kain, "Teachers, Schools, and Academic Achievement," *Econometrica* 73, no. 2 (2005): 417–58; Jonah Rockoff, "The Impact of Individual Teachers on Student Achievement: Evidence from Panel Data," *American Economic Review* 94, no. 2 (2004): 247–52.
152. Foote, *Relentless Pursuit*, 39.
153. Ibid., 39.
154. Deborah Ignagni, personal communication, December 17, 2008.
155. Williams, "Teach For America on Hot Seat."
156. Ibid.
157. Teach for America, "Major Foundations Pledge $30 Million for Teach For America's Growth Plan," press release, October 7, 2005.
158. Darling-Hammond et al., "Does Teacher Preparation Matter?"
159. Boyd et al., "How Changes in Entry Requirements Alter the Teacher Workforce and Affect Student Achievement," 212.
160. Julie Mikuta and Arthur Wise, "Teachers for America," *Education Next* 8, no. 2 (2008).
161. Kopp, "An Argument and Plan."
162. Shaper, "'Teach for America' Seeks Young Graduates," 13.

163. Megan Hopkins, "A Vision for the Future: Collective Effort for Systemic Change," *Phi Delta Kappan* 89, no. 10 (2008): 737–40.

164. Virginia Richardson, Toni Griego-Jones, and Georgea Langer, "Evaluation of Teach For America: Summer Institute" (unpublished research paper, 1996).

165. Foote, *Relentless Pursuit*, 195.

166. Knowles, personal communication.

167. Hodges-Biglan, personal communication.

168. Foote, *Relentless Pursuit*, 194.

169. Ibid.

170. Ibid., 195.

171. Teach For America, "Major Foundations Pledge $30 Million for Teach For America's Growth Plan."

172. Ibid.

173. U.S. Department of Education, "Teach for America Awarded $1 Million to Extend Its Reach."

174. Teach For America, "Major Foundations Pledge $30 Million for Teach For America's Growth Plan."

175. Ness, *Lessons to Learn*, 217.

CHAPTER 4

1. Susan Walton, "U.S. Pupils Rank Low in 8-Nation Test," *Education Week*, December 21, 1983, accessed January 6, 2011, *www.edweek.org/ew/articles/1983/12/21/05270011.h03.html?qs=international+test+scores*; Robert Rothman, "U.S. Pupils Earn Familiar Low Scores on International Math, Science Tests," *Education Week*, February 8, 1989, accessed January 6, 2011, *www.edweek.org/ew/articles/1989/02/08/08160046.h08.html?qs=international percent20test percent20scores*.

2. Jay R. Campbell, Catherine M. Hombo, and John Mazzeo, *NAEP 1999: Trends in Academic Progress,* NCES 2000-469 (Washington, DC: National Center for Education Statistics, Office of Educational Research and Improvement, U.S. Department of Education, 2000).

3. Joe Berger, "Demoting Advanced Placement," *New York Times*, October 4, 2006.

4. *General Education in School and College: A Committee Report by Members of the Faculties of Andover, Exeter, Lawrenceville, Harvard, Princeton, and Yale* (Cambridge, MA: Harvard University Press, 1952), 1.

5. "Summary of the Rockefeller Brothers Fund Report on U.S. Educational Needs," *New York Times*, June 23, 1958, 16.

6. Jerome S. Bruner, *In Search of Mind: Essays in Autobiography* (New York: HarperCollins, 1983), 179–80.

7. Ibid.

8.   Ibid., 181.
9.   School and College Study of College Admission with Advanced Standing, *Announcement and Bulletin of Information* (1954), 3.
10. School and College Study of Admission with Advanced Standing, *Bulletin of Information* (Philadelphia, 1952), 5.
11. School and College Study of Admission with Advanced Standing, *Bulletin of Information*, 5–6.
12. James B. Conant, *Slums and Suburbs* (New York: McGraw-Hill, 1961), 111.
13. School and College Study of Admission with Advanced Standing, *Bulletin of Information*, 7–8.
14. John A. Valentine, *The College Board and the School Curriculum: A History of the College Board's Influence on the Substance and Standards of American Education, 1900–1980* (New York: College Entrance Examination Board, 1987), 84.
15. David A. Dudley, "The Advanced Placement Program," *NASSP Bulletin* 42 (December 1958): 1.
16. Gordon Gould, "Your Johnny Is Different," *Chicago Daily Tribune*, October 20, 1957, C38.
17. In the year before Sputnik, NSF appropriation had leveled at $40 million. The following year, the NSF's budget grew to $134 million; ten years later, it had ballooned to nearly $500 million.
18. Robert L. Hampel, *The Last Little Citadel: American High Schools since 1940* (Boston: Houghton Mifflin, 1986), 73.
19. Hampel, *The Last Little Citadel*, 59.
20. Dudley, "The Advanced Placement Program."
21. Harold B. Gores and Leo Barry, "College-Level Courses in Secondary School," *College Board Review* 28 (1956): 7.
22. Hampel, *The Last Little Citadel*, 33.
23. Richard Pearson, "Advanced Placement Program: Opportunities Ahead," *College Board Review* 39 (1959): 24.
24. Chesly Manly, "Colleges Use Entrance Tests to Weed Out Potential Failures," *Chicago Tribune*, April 29, 1963, A2.
25. Gordon Gould, "Our Bright Kids Get a Break," *Chicago Daily Tribune*, April 20, 1958, C24.
26. Henry W. Bragdon, "Advanced Placement: Rising Tide with Breakers Ahead," *College Board Review* 42 (1960): 19.
27. Joan Beck, "Life in the Pre-College Pressure Cooker," *Chicago Tribune*, May 14, 1967, G8.
28. Hampel, *The Last Little Citadel*, 66.
29. Conant, *Slums and Suburbs*, 92.
30. "Theobald Asks Expansion of Advanced Courses Plan," *New York Times*, August 18, 1962, 22.

31. Gores and Barry, "College-Level Courses in Secondary School," 7.
32. Bragdon, "Advanced Placement: Rising Tide with Breakers Ahead," 20.
33. Patricia L. Casserly, "What's Really Happening in Advanced Placement?—II," *College Board Review* 59 (1966): 19.
34. Milton J. Cohler, "The Inner City," *Chicago Tribune*, November 10, 1963, H29.
35. Bragdon, "Advanced Placement: Rising Tide with Breakers Ahead," 20.
36. John R. Thelin, *A History of American Higher Education* (Baltimore: Johns Hopkins University Press, 2004), 294.
37. Beck, "Life in the Pre-College Pressure Cooker," G8.
38. Casserly, "What's Really Happening in Advanced Placement?—II," 19.
39. Eric Rothschild, "Four Decades of the Advanced Placement Program," *History Teacher* 32, no. 2 (February 1999): 185.
40. Hampel, *The Last Little Citadel*, 137.
41. William R. Hochman, "Advanced Placement: Can It Change with the Times?," *College Board Review* 77 (1970): 16.
42. "B. H. High Again Leads in Advanced Studies," *Los Angeles Times*, October 17, 1968, B8C.
43. Hochman, "Advanced Placement: Can It Change with the Times?," 16.
44. Lee Austin, "Schools Face Dilemma of Segregated Classes," *Los Angeles Times*, June 6, 1971, SG3.
45. Gene I. Maeroff, "Two Ideals at Issue," *New York Times*, May 22, 1974, 89.
46. Hochman, "Advanced Placement: Can It Change with the Times?," 17.
47. Aurelia Spurlark, "Education in Black and White," *Chicago Tribune*, December 8, 1968, A6.
48. Sidney P. Marland, "Advanced Placement," *Today's Education,* January–February 1976, 44.
49. College Board, *Annual AP Program Participation 1956–2007* (New York: College Entrance Examination Board, 2007), accessed January 6, 2011, *apcentral.collegeboard.com/apc/public/repository/2007_Annual_Participation.pdf.*
50. Hampel, *The Last Little Citadel*, 148.
51. Goodlad, *A Place Called School*, 244.
52. Ibid., 291.
53. University of California, "May 5, 1982, Academic Senate, Northern Section: Notice of Meeting of the Representative Assembly" (Berkeley: UC Academic Council, 1982).
54. Bob Riddle, personal communication, March 21, 2007.
55. James Feron, "The Class of '77," *New York Times*, June 26, 1977, 176.
56. Sheppard Ranbom, "Schools' Interest in Advanced-Placement Classes Increases," *Education Week*, April 13, 1983.
57. Ranbom, "Schools' Interest in Advanced-Placement Classes Increases."

58. David Savage, "Record Number of Students Take Advanced Tests," *Los Angeles Times*, December 10, 1984, B27.

59. Frank del Olmo, "Scoring Controversy Tests Latino Community Pride," *Los Angeles Times*, December 16, 1982, H7.

60. Arthur W. Steller and Walter K. Lambert, "Advanced Placement: Helping to Achieve Systemwide Reform in Urban Schools," *NASSP Bulletin* 80, no. 576 (January 1996): 100.

61. Ravitch was one of two lead authors, along with Charlotte Crabtree.

62. Charles J. Sykes, *Dumbing Down Our Kids* (New York: Macmillan, 1995), 246. For a example of support for AP from other supporters of standards and accountability, see Chester E. Finn Jr. "Things Are Falling Apart," *Education Next* 6, no. 1 (2006).

63. Ambrose Brodus, "'Tracking' or 'Equity': Schools Struggle with Best Way to Place Students," *Los Angeles Times*, December 16, 1984, SD2.

64. Elavie Ndura, Michael Robinson, and George Ochs, "Minority Students in High School Advanced Placement Courses: Opportunity and Equity Denied," *American Secondary Education* 32, no. 1 (2003).

65. Casey Banas, "Pre-College Tests Show Small Count of Success," *Chicago Tribune*, March 28, 1979, B2.

66. Rothschild, "Four Decades of the Advanced Placement Program," 198.

67. College Board, *AP Grade Distributions—All Subjects 1986–2005* (New York: College Entrance Examination Board, 2005), accessed January 6, 2011, *apcentral.collegeboard.com/apc/members/repository/gradedistall_47029.pdf*.

68. Rothschild, "Four Decades of the Advanced Placement Program," 198.

69. Edward Wiley III, "Advanced Placement Could Spell Benefits for Minorities," *Black Issues in Higher Education* 5, no. 21 (1989): 1.

70. Steller and Lambert, "Advanced Placement: Helping to Achieve Systemwide Reform in Urban Schools," 103.

71. Kristin Klopfenstein, "Advanced Placement: Do Minorities Have Equal Opportunity?," *Economics of Education Review* 23, no. 2 (2004): 119.

72. Harlan P. Hanson, "Reflections on Thirty Years of AP," *College Board Review* 135 (1985): 11.

73. Jay Mathews, "Low-Income Pupils Find Exam Fees a Real Test," *Washington Post*, April 25, 1991, A3.

74. Nina Hurwitz and Sol Hurwitz, "Is the Shine off the AP Apple?," *American School Board Journal* 190, no. 3 (2003): 14–18; Susan P. Santoli, "Is There an Advanced Placement Advantage?," *American Secondary Education* 30, no. 3 (2003): 23–35; Education Commission of the States, "Advanced Placement," *State Notes*, accessed January 6, 2011, *mb2.ecs.org/reports/Report .aspx?id=922*.

75. Maria Estela Zarate and Harry P. Pachon, *Equity in Offering Advanced Placement Courses in California High Schools, 1997–2003* (Los Angeles:

University of Southern California, Tomás Rivera Policy Institute, 2006), accessed January 6, 2011, *www.trpi.org/PDFs/ap_2006.pdf.*

76. Anne C. Lewis, "An Overview of the Standards Movement," *Phi Delta Kappan* 76, no. 10 (1995).

77. Ndura, Robinson, and Ochs, "Minority Students in High School Advanced Placement Courses," 21–38.

78. William Lichten, "Whither Advanced Placement—Now?," in *AP: A Critical Examination of the Advanced Placement Program*, ed. Philip M. Sadler, Gerhard Sonnert, Robert H. Tai, and Kristin Klopfenstein (Cambridge, MA: Harvard Education Press, 2010), 233; "Notices," *Federal Register* 65, no. 28 (2000): 6872.

79. U.S. Department of Education, "Awards—Advanced Placement Incentive Program Grants," accessed January 6, 2011, *www2.ed.gov/programs/apincent/awards.html.*

80. The AVID Center and College Board Collaborative Professional Development in Teaching, Learning, and Leading, "A Model for School Reform" (unpublished research report, June 2004), accessed November 10, 2009, *www.avidonline.org/info/?ID=1188&tabID=0.*

81. Rothschild, "Four Decades of the Advanced Placement Program," 194–95; Jay Mathews, "More College-Bound Minorities Using Advanced Placement Tests," *Washington Post*, December 12, 1988, A3.

82. College Board, *California and National Summary Reports* (New York: College Entrance Examination Board, 1997).

83. David Hill, "Test Case," *Teacher Magazine* 11, no. 6 (2000).

84. College Board, *AP Grade Distributions—All Subjects 1986–2005.*

85. For an example of criticism of AP Calculus, see David M. Bessoud, "The Rocky Transition from High School Calculus," *Chronicle of Higher Education*, January 17, 2010, accessed January 6, 2011, *chronicle.com/article/High-School-Calculus-The/63533/.*

86. College Board, *National Summary Reports* (New York: College Entrance Examination Board, 1999).

87. College Board, *National Summary Reports.* In 2008 the average AP exam score among white students was 2.96. Among African American and Mexican American students, the average scores were 1.91 and 2.38, respectively.

88. Jeff K. Lowenstein, "A View from Inside the Gates: What AP Means to Admissions Officers," *College Board Review* 206 (2005): 43.

89. Jay Mathews, "What's Wrong (and Right) with America's Best Public High Schools?," *College Board Review* 185 (1998): 6.

90. Kit Lively, "More States Encourage Advanced Placement Courses," *Chronicle of Higher Education*, May 26, 1993, 22. For an example of an earlier criticism of the program, see Gary A. Olson, Elizabeth Metzger, and Evelyn

Ashton-Jones, *Advanced Placement English: Theory, Politics and Pedagogy* (Portsmouth, NH: Boynton/Cook-Heinemann, 1989).

91. William Celis, "Advanced Placement Exams Suffering an Erosion in Value," *New York Times*, December 28, 1994, A1.

92. Karen W. Arenson, "Study Faults Advanced-Placement Courses," *New York Times*, February 15, 2002, A14.

93. Rachel Friis Stettler and Joseph Algrant, "Changing Course for the Better," *Independent School Magazine*, Winter 2003, accessed January 6, 2011, *www.nais.org/publications/ismagazinearticle.cfm?Itemnumber=144300&sn .ItemNumber=145956&tn.ItemNumber=145958*.

94. Choate Rosemary Hall, *History, Philosophy, Religion, and Social Sciences Curriculum* (Wallingford, CT: Choate Rosemary Hall, 2007).

95. Deerfield Academy, *Deerfield Academy Calendar 2007–2008* (Deerfield, MA: Deerfield Academy, 2007).

96. Edward J. Shanahan, "Changing with the Times, Maintaining Rigor," *College Board Review* 206 (2005): 20; Commission on the Future of the Advanced Placement Program, *Access to Excellence: A Report of the Commission on the Future of the Advanced Placement Program* (New York: College Entrance Examination Board, 2001), accessed January 6, 2011, *professionals.collegeboard.com/data-reports-research/cb/access-to-excellence*.

97. Andrew E. Carlan, "Programs for the Gifted: Another View," *New York Times*, June 26, 1983, LI21.

98. Joan Kernan Cone, "Untracking Advanced Placement English: Creating Opportunity Is Not Enough," *Phi Delta Kappan* 73, no. 9 (May 1992): 713.

99. Lynn H. Dodd, "Adopting AP as a Beacon for All Students," *College Board Review* 206 (2005): 21.

100. Steve Farkas and Ann Duffett, *Growing Pains in the Advanced Placement Program: Do Tough Trade-offs Lie Ahead?* (Washington, DC: Thomas B. Fordham Institute, 2009), 9.

101. Justin Ewers, "Is AP Too Good to Be True?," *U.S. News and World Report*, September 15, 2005, accessed January 6, 2011, *www.usnews.com/usnews/edu/ articles/050919/19advanced.htm*.

102. Kristin Klopfenstein and M. Kathleen Thomas, *The Link between Advanced Placement Experience and College Success* (Fort Worth: Texas Christian University, Department of Economics, 2005), 1.

103. For a fuller discussion of the causal impact of the AP Program, see Chrys Dougherty, Lynn Mellor, and Shuling Jian, *Orange Juice or Orange Drink? Ensuring That "Advanced Courses" Live Up to Their Labels* (Austin, TX: National Center for Educational Accountability, 2006).

104. Klopfenstein and Thomas, *The Link between Advanced Placement Experience and College Success*, 15.

105. Saul Geiser and Veronica Santelices, *The Role of Advanced Placement and*

Honors Courses in College Admissions, Research and Occasional Paper Series, CSHE-4-04 (Berkeley: Center for Studies in Higher Education, University of California–Berkeley, 2004), accessed January 6, 2011, *repositories.cdlib .org/cshe/CSHE-4-04*; Klopfenstein and Thomas, *The Link between Advanced Placement Experience and College Success*.

106. Vasugi V. Ganeshananthan, "Advanced Placement Program Faces New Criticism over Its Testing Standards," *Chronicle of Higher Education*, July 14, 2000.

107. Janet Gilmore, "Fall 2007 Freshman Admissions Data Released," press release, University of California–Berkeley, April 5, 2007, accessed January 6, 2011, *berkeley.edu/news/media/releases/2007/04/05_admissions.shtml*; College Board, "The 200 Colleges and Universities Receiving the Greatest Number of AP Grades," 2007, accessed January 6, 2011, *apcentral.collegeboard.com/ apc/public/repository/2007_200_Top_Colleges.pdf*; figures from Stanford University and Harvard University admissions offices.

108. John H. Pryor, Sylvia Hurtado, Victor B. Saenz, Jessica S. Korn, Jose Luis Santos, and William S. Korn, *The American Freshman: National Norms for Fall 2006* (Los Angeles: Cooperative Institutional Research Program, 2007), 2.

109. Wayne Camara, Neil J. Dorans, Rick Moran, and Carol Myford, "Advanced Placement: Access Not Exclusion," *Education Policy Analysis Archives* 8, no. 40 (2000), accessed January 6, 2011, *epaa.asu.edu/epaa/v8n40.html*; Dodd, "Adopting AP as a Beacon for All Students," 21; Rick Morgan and Len Ramist, *Advanced Placement Students in College: An Investigation of Course Grades at 21 Colleges*, report no. SR-98-13 (Princeton, NJ: Educational Testing Service, 1998), accessed January 6, 2011, *www.collegeboard.com/ap/ pdf/sr-98-13.pdf*; Renee H. Shea, "Stronger Than Ever at 50," *College Board Review*, no. 206 (2005): 14–19.

110. Celis, "Advanced Placement Exams Suffering an Erosion in Value," A1.

111. William Lichten, "Whither Advanced Placement?," *Education Policy Analysis Archives* 8, no. 29 (2000), accessed January 6, 2011, *epaa.asu.edu/epaa/ v8n29.html*.

112. Ganeshananthan, "Advanced Placement Program Faces New Criticism"; Lichten, "Whither Advanced Placement?"; Laura Pappano, "The Incredibles," *New York Times*, January 7, 2007.

113. Pappano, "The Incredibles."

114. Klopfenstein and Thomas, *The Link between Advanced Placement Experience and College Success*; Philip M. Sadler and Robert H. Tai, "Advanced Placement Exam Scores as a Predictor of Performance in Introductory College Biology, Chemistry and Physics Courses," *Science Educator* 16, no. 2 (2006): 1–19.

115. Shanahan, "Changing with the Times, Maintaining Rigor," 20.

116. Anne Marie Chaker, "Standards Tighten for Advanced Placement Courses," *Wall Street Journal*, August 11, 2005, D1.

117. College Board, "AP Course Audit Information," accessed November 10, 2009, *apcentral.collegeboard.com/apc/public/courses/teachers_corner/46361 .html.*

118. Theresa Crapanzano, "A Frenzy for Admission into the Top Colleges," *New York Times*, July 2, 2000, CT7.

119. Mark Oberjuerge, "Raising the Bar: Historically Disadvantaged Students Can Meet the AP Challenge," *History Teacher* 32, no. 2 (February 1999): 265.

120. Oberjuerge, "Raising the Bar," 265.

121. Berger, "Demoting Advanced Placement."

122. Eric Neutuch, "Advanced Placement United States History: A Student's Perspective," *History Teacher* 32, no. 2 (February 1999): 245.

123. Hunter Breland, James Maxey, Renee Gernand, Tammie Cumming, and Catherine Trapani, *Trends in College Admission 2000* (Tallahassee, FL: Association for Institutional Research, 2002).

124. Yilu Zhao, "High School Drops Its A.P. Courses, and Colleges Don't Seem to Mind," *New York Times*, February 1, 2002, B1.

125. Walter M. Stroup and Owen Priest, "How Advanced Is Advanced Placement?," *Independent School*, Winter 1992.

126. Patty Hager, "Taking a Hard Look at Advanced Placement," *Concord Academy Magazine*, Fall 2006, accessed January 6, 2011, *www .concordacademy.org/data/files/Gallery/SchoolPublications/FallMag06AP.pdf.*

127. Ibid.

128. Ret Talbot, "Replacing AP," *Education Week*, May 16, 2007, 29.

129. John D. Bransford, Ann L. Brown, and Rodney R. Cocking, eds., *How People Learn: Brain, Mind, Experience, and School* (Washington, DC: National Academy Press, 1999), accessed January 6, 2011, *books.nap.edu/ html/howpeople1/.*

130. Mitchell Landsberg and Rachana Rathi, "Elite School Will Expel AP Classes," *Los Angeles Times*, May 5, 2005.

131. Hager, "Taking a Hard Look at Advanced Placement."

132. Ibid.

133. Pappano, "The Incredibles."

134. Landsberg and Rathi, "Elite School Will Expel AP Classes."

135. See, for example, Finn, *Troublemaker*, 304.

136. Banas, "Pre-College Tests Show Small Count of Success," B2.

137. Mark Klimesh, personal communication, June 5, 2009.

138. Chicago Public Schools, *Advanced Placement 5-Year Summary* (unpublished research report, August 18, 2008).

139. Klimesh, personal communication.

140. Jordan H. Rickles, "Access to Advanced Placement Courses across LAUSD Schools" (unpublished research paper, Program Evaluation and Research Branch, Los Angeles Unified School District), 1–2, accessed November 10, 2009, *notebook.lausd.net/pls/ptl/docs/page/ca_lausd/fldr_organizations/fldr_plcy_res_dev/par_division_main/research_unit/publications/policy_reports/ap_access_final.pdf.*

141. Sam Wineburg, "A Sobering Big Idea," *Phi Delta Kappan* 87, no. 5 (2006): 401–2.

142. Michael Riley, "AP as the 'Common Curriculum,'" College Board AP Central, 2005, accessed January 6, 2011, *apcentral.collegeboard.com/apc/public/features/18762.html.*

143. Jan Davis, personal communication, December 18, 2008.

144. Barbara Caldwell, personal communication, March 8, 2007.

145. Friends Central School, Friends Select School, Germantown Friends School, and Westtown School.

146. Tamar Lewin, "The Two Faces of AP," *New York Times*, January 8, 2006, 24.

147. "Retreated Placement," *Education Gadfly* 9, no. 21 (June 11, 2009).

148. Hurwitz and Hurwitz, "Is the Shine off the AP Apple?"

149. Richard Atkinson, "Standardized Tests and Access to American Universities" (The 2002 Robert H. Atwell Distinguished Lecture, Annual Meeting of the American Council on Education, Washington, DC, 2001), accessed January 6, 2011, *works.bepress.com/richard_atkinson/36.*

150. George Madaus quoted in George Judson, "Taking a Tougher Route to College, *New York Times*, January 10, 1993, 26.

CONCLUSION

1.   Toch, *In the Name of Excellence*, 275.

2.   James Fallows, "How America Can Rise Again," *Atlantic*, January 1, 2010.

3.   "Schools in Chicago Are Called the Worst by Education Chief," *New York Times*, November 8, 1987, 38; Civic Committee of the Commercial Club of Chicago, *Still Left Behind: Student Learning in Chicago's Public Schools* (Chicago: Commercial Club of Chicago, 2009).

4.   Civic Committee of the Commercial Club of Chicago, *Still Left Behind.*

5.   Louis Cohen, Lawrence Manion, and Keith Morrison, *Research Methods in Education* (New York: Routledge, 2007), 274.

6.   Barker and Gump, *Big School, Small School*, 202.

7.   Vander Ark, "America's High School Crisis."

8.   Donald A. Erickson, "How Valid Are Coleman's Conclusions," in *The Great School Debate: Which Way for American Education*, ed. Beatrice Gross and Ronald Gross (New York: Simon and Schuster, 1985), 462.

9.   David Hill, "Test Case," *Teacher Magazine* 11, no. 6 (March 2000).

10. Charles M. Payne, *So Much Reform, So Little Change: The Persistence of*

Failure in Urban Schools (Cambridge, MA: Harvard Education Press, 2008), 6.

11. Nel Noddings, *When School Reform Goes Wrong* (New York: Teachers College Press, 2007), 36.

12. According to Ugo Pagano, "It is possible to consume a positional good only if it is unequally consumed. . . . Whereas we must consume equal amounts of public goods and we can consume equal amounts of private goods, we must consume unequal quantities of positional goods." Ugo Pagano, "Is Power an Economic Good?," in *The Politics and Economics of Power*, ed. Samuel Bowles, Maurizio Franzini, and Ugo Pagano (London: Routledge, 1999), 64.

13. Frederick M. Hess and Michael J. Petrilli, "Obama, Failing to Learn from Bush's Lessons?," *Education Gadfly* 9, no. 27 (July 30, 2009).

14. Larry Cuban, *Why Is It So Hard to Get Good Schools?* (New York: Teachers College Press, 2003), 6.

15. David Tyack, *The One Best System.*

16. David Bridges, "Educationalisation: On the Appropriateness of Seeking or Offering a Response by Educational Institutions to Social and Economic Problems," *Educational Theory* 58 (2008).

17. Peter Schrag, "Schoolhouse Crock," *Harpers Magazine*, July 2007, 42.

18. Barack Obama, Press Conference, September 10, 2010.

19. "We cannot continue to tinker in high schools that are little more than 'dropout factories' where students fall further behind, year after year." From U.S. Department of Education, "Secretary Arne Duncan's Remarks to the National Council of La Raza," press release, July 28, 2009, accessed January 6, 2011, *www.ed.gov/news/speeches/secretary-arne-duncans-remarks-national-council-la-raza*.

INDEX